English Words

THE LANGUAGE LIBRARY

Series editor: David Crystal

The Language Library was created in 1952 by Eric Partridge, the great etymologist and lexicographer, who from 1966 to 1976 was assisted by his co-editor Simeon Potter. Together they commissioned volumes on the traditional themes of language study, with particular emphasis on the history of the English language and on the individual linguistic styles of major English authors. In 1977 David Crystal took over as editor, and *The Language Library* now includes titles in many areas of linguistic enquiry.

The most recently published titles in the series include:

Ronald Carter and Walter Nash   *Seeing Through Language*
Florian Coulmas   *The Writing Systems of the World*
David Crystal   *A Dictionary of Linguistics and Phonetics*, Fifth Edition
J. A. Cuddon   *A Dictionary of Literary Terms and Literary Theory*, Fourth Edition
Viv Edwards   *Multilingualism in the English-speaking World*
Geoffrey Hughes   *A History of English Words*
Walter Nash   *Jargon*
Roger Shuy   *Language Crimes*
Gunnel Tottie   *An Introduction to American English*
Ronald Wardhaugh   *Investigating Language*
Ronald Wardhaugh   *Proper English: Myths and Misunderstandings about Language*
Heidi Harley   *English Words: A Linguistic Introduction*

English Words

A Linguistic Introduction

Heidi Harley

Blackwell
Publishing

PE
1175
.H43
2006

BLACKWELL PUBLISHING
350 Main Street, Malden, MA 02148-5020, USA
9600 Garsington Road, Oxford OX4 2DQ, UK
550 Swanston Street, Carlton, Victoria 3053, Australia

First published 2006 by Blackwell Publishing Ltd

1 2006

Library of Congress Cataloging-in-Publication Data

Harley, Heidi.
    English words : a linguistic introduction / Heidi Harley.
        p. cm. (The language library)
    Includes bibliographical references and index.
    ISBN-13: 978-0-631-23031-1 (alk. paper)
    ISBN-10: 0-631-23031-9 (alk. paper)
    ISBN-13: 978-0-631-23032-8 (pbk. : alk. paper)
    ISBN-10: 0-631-23032-7 (pbk. : alk. paper)   1. English language—Word formation.   2. English language—Morphology.   3. English language—Phonology.   4. English language—Semantics.   I. Title.   II. Series.

    PE1175.H43 2006
    425—dc22
                                                                    2005028556

A catalogue record for this title is available from the British Library.

Set in 10/12¹/₂ pt Palatino
by Graphicraft Limited, Hong Kong
Printed and bound in Singapore
by C.O.S. Printers Pte Ltd

The publisher's policy is to use permanent paper from mills that operate a sustainable forestry policy, and which has been manufactured from pulp processed using acid-free and elementary chlorine-free practices. Furthermore, the publisher ensures that the text paper and cover board used have met acceptable environmental accreditation standards.

For further information on
Blackwell Publishing, visit our website:
www.blackwellpublishing.com

6187963

This book is dedicated to my father, Peter Harley, who takes words seriously.

Contents

Preface

This textbook is intended as a thorough introduction to the study of English words from a linguistic perspective. It introduces students to the technical study of words in several areas: phonology, morphology, syntax, semantics, language acquisition and historical linguistics, in that order. Some introductory material is covered in each section, to give students the theoretical tools they will need to proceed, and then those tools are employed to analyze the English vocabulary.

This book will be of interest to students who have a general interest in words – people whom Richard Lederer smilingly calls "verbivores." They enjoy reading tidbits of word facts in language mavens' columns, word games and etymologies, but have never taken a linguistics or structure of language course.

The text is designed to give students a command of the basic theory in each area, skill in analyzing and understanding English words, and the grounding needed for more advanced study in linguistics or lexicology. Ultimately, however, the aim is to provide students who will never take another linguistics-related course with a grasp of some of the basic methods and questions of the field, viewed through the window of words.

Acknowledgments

This book would not have been possible without the help of a great many people. It wouldn't exist had Andrew Carnie not suggested that I submit a proposal for it, building on my lecture notes for the cross-listed Linguistics/English 322 course, "The Structure and

Meaning of Words." My students and colleagues at the University of Arizona provided invaluable feedback and expertise in many moments of uncertainty. I would especially like to thank Michael Hammond, Adam Ussishkin, Diane Ohala and Andrew Carnie for reading and commenting on portions of the manuscript. Several teaching assistants I have had over the years also provided feedback, including Bob Kennedy, Jason Haugen, Sarah Longstaff, Gwanhi Yun and Xu Xu. Thanks especially to Xu Xu for preparing the IPA transcription key. The three anonymous reviewers of the manuscript for Blackwell provided exhaustive comments that improved it considerably and also saved me from many mistakes; I am very grateful to them. The linguistics editors at Blackwell, first Tami Kaplan and then Sarah Coleman and Ada Brunstein, have exhibited a combination of patience, persistence and tact that both reassured and motivated a fairly skittish author. I also have very much appreciated Sarah's and Margaret Aherne's guidance and hard work throughout the publication process.

Last but far from least, both my parents, Carolyn and Peter Harley, read through the entire first draft manuscript and provided detailed comments that have helped me no end. My husband, Art Torrance, read through the manuscript not once, but twice, thinking through each analysis and transcription, paying sharp attention to every comma and apostrophe, and saving future students from a great deal of unnecessary confusion. He also has supported me throughout the process with encouragement, snacks and late-night cups of hot chocolate. I cannot express my gratitude to him and them enough.

Needless to say, the many flaws that doubtless remain are entirely my responsibility!

Heidi Harley
April, 2005

IPA Transcription Key

Consonants of English   ☐ voiceless   ▨ voiced

manner \ place	labial		labio-dental		inter-dental		alveolar		palatal		velar		glottal	
stops	p	b					t	d			k	g	ʔ	
fricative			f	v	θ	ð	s	z	ʃ	ʒ			h	
affricates									t͡ʃ	d͡ʒ				
nasal		m						n				ŋ		
liquids (lateral) (non-lateral)								l ɹ						
glides		w								j				

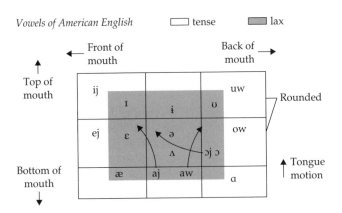

Vowels of American English   ☐ tense   ▨ lax

← Front of mouth   Back of mouth →

Top of mouth   ij   ɪ   ɨ   ʊ   uw   ⌐ Rounded

ej   ɛ   ə   ow

ʌ   ɔj ɔ

Bottom of mouth   æ   aj   aw   ɑ   ↑ Tongue motion

Transcription of British English

As discussed briefly on page 41, there are many dialects of English with correspondingly many transcription systems. One of the most widely used and taught Englishes is the broadcasting standard of the United Kingdom, called 'Received Pronunciation', or RP for short.

In the text we use a transcription suited to American English, but for the benefit of readers who are interested in using the RP transcription system, the vowel symbols are presented in summary below (the consonants are essentially the same as those presented in the text). Also provided below are RP transcriptions corresponding to all the American English transcriptions in the text, organized by page number.

Most of the differences between the two transcriptions have to do with the different pronunciations of the two dialects, but a few differences are simply notational. For instance, rather than use the upside-down symbol /ɹ/ for the retroflex liquid, the more usual symbol /r/ is used. Similarly, rather than representing the affricates in 'church' and 'judge' with a ligature arc over the two symbols which make up their pronunciation, the RP custom is to print the two symbols closer to one another – that is, rather than /t͡ʃ/ and /d͡ʒ/, the RP transcription uses /tʃ/ and /dʒ/.

RP vowel	Transcription
sea, feet, me, field	iː
him, big, village, women	ɪ
get, fetch, head, Thames	e
sat, hand, ban, plait	æ
sun, son, blood, does	ʌ
calm, are, father, car	ɑː
dog, lock, swan, cough	ɒ
all, saw, cord, more	ɔː
put, wolf, good, look	ʊ
soon, do, soup, shoe	uː
bird, her, turn, learn	ɜː
the, butter, sofa, about	ə
ape, waist, they, say	eɪ
time, cry, die, high	aɪ
boy, toy, noise, voice	ɔɪ
so, road, toe, know	əʊ
out, how, house, found	aʊ

deer, here, fierce, near   ɪə
care, air, bare, bear   eə
poor, sure, tour, lure   ʊə

RP transcriptions corresponding to American transcriptions in text, indexed by page number:

1   wɒt ɪz ə wɜːd
21   saʊnd ən 'fjʊərɪ 'ɪŋglɪʃ fə'nɒlədʒɪ
33   'nʌʧel, 'ʧeləʊ
43   'teɪkn̩, lɪtl̩
44   'pəʊlɪʃ, 'pɒlɪʃ
44   Exercise 2.7
      ðə 'bændɪʤ wəz waʊnd ə'raʊnd ðə wuːnd
45   Exercise 2.7, continued
      ðeɪ wə tuː kləʊs tə ðə dɔː tə kləʊz ɪt
      ðə bʌk dʌz 'fʌnɪ θɪŋz wən ðə dəʊz aː 'prezn̩t
      tə help wɪð 'plɑːntɪŋ ðə 'fɑːmə tɔːt ɪz saʊ tə səʊ
      ðə wɪnd wəz tuː strɒŋ tə waɪnd ðə seɪl
      'ɑːftər ə 'nʌmbə əv ɪn'ʤekʃn̩z maɪ ʤɔː gɒt 'nʌmə
      ə'pɒn 'siːɪŋ ðə teər ɪn maɪ kləʊðz aɪ ʃed ə tɪə
      aɪ hæd tə səb'ʤekt ðə 'sʌbʤɪkt tuː ə 'sɪəriːz əv tests
51   – Study Problem 1
    a.   'preʃəs, ə'bɪlɪtɪ, 'waɪəlɪs, ɪn'telɪʤəns, pə'laɪt, 'kaʊəd,
       saɪ'kɒlədʒɪ, ɪn'kredəbl̩', 'nekləs
    b.   nʌm, kəm'pjuːtə, ʃæm'peɪn, 'nɒlɪʤ, æŋ'zaɪətɪ, ʤuː'dɪʃəs,
       'pɪkpɒkɪt, 'sɪzəz, jʌŋ
    c.   'rɪstwɒʧ, waɪnd, fən'ɒlədʒɪ, traʊt, 'ʧɪlɪŋ, bɪ'jɒnd, dɪ'leɪ,
       'deɪlɪ, 'θaʊzn̩d, fʌʤ
    d.   naɪf, ˌrepɪ'tɪʃəs, 'plaɪəz, raɪd, 'æŋkə, 'dɪfθɒŋ, krʌm,
       'pɑːθweɪ, ˌkɒmplɪ'mentrɪ, 'eksəsaɪz
52   – Study Problem 3
      lɪtl̩ bɪliːz fɪfθ greɪd tiːʧə kɔːld ɪz faðə wʌn iːvnɪŋ. "aɪm sɒrɪ tə
      tel juː ðɪs," ʃiː sed, "bət bɪliː ʧiːtɪd ɒn ɪz kwɪz tədeɪ. hiː kɒpiːd
      frɒm ðə gɜːl sɪtɪŋ nekst tə hɪm."
      "aɪ dəʊnt bəliːv ɪt," ɪz faðə sed. "haʊ də jə neʊ ðə gɜːl dɪdn̩t
      kɒpɪ ðiː ænsəz ɒf əv bɪliːz test?"
      "wel," sed ðə tiːʧə, "bəʊθ sets əv ansəz wɜː ðə seɪm ɔːl ðə weɪ
      daʊn ðə peɪʤ, eksept fə ðə last wʌn. fɔː ðæt wʌn ʃɪ reʊt aɪ
      dəʊnt nəʊ, ən bɪliː rəʊt miː niːðə"
54   fəʊnə'lɒdʒɪkl̩ wɜːdz 'kɔːlɪŋ ɔːl 'skræbl̩' 'pleɪəz

60   hiː, strɪŋ, teksts
62   trʌk, drɒp
63, 64   'meni
65   stɪk, traɪ
66   kaʊ, laɪ
68   læmp, spæmd, dæmz, ruːʒd, bʌzd, dʒʌdʒd
70   bɜːpt, bɜːps
71   duː, biː, səʊ
72   siː, aɪsiːðə'dɒgiː, siːð, aɪs
73   'fɪŋgə, 'æŋgə, 'tɪŋglɪ, 'ɪŋglɪʃ,
74   aɪ wɪn geɪmz, θɪn 'gruːəl, paɪn grəʊsbiːk
77   'mʌðə, ə'pɪə
78   dʒɒn ɪz 'ærəgənt, rəgənt
79   bɪl ɪz 'baɪɪŋ ə gɪ'taː, taː
82   beɪelzəbʌbhæzədevɪlpʊtəsaɪdfəmiː, bɪl ɪz 'baɪɪŋ ə gɪ'taː, kɪs ðə
     skaɪ, kɪs ðɪs gaɪ
87   liːf, kə'lekt, ɪn'heɫ, pə'liːs, 'fɪɫtə, səʊɫd, læp, 'mɪɫkɪŋ, 'letə
88   fiːw, 'teɪbu
     Exercise 4 is specifically about the pronunciation of American
     English, so no RP transcriptions are given.
90   weə duː wɜːdz kʌm frɒm
95   ɒlədʒɪ
96   ɪ'lɪzəbəθ, eɪdz, saːz, diːəʊei
108   biːnə
111   priː ænd 'sʌfɪksɪz ɪŋglɪʃ mɔː'fɒlədʒɪ
112   kæt, kɪk ðə 'bʌkɪt, əd
118   ən 'æpl, ə letə tə dʒɒn, sɪks əv wʌn
119   iːləktr, tɒks, əmfæt
133   wæg, wægɪd, snɪft, 'bɒksɪz, wægd, pæt, weɪdəd, weɪd
134   snɪft, kuːd, pleɪd, weɪvd
136   ɪn griːn, ɪŋglɪʃ, ɪn prɪnt, 'ɪmprɪnt
143   'lɪtḷ
144   ˌmɔːfə'lɒdʒɪkḷ ˌɪdiːəʊ'sɪŋkrəsiːz
148   ɪz
151   eɪʃn̩, keɪʃn̩, ɪŋ
152   ə'sɪst, ə'sɪstənt, ə'sɪstənts
154   et, iːt, dʌkt, 'djuːs
157   eɪdʒd, eɪdʒɪd
159   haʊs, 'haʊzɪz, 'faːðə, waɪvz, naɪvz, wʊlvz, kaːvz
163   ə'fɪʃḷ, əˌfɪʃə'liːz, 'tɒnsɪl, ˌtɒnsɪ'laɪtɪs
164   'kɒmplɪmənt, ˌkɒmplɪ'mentrɪ, kə'neɪdiən, 'kænədə

169 ɪfaɪ, 'sɒlɪd, sə'lɪdɪfaɪ
172 'kjuːdɒs
174 ɑː, wɜː, ɪz, biː, ɡʊd, 'betə, wel, bæd, wɜːs
179 'ænəlaɪz, ə'næləsɪs, 'eɪn̩l
180 'mædʒɪk, 'ekspɪdaɪt, 'ɑːtɪfɪs, 'mælɪs, mə'dʒɪʃn̩, 'ekspɪ'dɪʃəs,
    'ræʃn̩, ˌɑːtɪ'fɪʃl̩, mə'lɪʃəs
185 'leksɪkl̩ sɪ'mæntɪks ðə 'strʌktʃər əv 'miːnɪŋ ðə 'miːnɪŋ əv
    'strʌktʃə
193 'evrɪ, ðə
196 ðæt, 'weðə
199 braʊn
218 'tʃɪldrən 'lɜːnɪŋ wɜːdz
222 'ræbɪt, ɡævəɡaɪ
224 'ræbɪt, maʊs
225 maʊs, ɡreɪ, 'ræbɪt, 'rəʊdn̩t, ɪə
226 'ænɪməl, ɪə, fɜː, 'piːtə
227 'ræbɪt, 'piːtə
228 'piːtə, 'ræbɪt
229 tə'mɒrəʊ
232 fɪə
239 'æksɪdənts əv 'hɪstriː ɪŋɡlɪʃ ɪn flʌks
270 fiːt, feɪt, faɪt
271 iː aɪ uː
272 kiːn
273 kaɪt, reɪt, kɪt, ræt, 'reɪtɪŋ, 'rætɪŋ
276 'kændl̩, ˌʃændə'lɪə, kæp, ˌʃæpə'reʊn, 'kɑːsl̩, 'ʃætəleɪn, tʃeə, ʃeɪz
    lɒŋ, 'tʃerɪ, sə'riːz, tʃeɪn, 'ʃiːnjɒn, kætʃ, tʃeɪs

1

What Is a Word?

/ˈwʌt ɪz ə ˈwəɹd/

In this chapter, we look at the intuitive notion of what a word is and see that there are several perspectives on wordhood. A word has different properties depending on whether you're looking at it phonologically, morphologically, syntactically or semantically. Essentially, we end up with two different notions of word: a *listeme* – a sound–meaning correspondence – and a *phonological word*, a sound unit on which the spacing conventions of written English are based. Finally, we distinguish between necessary and conventional aspects of wordhood.

1.1 Explaining *Word* in Words

Stop. Before reading any further, get out a sheet of paper and a pencil (or fire up a word processor, or just introspect), and try to compose a definition of the word *word*.

Exercise 1.1 Compose a definition of *word*.

Throughout this text, there will occasionally be exercises inserted in the middle of discussion. You should stop and try to answer them before reading on. Answers to the exercises are often given in the text immediately below; you'll be able to compare the response you came up with to the discussion in the text, and think about any differences between the answer in the text and your own answer.

What Is a Word?

Here's one possible first try:

Definition 1
word: a sequence of letters that we write consecutively, with no spaces.

How does that definition compare with your own? Yours is probably better. One thing that is obviously wrong with this one is that it depends crucially on the conventions of writing. Languages have words before they're written down. Let's try again, trying to eliminate the reference to writing:

Definition 2
word: a sequence of sounds that we pronounce consecutively, with no pauses.

Hang on a minute – when we're talking, there's not usually any pauses between words. (Try listening for a moment to someone talking. Is there a pause before and after every word? Where *are* the pauses?) We do know, though, that it is at least possible to put pauses between words when talking. Imagine you are speaking to someone for whom English is a second language, and who is hard of hearing besides. To give them the best chance of understanding you, you . . . would . . . probably . . . talk . . . rather . . . like . . . this, inserting big spaces between words. (People talk like this when dictating, as well.) You certainly wouldn't insert spaces inside them. No one would say "y . . . ou . . . wou . . . ld . . . pro . . . b . . . abl . . . y . . ." etc. Maybe we can use the *possibility* of spaces in our definition:

Definition 3
word: a sequence of sounds which *can* be pronounced on its own, with pauses on either side.

Hang on again! A word is not just any old sequence of sounds that can be pronounced on its own. According to that definition, *spimble* or *intafulation* or *pag* are words, and so are *raise your arm* or *how are you* (you can pronounce them with space on either side, can't you?). The former, however, are sequences of sounds that don't have any meaning associated with them, and the latter are sequences of sounds that have too much meaning associated with them. Intuitively, the former are not words, and the latter are groups of words.

2

To help make the text clearer, when we're discussing the linguistic properties of some word, the word will appear in italics. This indicates that the word is just being mentioned – that is, being discussed – rather than being actually used. This mention/use distinction is hard to keep track of when it's not indicated by some distinguishing feature, such as italics.

It seems fairly clear that we have to include meaning in our definition. The sounds that make up, for instance, the word *word* have a certain meaning in combination that they don't have by themselves, or when they appear in other words (like <u>wa</u>ter or <u>murder</u>). So the *w* sound in *word* doesn't mean anything by itself, nor does the *-ord* sequence, but together, they have a meaning, even if it's a meaning that's hard to pin down. So for our final try, let's look at the relevant definition in the *Oxford English Dictionary* (**OED**), which is listed as definition number 12a in their entry for the word *word*:

Definition 4 (final)
word: A combination of vocal sounds, or one such sound, used in a language to express an idea (e.g. to denote a thing, attribute, or relation), and constituting an ultimate minimal element of speech having a meaning as such; a vocable.

This is probably fairly close to the definition you came up with, albeit perhaps with a few extra elements. The crucial part that we didn't have in our earlier versions is the bit about the "ultimate minimal unit of speech having a meaning as such."

So consider our example word, *word*. The *w* doesn't have a meaning by itself, nor does any other individual sound. The first three sounds, which we spell *wor* in the word *word*, do have a meaning of their own (spelled *were*, the past plural of the verb *to be*), but that meaning is not a part of the meaning of *word* – that is, the meaning of *word* does not include the meaning of *were*. Other subsets of the sound sequence (*or, rd, ord*) are similarly unrelated in meaning or meaningless. *Word*, then, is a minimal unit of speech having a meaning.

This definition works to eliminate our counterexamples above from consideration as possible "words." *Spimble, intafulation* and *pag* are units of speech that don't express any idea, and *raise your arm* and *how are you* are units of speech that have a meaning, but they aren't minimal – their meaning is made up of the meanings of the smaller elements within them, each of which contributes its own meaning to the meaning of the whole expression in a consistent way. So although the meaning of *were* is not part of the meaning of *word*, the meaning of *raise* IS a part of the meaning of *raise your arm*.

Nonetheless, we'll see that this definition of *word* does not correspond with the everyday sense of the word *word* in English.

Exercise 1.2   Can you figure out why this definition doesn't match the usual meaning of "word" before reading Section 1.3? Try to think of English words or expressions which are counterexamples.

Before we do that, however, let's look at basic design of language, in order to understand the central role that words play every day in the dance of communication.

1.2   Language Is a Secret Decoder Ring

Language lets us see into other people's minds, and lets other people see into ours. If we speak the same language, then just by talking I can cause you to have an idea that I have had, or at least a close approximation of it. If we speak different languages, no amount of talking will let me share my idea with you. It's as if learning a language is like getting a secret decoder ring that lets you encrypt thoughts and feelings and transmit them to someone with the same decoder ring. What's especially great about this encryption device that we all carry around in our heads is that it's more or less automatic. You don't (usually) have to *consciously* identify and match up the symbols (the spoken words) to the ideas; it happens automatically, both on the sending end and the receiving end.

Consider the stick figures modeling the communication process in Figure 1.1. The skirted figure has an idea to communicate (panel 1). She encodes it into a linguistic form (panel 2) – ultimately, a string of instructions transmitted by her nerves to her vocal cords, lips, and tongue – and creates some sound waves (panel 3). The stick figure she's talking to hears the sound waves (panel 3), translates them back into an abstract linguistic form (panel 4), and ultimately, back into the idea (panel 5).

Even though it doesn't take very long to accomplish the encryption in step 2 and the decryption in step 4 of this process, it's an incredibly

Figure 1.1 Communicating using language

complicated business. (This book is mostly about just one sub-part of what's involved during this process, the part that has to do with words.)

The encryption system has two basic parts. The first part is a set of symbols which stand for concepts, like the English word *dog* is a symbol standing for the concept DOG. (Note that in French, the word *chien* stands for the concept DOG, in Spanish, *perro* stands for the concept DOG, and in Hiaki, a language spoken in southern Arizona and northern Mexico, the word *chu'u* is the symbol that stands for DOG.) These symbols are, of course, words. In spoken language, words are made up of sounds produced by the vocal cords, lips and tongue, but they don't have to be: sign languages use certain handshapes and motions as the building blocks of words. Any symbol can behave like a word if it's associated with an appropriate meaning.

You can get pretty far, communication-wise, with just words, even without the second part of the encryption system. Chimpanzees trained in sign language can do pretty well at communicating ideas about their likes and dislikes, needs and wants, and about things in the immediate environment, using unstructured clusters of words. The second part of the encryption system, though, is what makes it infinitely versatile. There's a procedure for sticking symbols together to make up complex units that correspond to complex ideas: the meanings of the complex units derive from both the meanings of the symbols (part one) AND the rule used to combine them (part two). Crucially, these combining rules are *recursive*: they can construct complex units that contain other

5

complex units of the same type (*this is the cat that chased the rat that ate the malt that lay in the house that Jack built*). Because they are recursive, these rules can create infinitely long and complex sentences. The rules are called *syntax*. By combining meaningful symbols in a structured, hierarchical way, syntax allows us to communicate about our plans, our beliefs, our hopes and fears, and our procedure for replacing a timing belt in a 1999 Toyota pickup truck.

So the skirted figure in step 2 of Figure 1.1 is doing two things: (1) selecting the right words for the concepts that make up the sub-parts of our idea; and (2) selecting the right combination of rules to stick the words together so that they add up to the idea she's trying to get across. The syntactic rule system is what lets us encode and understand the differences between *a dog is barking* and *a dog that is barking* and *a barking dog* and *there is a barking dog* and *there is a dog that is barking* and *the dog that is barking is barking* and *a barking dog is barking* and *a barking dog that is barking is barking* . . . and so on.

Compare the following two strings of words:

(1)   The dog that is barking

(2)   The dog is barking.

The only difference between them, word-wise, is that the first group of words has one more word in it than the second. Nonetheless, they mean fundamentally different things to an English speaker: the second one is a complete sentence describing an event that is happening right now, while the first one is a phrase that refers to a particular being in the world – a noun phrase – but it is not a complete sentence.

Now compare these two strings of words:

(3)   *Is dog the barking that

(4)   *Is dog the barking.

Here and throughout this book we will use the asterisk symbol * in front of examples to indicate that they are ill-formed, or *ungrammatical* in the linguist's sense. (In this use, the symbol is called a "star.") Examples marked with a * sound funny. It's not that they are stylistically disfavored, like *ain't* or *Where did the cockroach run to?* They are simply not produced by the linguistic system of a speaker of English.

These two strings are made up of exactly the same words as the first two, and differ in exactly the same way, word-wise – (3) has one more word in it than (4). However, the extra word – "that" – has much less effect in these two strings of words than in the first two: both of them are just gibberish, with or without the "that." You can recognize that the individual words mean something, but it's hard to tell whether the whole string of words means anything at all, let alone whether (3) means something different from (4). This is the effect of the second part of the encryption system. It is the way the words are put together – their syntax – that makes the sequences in (1) and (2) so different from the sequences in (3) and (4).

We'll learn more about both parts of the system as we go along, and how the parts interact, but for now, let's get back to our central question for this chapter. What's the problem with defining a "word" as "the minimal unit of speech with its own meaning"?

1.3 Wordhood: The Whole Kit and Caboodle

1.3.1 Minimal units with meaning that are smaller than "words"

Here's the problem: there are many cases where an "ultimate minimal element of speech having a meaning" is *smaller* than the units we put spaces around when we're writing or talking slowly, i.e. the ultimate minimal unit of meaning can be smaller than the things we normally refer to as "words." Let's take a fairly straightforward case first. Read the sentences below aloud to yourself:

(5) a. I'm mad at you.
  b. Don't take candy from strangers.
  c. Why couldn't you carry it more carefully?
  d. You aren't going out dressed like that, are you?
  e. You're not going out dressed like that, are you?

Exercise 1.3 What is it about these sentences that poses a problem for defining "word" as an "ultimate minimal unit of speech having a meaning"?

In each of (5)a–e, it should be clear that there is an element that is surrounded by space on both sides (and that can be pronounced as a word on its own), but that single element contains two concepts – two units of meaning. That is, as pronounced (and written), they count as single words, but they are combinations of two elements as far as meaning is concerned. The items in question in (5)a–e, plus several other common examples, are listed in (6):

(6)   I'm, don't, couldn't, aren't, you're, he's, they've, we're . . .

Of course, you might argue, these aren't true counterexamples to the definition, because they are **contractions**, squeezed-together versions of two real words, both of which constitute minimal units of speech with meaning in their own right. *I'm* corresponds to *I am*, *don't* is *do not*, *you're* is *you are*, *aren't* is *are not*, etc. On some level, then, these are truly separate words, and this is reflected in that they *can* be pronounced as separate words. At some point during linguistic processing and before actual pronunciation (in panel 2 in Figure 1.1), the two words get pushed together and are pronounced as a single unit. In order to make the OED definition match up to our everyday sense of "word," then, it needs to be altered. What if we say that a "word" isn't *always* a sequence of sounds that is pronounced separately (an "ultimate minimal element of speech"), but rather, it's a phonological unit that *could* be pronounced as a separate sequence of sounds, as we did in our third definition revision above? Then in the sentences above, *n't*, *'re*, and *'m* would count as words, because they could have been pronounced *not*, *are* and *am* instead.

If we make that move, we take care of another troublesome class of words: *compounds*, words made up of two words in combination. Some good examples are *homeowner, blackbird, man-eater, greenhouse, overhead, pickpocket*, etc.

This revision isn't enough, however. Contractions and compounds are not the only ways that two meanings, attached to two sets of sounds, can be packaged up into a single word. Consider the word *dog*, which is a word that satisfies the definition: none of the possible minimal units contained within the word (*d, do, o, og, g*) have any meaning of their own (or no meaning that contributes to the meaning of the whole), so *dog* is a minimal unit of speech with its own meaning – it doesn't get any of its meaning from some smaller unit within it. Now, what about the word *dogs*? Its overall meaning appears to be made up of two elements: the word *dog* that we just saw, plus a **suffix** -*s*. As a speaker of English, you will know that the -*s* suffix, applied to **nouns**, indicates plurality – it means, roughly, "more than one X," where X is the noun it's attached to. In the dictionary, that could even be its definition, like this:

-*s*: More than one X (where X is the noun -*s* is attached to)

So here we have a sound unit, -*s*, which has its own meaning, PLURAL, and yet it's certainly not anything that we would call a "word" on its own – it can't be pronounced by itself in answer to a question, for example:

(7) *Jack*: How many of them did you see?
    Jill: * S. (*intended meaning*, "More than one.")

Of course, any suffix with a regular meaning falls into this category. In (8) we see some groups of words with prefixes and suffixes, whose meanings are regular combinations of the meanings of their various parts:

(8) a. iconic, acrobatic, idealistic, photographic, idyllic, robotic
    b. writing, hammering, presenting, kissing, analyzing, shivering, thinking
    c. bendable, breakable, manageable, loveable, fixable
    d. unbeaten, unhappy, un-American, unwanted, undefined, unremarkable
    e. writer, gardener, clipper, timer, greeter, cleaner, washer, dryer

---

Exercise 1.4 Based on these lists of words, see if you can come up with a definition for each of the affixes -*ic*, -*ing*, -*able*, *un*- and -*er* shown in (8)a–e, on the model of the definition given above for -*s*.

So, there are minimal sound sequences that have meaning that cannot stand on their own. Such sound sequences are not words as we use the term in everyday language – we don't write them with spaces on either side, like this: *dog s, icon ic, bend able* – nor, if we are spacing "words" apart and speaking slowly, do we include pauses between the pieces.

> **phonology,** *n.* From the Greek roots *phono-,* "voice, sound" and *-logy* "saying, speaking." 1. The study of spoken sounds. 2. The system of sounds in a language. **phonological,** *adj.* relating to phonology.

A *phonological word* is sequence of sounds which is identified as a unit on the basis of how it is pronounced – a collection picked out by the phonology of a language. *Can't, bendable* and *dogs* are phonological words.

1.3.2 Phonological words that don't carry any meaning whatever

In addition to the problem posed by affixes, above, there's another problem for the definition we're considering, although examples are somewhat harder to come by. Consider the following phrases:

(9) a. Jill took it all, *kit and caboodle*
    b. Jack walked *to and fro*
    c. If I *had my druthers*, the party would be on Saturday.
    d. The responses *ran the gamut* from brilliant to insane.

While it's clear to most speakers of English what the phrases *kit and caboodle, to and fro, have (one's) druthers*, and *run the gamut* mean (respectively, "everything," "back and forth," "get one's way," and "vary as widely as possible"), hardly any speakers know what the words *caboodle, fro, druthers*, or *gamut* mean in these expressions (no one would ever say "Do you like John's druthers?" or "She made it clear she wanted the caboodle."). Perhaps a guess can be made about the meaning of *fro*, since the phrase is so much like *back and forth* in structure and meaning: it seems like it must mean the same thing as *forth*. Yet, *to and forth* is nonsensical, and *forth* in other uses cannot be replaced by *fro*. Who ever heard of a knight going fro on a quest? Yet, *fro, caboodle*, etc. clearly are phonological words, shown by the fact that they can be pronounced, and are written, with spaces on either side. Essentially, what these examples show is that there can be phonological words which don't have a meaning associated with them at all, but only acquire meaning in conjunction with other phonological words. According to the OED definition, however, *kit and caboodle* is one "word," as it is a minimal unit of speech having a meaning. Do you agree?

It's not simply that there are some phonological words that have no meaning. There's an enormous class of expressions made up of several phonological words that do have meanings but whose meanings have nothing to do with the meaning of the whole expression. Consider the examples in (10):

(10) a. Bill *kicked the bucket* last night.
  b. The promotion is a real *feather in her cap*.
  c. Fred was suffering from an attack of *the green-eyed monster*.
  d. He wouldn't stop complaining, but he was *flogging a dead horse*.

There's no actual, or even metaphorical, bucket involved in (a), no feather, monster or horse in (b), (c) and (d). These phrases are **idioms**, expressions whose meaning must be learned by rote, just as one would learn the meaning of *pith* or *reimburse*. As they occur within these expressions, these phonological words have no meaning associated with them at all: the only meaning around is associated with the larger phrase of which they form a part. Since these phrases are minimal units of meaning, but are composed of many smaller, easily identifiable phonological words – minimal units of speech – they too show that "word" cannot be defined as something that correlates a minimal unit of speech with a minimal unit of meaning.

1.4 Two Kinds of Words

There's an easy way out of this dilemma. On one view, the meaning of "word" has mainly to do with semantics – the part of the definition that refers to the "minimal meaningful unit," that is, an element of the list of sound–meaning correspondences that is one of the two fundamental elements of language. The other, more everyday interpretation of the meaning of "word" has mainly to do with **phonology**: the fact that we call whatever we can pronounce in isolation a "word." The latter we have simply labeled: *phonological word*. We'll learn some of the properties that English requires of its phonological words in Chapter 2. The former, the true *minimal meaningful unit*, which includes affixes, like -*s* and *un*-, and idioms like *kick the bucket*, we will call *listemes*.

11

Listemes are often equivalent to what linguists call *morphemes*. We'll learn more about morphemes soon, and discuss why in this volume we distinguish listemes from morphemes. Another technical word that has a related meaning is *lexeme*. It could be useful to look these terms up in several different linguistic encyclopedias, dictionaries, or glossaries and compare their definitions and uses.

Why "listemes"? Since these sound–meaning combinations are *arbitrary*, the connection must be *listed* in the speaker's (your) head somewhere. We know that listemes are arbitrary because languages use different words for the same concept (as we saw in the names *perro, dog, chien,* and *chu'u* for the concept DOG, above). Indeed, any group of people – say, a children's secret club – could just get together and decide: "We won't call this a *dog* anymore, it's now a *spimble*." Similarly, while it would be considerably more difficult to stick to, a secret club could equally decide that they wouldn't make plurals with -*s* anymore; rather, they'd use -*int*. ("Mom! Where's my box of colored pencilint?") Ferdinand de Saussure called this property *the arbitrariness of the sign* (Saussure, [1916] 1959). Another way of putting it is that there is no "right" name for any concept, except what speakers of a language happen to agree on. This list of sound–meaning connections is what learners of second languages spend hours memorizing, and it's what dictionary makers try to replicate. (Look in any college or unabridged dictionary. It includes not only phonological words *per se*, but also many affixes and idioms: there'll be an entry for -*ed*, one for *un-*, one for -*ing*, etc.). This book is about phonological words and listemes, and their love–hate relationship.

1.5 The Anatomy of a Listeme

Stop again. Before reading any further, make a list of the *minimum* amount of information you think it is necessary to know in order to know the (most common meaning of the) word *nice* and use it like an English speaker. (No looking in the dictionary, now. What do *you* know about it? Imagine you had to explain this word to someone learning English so that they could use it in speech.)

Exercise 1.5   Make a list of the minimum amount of information it is necessary to know in order to "know" the word *nice*.

Here are some things that all English speakers know about *nice*:

1   **Pronunciation.** You know how to pronounce it. A set of instructions for pronouncing the word *nice* might go like this: First, press the tip of your tongue to the roof of your mouth behind the tongue, blocking off all air exiting through the mouth Create a sound by allowing air to escape through your nose while simultaneously tightening your vocal folds so that the air passing over them causes them to vibrate. Then, continuing to vibrate your vocal cords, open your mouth with your tongue almost flat, allowing air to escape. Raise your tongue up and forward somewhat, vibrating your vocal cords all along. Finally, bring your tongue nearly all the way to the top of your mouth behind the teeth, creating a narrow opening. Stop vibrating your vocal cords and allow air to pass through the opening, making a hissing noise as it does so. (Isn't it lucky we don't have to have this kind of instruction to learn to talk? In any case, it's clear that all of this is information you know about *nice*.)

2   **Meaning.** You know what it means: something like "pleasant, agreeable."

3   **Category.** You know that it is an **adjective**. That is to say, even if you've never heard the word *adjective*, you know that *nice* can modify nouns (*a nice picture*). *Adjective* is just a term that means roughly "a word that can modify a noun." Speakers of some dialects of English also use it as an adverb, to modify verbs (*he sings nice*), so if you speak such a dialect, you can list "adverb" next to "adjective" as something that you know about *nice*.

4   **Other forms.** You know that it consists of a single, stressed syllable, and hence that it has a **comparative** form *nicer*, and a **superlative** *nicest*. (This is not true of all adjectives: compare *nicer* to the comparative form of *aware*: *more aware*, not **awarer*). If you speak a dialect like Standard American English that doesn't allow *nice* as an adverb, you can also list the adverbial form *nicely* as something you know about *nice*.

How much of the above was in your list? You might have spent the most time on 2, and you might have omitted to mention any of 1, 3, and 4 entirely. Nonetheless, anyone who speaks English and has the word *nice* in their vocabulary certainly knows all of the above. All of this information must be in your head somewhere.

In traditional linguistic study, the information in 1, about pronunciation, is part of **phonology**. In 2, the information about meaning is part of **semantics**. In 3, the information about category is part of **syntax**. And finally in 4, the information about affixes and the internal structure of the word is **morphology**. When a child (or anyone) learns a new listeme, they learn (or figure out) at least some information from all of the above categories. They *have* to; that's what it means to learn a word.

1.6 What *Don't* You Have to Learn When You're Learning a Word?

Many of you might know a great deal more about the word *nice*. For instance, I'm fairly sure that everyone reading this textbook knows how to *spell* the word nice. Stop and consider a moment, however. Is it necessary to know how to spell a word to "know" it? Consider a 5-year-old, who can't read or write. After hearing his mother read *Jack and the Beanstalk*, he says, "That was a nice story." He certainly can't *spell* the word "nice," but would you say he doesn't know the word "nice"? It seems clear that he *does* know it, enough to pronounce it correctly and use it accurately.

Some of you might know something about the history of *nice*. It was borrowed by English speakers from Old French in about 1300 AD, and originally meant "stupid or foolish," which is what it meant at the time in Old French. Over the years, it went through many permutations of meaning: from "foolish" to "loose-mannered, wanton," and from there to "lazy, indolent, slothful." From "lazy" it permuted to "not able to endure much, delicate," and thence to "over-refined." Then it was a short step to meaning "fastidious, difficult to please," which became, "precise, finely discriminating," which became "refined," and, applied to food, "dainty, appetizing," which finally led to our modern sense, "agreeable, pleasant" (with several side-shoots of meaning that I haven't mentioned).

In Old French, *nice* had developed over the years from the Latin word *nescius*. *Nescius* in Latin was originally a contraction of the phrase *ne scire*, "not to know" (hence, "stupid, foolish"). The Latin verb *scire*, meaning "to know," is also the root of the English word *science*, as well as *prescient, conscientious, omniscient,* and *conscious*, although these were borrowed by English at a much later date than *nice* was.

Some of you might know that *nice*, while quite a nice word, is used so frequently that some sophisticated writers of English consciously try to avoid it: a sentence that is stylistically strong and descriptively gripping doesn't usually have the word *nice* in it. If you're a speaker of a dialect of English which allows *nice* as an adverb, as in *She sings nice*, you may also know that Standard English – the English you are expected to use in written work at school or in professional settings – does not permit *nice* to be used as an adverb.

The above information, while interesting and true, is not part of what anyone automatically learns when they're first learning the word *nice*. We'll be learning about both types of knowledge in this book: the complex information about words that all English speakers carry around in their heads, and the historical and social information about words that is the result of accidents of history and language change. The former information tells us about the nature of our minds, giving us a window onto the computation that goes into the utterance of the simplest English sentence; the latter information can give us an insight into the history and culture of the people who have spoken and written English over the past 10 centuries. We'll be talking about both kinds of information, but we'll be taking care not to get them mixed up. The first kind of information belongs to the study of psychology of language, and the latter to the study of the history of language. Keep the distinction in mind as we go on. If you're wondering which category a certain kind of information falls into, ask yourself: is this something that children who speak English know?

The study of the psychology of language and study of the history of language are connected by the study of the *sociology* of language, the study of how and why people end up speaking the way they do. Psycholinguistics, historical linguistics and sociolinguistics are all subdisciplines of linguistics, areas in which a linguist can choose to specialize.

1.7 A Scientific Approach to Language

In this book, we will be studying English words in the same way an entomologist would study a species of insect, the same way a geologist would study layers of rock, the same way a meteorologist would study weather patterns. We will look at English, describe what we see, and then try to develop an analysis that explains any patterns or regularities that we find.

We won't be concerned, in our study, with "correct" or "proper" ways of speaking and writing English, except insofar as they are relevant to our discussion of how people actually do speak or write. Teaching English speakers to adhere to certain rules of grammar, or punctuation, or style, is undertaken by people interested in a *prescriptive* approach to English, who are interested in ensuring conformity among speakers of English for some purpose. We here taking a *descriptive* approach: trying to discuss what English speakers actually do, not what they "should" do.

If you are a second language learner of English, this book will be useful in your study of English: it is full of information about what native English speakers actually do when they're speaking English. If you are a native speaker of English, you will find that this book tells you about *how* you speak English, and something about *why* modern English is the way it is – but it won't teach you anything about how you *ought* to speak English. We'll leave that up to the language mavens and your own good judgment.

With those preliminaries completed, onward to our first topic: the sounds of English.

Appendix: Basic Grammatical Terms

Although this book is intended for people with no background in linguistics, I have assumed that most of you will know terms such as "noun," "verb," "subject," "suffix" and "prefix" already, or at least have a general idea of how they are used. Often these terms are used more generally or loosely in everyday speech than we will be using them here, so here are some rough-and-ready definitions and a few problem sets to help cement your familiarity with a few basic terms. These definitions also show up in the glossary at the end of the book, but you should be sure you understand them fully now, before reading further:

Affix A covering term for both suffixes and prefixes.

Parts of speech Parts of speech are also often called *syntactic categories*, or word classes. Just as we can say things like "The part of speech of *dog* is 'noun'," we could say "The syntactic category of *dog* is 'noun'." All words have a part of speech – sometimes more than one. Here we'll look at just a few of the most basic; for more discussion, see Chapter 6.

Nouns are often defined as "people, places or things," and verbs as "actions, states or states of being," but this is definitely not adequate for our purposes. For instance, *attraction* is a noun, but it would be pretty crazy to call it a person, place or thing! Similarly, an *incantation* is an action, but it would be pretty crazy to call it a verb. Parts of speech are not defined by their meaning, but by their distribution – where they show up in a sentence, and what kinds of other words or affixes can go with them.

Noun A listeme that:
- can be used as the subject of a sentence;
- can occur immediately following determiners (a.k.a. "articles") such as *the, one, some, any, this, a, many*, etc., or possessive pronouns such as *his, her, our* etc., with no other word in the phrase (see Chapter 6 for more discussion of these);
- can usually be marked with the plural suffix *-s*;
- can be modified with adjectives such as *pretty, happy, lucky, fortuitous*.

Verb A listeme that
- can be marked for past tense (usually by putting *-ed* on it);
- can be suffixed with *-ing*;
- can be modified with words like *again, sometimes, often*;
- can occur immediately following auxiliaries, like *can, may, might, would, will*; also after negation (*not, can't, won't*), or the infinitive marker *to*.

Adjective A listeme that
- can appear between a determiner and its noun, as in *the lucky cat*, modifying the noun;
- often ends in *-y, -ish, -ous*; often can be prefixed with *un-*;
- can be modified by words like *very* or *extremely*, as in *the very lucky cat*.

Adverb A listeme that
- can modify a verb;

- often ends in *-ly*;
- can be modified by words like *very* or *extremely*, as in *extremely quickly*.

Prefix   A smaller-than-phonological-word-sized listeme that attaches to the beginning of another listeme: *un-* in *unhappy* is a prefix, *re-* in *refill* is a prefix, *dis-* in *disentangle* is a prefix.

Suffix   A smaller-than-phonological-word-sized listeme that attaches to the end of another listeme: *-s* in *dogs* is a suffix; *-ed* in *patted* is a suffix; *-ion* in *attraction* is a suffix.

Study Problems

1. Identify all the suffixes and prefixes in the following sentences. If you think something might be an affix but you're not sure, explain why you think it might be and also what it is that makes you unsure:

    a. It is often written that *antidisestablishmentarianism* is the longest word in the English language, but it isn't.

    b. Calamities are of two kinds: misfortune to ourselves, and good fortune to others. (Ambrose Bierce)

    c. If you want to know what God thinks of money, just look at the people he gave it to. (Dorothy Parker)

    d. It is difficult to produce a television documentary that is both incisive and probing when every twelve minutes one is interrupted by twelve dancing rabbits singing about toilet paper. (Rod Sterling.)

2. In each quote below, identify the nouns, verbs and adjectives that are employed. Again, if you think a particular word is being used as a noun, verb or adjective but are not sure, explain why you think it might be, and what it is that makes you unsure.

    a. The way to write American music is simple. All you have to do is be an American and then write any kind of music you wish. (Virgil Thompson)

    b. Do not, for one repulse, forego the purpose that you resolved to effect! (William Shakespeare, *The Tempest*)

    c. Men who are unhappy, like men who sleep badly, are always proud of the fact. (Bertrand Russell)

    d. It is a common delusion that you make things better by talking about them. (Dame Rose Macaulay)

3. Identify whether each of the following words is a noun, verb, adjective, or adverb. Some belong, or can belong, to more than one part of speech. For each word, write a sentence in which you illustrate it being used as that part of speech. If you identify it as having two or more parts of speech, write two or more sentences, one illustrating each part of speech you think it has:

publicly, love, government, bank, take, smart, sympathy, realistic, particularly, always, maturity, shelter, elegant, smooth, fast.

4. Two sets of English pronouns, the *object* pronouns and the *possessive* pronouns, are given below:

	Object pronouns		*Possessive pronouns*	
1st	me	us	my	our
2nd	you	you	your	your
3rd	him/her/it	them	his/her/its	their

Now consider the following subset (1st and 2nd person forms only) of another group of English pronouns, the *reflexive* pronouns:

	Reflexive pronouns	
1st	myself	ourselves
2nd	yourself	yourselves

a. These reflexive pronouns are made up of two parts. What are they? Describe them using the name of the appropriate family of pronouns given above.

b. State your description of the reflexive pronouns as a rule: "To create a reflexive pronoun, put a _____ pronoun together with the noun _____."

c. Following your rule, what should the (four) English 3rd person reflexive pronouns be?

d. What are the actual 3rd person reflexive pronouns in your dialect of English?

e. Some dialects of English use the reflexive pronouns you created in (c), but they are not the forms used in Standard American English. What would a prescriptive approach to language have to say about the forms in (c)? What about a descriptive approach? Which dialect of English is more "logical" in its formation of reflexive pronouns?

19

    f.   Describe some prescriptive attitudes to English that you have encountered, discussing their pros and cons.

Further Reading

On modern linguistics and what it's about:
Pinker, Steven (1994) *The Language Instinct*. New York: W. Morrow and Co.

On what modern linguistics is *not* about:
Bauer, Laurie and Trudgill, Peter (1998) *Language Myths*. London: Penguin Books.
Wardhaugh, Ronald (1998) *Proper English: Myths and Misunderstandings about Language*. Oxford: Blackwell.

On Saussure and the arbitrariness of the sign:
Holdcroft, David (1991) *Saussure: Signs, System, and Arbitrariness*. Cambridge: Cambridge University Press.
Saussure, Ferdinand de ([1916] 1959) *Course in General Linguistics*. Charles Bally and Albert Reidlinger, eds. Wade Baskin, trans. New York: Philosophical Library.

General useful reference:
Crystal, David (1995) *The Cambridge Encyclopedia of the English Language*. Cambridge: Cambridge University Press.
Huddleston, Rodney D. and Pullum, Geoffrey K. (2002) *The Cambridge Grammar of English*. Cambridge: Cambridge University Press.

2

Sound and Fury: English Phonology

/ˈsawnd ən ˈfjuɹij: ˈɪŋglɪʃ fəˈnalədʒij/

In this chapter, we look at English sound patterns. We learn about the distinct sounds that make up words (*phonemes*), and the mechanisms in the vocal tract that are employed to produce them. We learn a system of writing that can be used to accurately represent pronunciation, the *International Phonetic Alphabet*. We think about how sounds group into families, and consider one example of sound change from the prehistory of English. This groundwork will allow us, in future chapters, to understand restrictions on phonological words in English, to look at other historical changes that have altered the pronunciation of English words in the past, and to discuss differences between dialects of English spoken today. It will also enable us to analyze other kinds of processes in English words, when we look at *morphology*.

2.1 English Spelling and English Pronunciation

The first thing we have to do, when considering the pronunciation of English words, is find a way to represent their pronunciation accurately in print (since you can't hear me talking). English spelling is notoriously bad at this: probably, at least once in your life as a literate English speaker, you have mispronounced a word in speech that you learned from a book; that is, you've probably used a spelling pronunciation. (I certainly have.) The mismatch between spelling and pronunciation is the reason that English spelling is a hard thing to master.

> **orthography,** *n.* From Greek, via French and Latin, *orth-* "right, correct" [related to Sanskrit *urdhva,* "high, upright"], and *-graph,* "scratch, write" [English *carve* is also related to *-graph*]. A writing or spelling system.

Just consider the following sets of words:

(1) a. their   they're   there
     b. two   to   too
     c. right   write   rite
     d. prints   prince
     e. threw   through
     f. who's   whose
     g. principle   principal

Each set is pronounced the same way, but they are spelled differently: if you were an alien, or a child, looking at written English, you might reasonably surmise that they should sound different. And of course, there are similar problems in the other direction: the same spelling can be pronounced differently in different words:

(2) a. lead (*a metal*)   lead   (*to precede*)
     b. dove (*a bird*)   dove   (*jumped into water headfirst*)
     c. does (*the auxiliary verb*)   does   (*more than one female deer*)
     d. wound (*an injury*)   wound (*wrapped around*)

There's also a problem with the numbers of letters used to represent sounds. Often, a single sound needs two letters to represent it – the "th" and "ng" in *thing* both are two letters used for a single sound, as is the "ea" in *read* or the "oo" in *good.* Many letters are not pronounced in certain words – the "g" and the "h" in *through,* the *p* in *psychology,* the "b" in *numb, thumb, bomb* . . . In general, English spelling is only a fairly loose representation of pronunciation.

This fact about English orthography is very well known – everyone who has learned to write English knows it. Gerard Nolst Trenité, a Dutch teacher of English, wrote the following remarkable poem in 1922 to illustrate this point. Try reading it aloud to yourself. All the rhymes except one are valid in American English; if you hit a word you don't recognize, or that you don't believe rhymes, look it up in a good English dictionary.

Exercise 2.1 Read this poem aloud. Which rhyme only works in British English?

The Chaos
Dearest creature in creation, study English pronunciation.
I will teach you, in my verse, sounds like corpse, corps, horse, and
   worse.
I will keep you, Suzy, busy; make your head with heat grow dizzy.
Tear in eye, your dress will tear. So shall I! Oh hear my prayer.
Just compare heart, beard, and heard, dies and diet, lord and word,
Sword and sward, retain and Britain. (Mind the latter, how it's written.)
Now I surely will not plague you with such words as plaque and ague.
But be careful how you speak: Say break and steak, but bleak and
   streak;
Cloven, oven, how and low; script, receipt, show, poem, and toe.
Hear me say, devoid of trickery, daughter, laughter, and Terpsichore,
Typhoid, measles, topsails, aisles; exiles, similes, and reviles;
Scholar, vicar, and cigar; solar, mica, war and far;
One, anemone, Balmoral; kitchen, lichen, laundry, laurel;
Gertrude, German, wind and mind; scene, Melpomene, mankind.

Billet does not rhyme with ballet; bouquet, wallet, mallet, chalet.
Blood and flood are not like food, nor is mould like should and would.
Viscous, viscount, load and board; toward, to forward, to reward.
And your pronunciation's OK when you correctly say croquet,
Rounded, wounded, grieve and sieve, friend and fiend, alive and live.

Ivy, privy, famous; clamour – and enamour – rhyme with hammer.
River, rival, tomb, bomb, comb; doll and roll and some and home.
Stranger does not rhyme with anger, neither does devour with
   clangour.
Souls but foul, haunt but aunt; font, front, wont, want, grand, and grant,
Shoes, goes, does. Now first say finger, and then singer, ginger, linger,
Real, zeal, mauve, gauze, gouge and gauge; marriage, foliage, mirage,
   and age.

Query does not rhyme with very, nor does fury sound like bury.
Dost, lost, post and doth, cloth, loth. Job, nob, bosom, transom, oath.
Though the differences seem little, we say actual but victual.
Refer does not rhyme with deafer. Foeffer does, and zephyr, heifer.
Mint, pint, senate and sedate; dull, bull, and George ate late.
Scenic, Arabic, Pacific; science, conscience, scientific.

Liberty, library, heave and heaven, Rachel, ache, moustache, eleven.
We say hallowed, but allowed, people, leopard, towed, but vowed.
Mark the differences, moreover, between mover, cover, clover;
Leeches, breeches, wise, precise; chalice, but police and lice;
Camel, constable, unstable; principle, disciple, label.

Petal, panel, and canal; wait, surprise, plait, promise, pal.
Worm and storm, chaise, chaos, chair; senator, spectator, mayor.
Tour, but our and succour, four; gas, alas, and Arkansas.
Sea, idea, Korea, area; psalm, Maria, but malaria.
Youth, south, southern, cleanse and clean; doctrine, turpentine, marine.

Compare alien with Italian, dandelion and battalion.
Sally with ally, yea, ye, eye, I, ay, aye, whey, and key.
Say aver, but ever, fever; neither, leisure, skein, deceiver.
Heron, granary, canary, crevice and device and aerie.

So much for English orthography as a precise representation of pronunciation. (It is worth noting that although English orthography does not always directly reflect pronunciation, that does not necessarily make it a "bad" writing system. We will discuss this question more when we look at morphology (Chapters 4 and 5) and etymology (Chapter 9).)

In order to consider the phonological structure of words properly, we need a writing system which will allow us to represent English pronunciation accurately. We will use the International Phonetic Alphabet (**IPA**) to represent the individual sounds which make up English words. The IPA is a symbol system developed by linguists to represent the pronunciation of any human language. (We will mostly consider the symbols that represent the sounds of American English in this chapter; other languages and other dialects of English make use of different IPA symbols for sounds that are not present in American English.)

I'll introduce this new alphabet in groups of sounds according to the parts of the vocal tract involved in producing them, and the way in which they are produced. This will be useful in our discussions later, because it turns out that as the sounds of a language change over time, they tend to change in groups picked out by a particular pronunciation characteristic that they share. Similarly, it is families of sounds, not individual sounds, that are affected by the sound rules of a language.

2.2 The Voice Box

Before we get to the actual sounds and symbols, however, let's briefly consider the instrument that produces the actual sound that constitutes an individual's unique voice: the **larynx**, also called the **voice box**. The larynx is a triangular structure of cartilage situated at the exit of the windpipe (trachea), separating the windpipe from the oral cavity. (The triangle points forward, the tip making a small bump on the front of the neck of some men – the "Adam's apple"). Its crucial features are two flat, thin strips of tissue that are stretched across it like rubber bands, from front to back (see Figure 2.1), the vocal cords, or "vocal folds." At the back are muscles that can act to tighten or relax the vocal cords. When you're not speaking, your vocal folds are spread apart, as in Figure 2.1a, allowing air to pass freely back and forth as you inhale and exhale. When you're speaking, however, the folds are tensed and brought together, as in Figure 2.1b – but not too tightly. Air coming up from your lungs pushes on the closed vocal folds, and when a certain pressure is built up, they flap open. The air rushes out, causing a sudden pressure decrease, upon which they flap closed again, then the pressure builds up, they flap open, and so on, approximately 100 times per second, more or less.

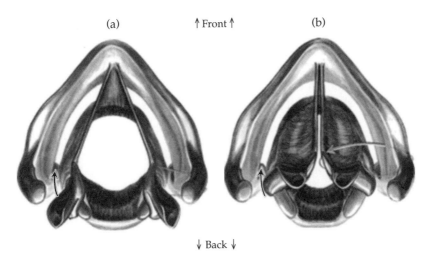

Figure 2.1 Larynx and vocal cords, top view

The drop in pressure associated with movement in a gas or liquid is called the *Bernoulli effect*, and it's responsible for the lift that holds an airplane up, the way your shower curtain swings inward when you turn the water on, and the rapidity with which your vocal cords snap shut after being blown open.

The vibrations in the air caused by the opening and closing of the vocal folds create the sound of your voice. This works in exactly the same way that your lips quickly flap open and closed when you're making a raspberry, and the same way that air escaping from the neck of a rubber balloon creates a buzzing noise. You can stretch the neck of the balloon to change the pitch of the buzz – this increases the frequency of the flapping rubber, which increases the frequency of the vibrations it creates. (If you play the trumpet, you know very well how this works – trumpeters do the same thing by compressing their vibrating lips.) A higher frequency corresponds to a higher pitch. In the same way, you change the pitch of your voice by moving a part of your voice box so that the vocal cords are stretched thinner and tighter, and flap faster. (Since men's voice boxes are somewhat bigger and their vocal cords somewhat thicker than women's, the cords flap more slowly, so the pitch of a typical man's voice is lower than the pitch of a typical woman's, just as a cello makes lower notes than a violin.)

If you touch your fingers to your Adam's apple – the point of the triangle in Figures 2.1a and b – and say *aaa . . . aaaa . . . aaaa*, you will feel the vibration produced by your vocal cords starting and stopping. This vibration is called *voicing*, and during speech you manipulate it to produce different kinds of consonants. (Try changing the pitch of your voice, too. In order to stretch the cords to make a higher noise, you move the front of your voice box upwards. Sing a scale and feel it move.)

When you were a child, you might have sometimes talked in a funny, strained voice, that can sound a little scary – it could be used to imitate a creaking door, or the way a ghost's voice might sound. That voice, called *creaky voice*, is produced by manipulating your vocal cord muscles so that just the front half vibrates, giving a sort of strange, staccato voicing vibration.

Now we are ready to see what the vocal tract does with that buzzing to turn it into the sounds of speech – the **phonemes** of English.

2.3   The Building Blocks of Words I: Consonants in the IPA

Consonants are produced when the airflow through the mouth is partially or completely obstructed. Some mobile part of your mouth moves to a certain position and blocks the airflow. Partial obstruction results in sustainable sounds, since airflow can be maintained, although it's restricted. These sustainable consonants are named **fricatives** (like the *s* sound in *sing*), **liquids** (like the *l* sound in *liquid*), or **glides** (like the *w* sound in *wave*), after the way they sound. Complete obstruction of the oral cavity produces **stop** consonants (like the *p* sound in *pet*), which are generally not sustainable sounds, since the oral cavity is, momentarily, completely blocked off. The exception is when air is allowed to flow through the nose, even though the mouth is completely obstructed; this produces the sustainable **nasal** stops (like *m* in *mother*). There are also a couple of combination stop/fricative consonants, called **affricates** (like the *ch* sound in *church*). Stop, affricate and fricative consonants involve a greater degree of obstruction of the oral cavity than liquids or glides; they are consequently called **obstruents**. Liquids, nasals, and glides are called **sonorants**. The six groups of consonants are illustrated in (3). We'll look at each of them in turn in a moment.

(3)   *Types of English consonants*

More obstruction of airflow			Example
		(oral) **stops**	*tall*
		affricates	*church*
	obstruents	**fricatives**	*sing*
	sonorants	**nasal stops**	*neither*
		liquids	*liquid*
Less obstruction of airflow		**glides**	*yell*

The mobile parts which create the crucial obstructions are the lips and different parts of the tongue. The lips and tongue are the **articulators**, and the different spots in the mouth at which they can create an

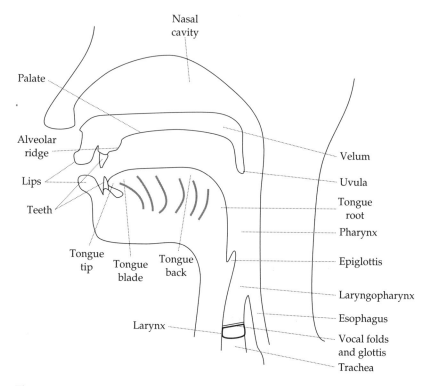

Figure 2.2 The vocal tract

obstruction are called **places of articulation**. Each distinct place of articulation creates a different consonant sound.

Exercise 2.2 Look at the diagram in Figure 2.2 as you're reading the next paragraph, and identify each of the parts as they're mentioned.

In English, obstructions can be created at the lips (**labial** consonants, like *b* in *boy*), at the teeth (**dental** consonants, like *th* in *thing*), just behind the teeth, at the **alveolar ridge** (**alveolar** consonants, like *d* in *dog*), or, farther back in the mouth, against the palate (**palatal** consonants, like *sh* in *shin*) and **velum** (**velar** consonants, like *g* in *goat*). The velum can also be lowered to allow air to pass through the **nasal cavity** and out the nose; this is how nasal consonants (and nasal vowels) are produced. We'll consider each of these places of articulation in turn.

> **consonant,** *n.* From Latin, via French, *con-* "together" + *sonāre* "to sound." An alphabetic or phonetic element other than a vowel. (Note also its adjectival meaning, "harmonious, in accord with.")

Consonants, then, are made up of several distinct features. They have a *manner* of articulation – the type of obstruction produced: fricative, liquid, glide or stop. They have a *place* of articulation – labial, dental, alveolar, palatal, or velar. Further, they can be produced while the vocal cords are buzzing, in which case they are *voiced*, or they can be produced without buzzing, by simply allowing the air to flow freely through the open larynx, in which case they are *voiceless*. Let's see how all this fits together to make the different consonant sounds of English.

2.3.1 Fricative consonants

Fricative consonants are the sounds created when airflow is restricted a great deal but not stopped completely. Air is escaping only through a small opening, and the resulting friction produces turbulence that gives these consonants a sort of hissing quality, hence their name. Table 2.1 gives the IPA symbol and the combination of articulators and voicing used to produce each of the fricatives of English, along with three example words in which the sound occurs.

> IPA symbols are enclosed between slashes, /.../, here and throughout the text, to differentiate them from normal English orthography.

To hear the difference voicing makes, make a long *sssssssssssss* noise. Without stopping, change to a *zzzzzzz* sound. Go back and forth, *sssszzssssszzzzsssszzz*. Notice that nothing changes in the position of your lips, teeth and tongue: the only difference is in whether the vocal cords are vibrating or not – put your finger on your Adam's apple and check it out. (You could also try putting your fingers in your ears while doing this – you can hear the voicing resonate inside your head.)

Table 2.1 Fricative consonants of English

Place, Articulator, Name	IPA symbols	Voicing	Example: word-initial	Example: word-medial	Example: word-final
Upper teeth, Lower lip, *Labiodental*	/v/	voiced	vine	ravel	of
	/f/	voiceless	fine	raffle	rough
Upper teeth, Tongue tip, *Interdental*	/ð/[1]	voiced	then	either	breathe
	/θ/[2]	voiceless	thin	ether	breath
Alveolar ridge, Tongue tip, *Alveolar*	/z/	voiced	zit	raisin	as
	/s/	voiceless	sit	racing	ass
Behind ridge, Tongue tip, lip rounding, *Palatal*	/ʒ/	voiced	—[3]	treasure	mirage
	/ʃ/[4]	voiceless	shuffle	ration	bush
Glottis,[5] *Glottal*	/h/	voiceless	half	behave	—

Notes

[1] This symbol is named "eth," or "edh" – the name of the symbol, of course, contains the voiced interdental fricative, not the voiceless one.

[2] This symbol is named "theta."

[3] This sound can occur at the beginnings of words in some other languages – English has even borrowed a couple of such words: *Dr. Zhivago, gendarme* – but no words that begin with /ʒ/ are native to English.

[4] This symbol is named "esh."

[5] The *glottis* is the name for the space between the vocal folds. The sound /h/ is produced without any closure anywhere in the mouth, just a small constriction of the vocal folds, giving it its breathy sound.

The palatal fricatives are two of the six English consonants that are produced with an additional articulation – they're pronounced with a distinct rounding of the lips. Try saying *shoe* to yourself, lingering over the initial voiceless palatal fricative, like a librarian

Table 2.2 Stop consonants of English

Place, Articulator, Name	IPA symbols	Voicing	Example: word- initial	Example: word- medial	Example: word- final
Upper and lower lips,	/b/	voiced	bile	rabid	mob
Labial	/p/	voiceless	pile	rapid	mop
Alveolar ridge,	/d/	voiced	den	adore	made
Tongue tip, *Alveolar*	/t/	voiceless	ten	attach	mate
Velum,	/g/	voiced	gum	bagging	dug
Tongue back, *Velar*	/k/	voiceless	come	backing	duck
Glottis *Glottal*	/ʔ/	voiceless	—	button	don't

shushing someone. Your lips are pushed forward and slightly rounded, right?

2.3.2 *Stop consonants (oral)*

In this group of sounds, the IPA symbols and the English spelling conventions match up almost one-to-one (see Table 2.2). Stops are formed when the passage of air from the lungs out through the mouth is completely blocked off at some point. (Stops are sometimes also called *plosives*.)

There's also a stop made with the vocal cords, just by shutting them off in the middle of a vowel sound. It doesn't occur too often in my dialect of standard American English, but it does show up now and then – in words like *button* or *fatten*, in the middle of the exclamation *uh-oh*, or at the end of the word *can't* in normal speech. It's written as /ʔ/ in IPA, and it is more widely used in other dialects of English, as we'll see.

31

2.3.3 Nasal stop consonants

These are all produced in exactly the same way as the voiced oral stops, above, but with the velum lowered, allowing air to escape out the nose. With the vocal cords vibrating, a sort of humming noise is produced. (There are no voiceless nasal consonants. With no vibration to produce a sound, a voiceless airflow out the nose sounds the same no matter what the place of articulation is. Try it and see: make an *mmmmm* sound, then stop the voicing and just let the air hiss out your nose – then do the same with an *ŋŋŋŋŋŋŋ* sound, like the last consonant in *sing*.) Nasal stops often lend a nasal quality to neighboring vowels, as the velum gets into the open position a little before the consonant is produced, and takes a moment to close again after the consonant is finished (see Table 2.3).

Table 2.3 Nasal stops of English

Place, Articulator, Name	IPA symbol	Voicing	Example: word-initial	Example: word-medial	Example: word-final
Upper and lower lips, *Labial*	/m/	voiced, nasal	**m**ow	re**m**ain	to**mb**
Alveolar ridge, Tongue tip, *Alveolar*	/n/	voiced, nasal	**kn**ow	i**n**ane	tu**n**e
Velum, Tongue back, *Velar*	/ŋ/[1]	voiced, nasal	—[2]	si**ng**able	to**ng**ue

Notes
[1] Called "eng" or "engma."
[2] Again, in English no words begin with this sound, but in some languages it is possible – a common Vietnamese name, for example, is Nguyen, pronounced /ŋwin/.

> The nasal stops are the consonants that sound funny when you
> have a cold and your nose is stuffed up. When your nose is
> stuffed up, airflow through the nasal passage is blocked, no mat-
> ter what you do with your velum. Consequently, you can't say
> something like *Lend me your pen* properly because all the nasals
> come out sounding like regular stops; you end up saying *Led be
> your ped.*

One thing that's important to understand about the velar nasal /ŋ/,
as in *sing*, is that it's a single sound, like /m/ or /n/. The spelling
system of English is confusing on this point, since it invariably represents the /ŋ/ sound with two letters, "ng." There is no "g" sound in
sing, in most dialects of English.

2.3.4 Affricates

In English, there are two consonants that are formed by combining a
stop and a fricative. These are called *affricates*. These sounds are produced by first pressing your tongue against the alveolar ridge, producing the /t/ portion of the affricate, and then sliding the tongue
back to the palate and producing the /ʃ/ portion. Try pronouncing
the voiceless affricate, usually spelled "ch," as in *church*, really slowly,
and you'll hear these two parts.

The affricates are two of the other six consonants that are produced
with lip-rounding – when you pronounce them, you push your lips
forward into a slightly rounded position. This is because the palatal
fricative part – the /ʃ/ and /ʒ/ part – is produced with lip-rounding.
The other two consonants in English with some rounding are the "r"
sound in words like *red*, and of course the "w" sound in words like
wet – see the next section on liquids and glides (see Table 2.4).

The affricate consonants are written with a curved line on top, join-
ing the two symbols together, to distinguish them from transcriptions
in which the two consonants which make them up occur separately.
For example, there are words where /t/ and /ʃ/ occur next to each
other, but are not part of the same consonant, as in the word *nutshell*.
Contrast that with the word *cello*, where the initial consonant is the
single affricate /t͡ʃ/. We'd transcribe *nutshell* like this, without the link-
ing line: /nʌtʃɛl/, and *cello* like this, using the line: /t͡ʃɛlow/.

Table 2.4 Affricate consonants of English

Place, Articulator, Name	IPA symbol	Voicing	Example: word-initial	Example: word-medial	Example: word-final
Behind ridge, Tongue tip (lip rounding), *Palatal*	/d͡ʒ/	voiced	**j**ump	ri**g**id	lo**dge**
	/t͡ʃ/	voiceless	**ch**ump	wre**tch**ed	la**tch**

2.3.5 *Liquids and glides*

Liquids and glides are consonants that are almost like **vowels**: /l/ as in *lateral* and /ɹ/ as in *ripper* are liquids, and the "y" and "w" sounds in *yell* and *water* are glides. Liquids involve considerably less airflow obstruction in the mouth than other consonants, and so these, like nasals, are nearly always voiced, since without obstruction, there wouldn't be enough turbulence to distinguish voiceless liquids.

Glides involve a small movement of the relevant articulator: the articulator (lips or tongue) starts out in one position which, if you held it longer, would produce a vowel sound, but it then quickly *glides* into another position. The vowel position is released so quickly that the resulting sound has consonantal qualities. Because of their close relationship to vowels, glides are sometimes called *semivowels*. (Remember "*A, e, i, o, u* and sometimes *y*"?)

The English liquid "r" is formed with the tongue blade, and has a secondary articulation as well: the lips are rounded, as with /ʃ/ and /ʒ/. In many dialects of English, "r" only occurs in the beginnings of syllables, but not at the ends – British English is like this, for instance. The syllable-final midwestern American English "r" in words like *bird, farm*, etc., is a comparatively rare sound cross-linguistically – a Spanish-style trilled "r" is much more usual. (This is why the IPA uses the regular right-side up /r/ for the trilled "r", and the odd upside-down /ɹ/ for the English kind.)

Table 2.5 Liquids and glides of English

IPA symbol	Place, Articulator, Name	Manner, Voicing	Example: word-initial	Example: word-medial	Example: word-final
/l/	Alveolar ridge, Tongue blade, *Lateral Alveolar*	liquid, voiced	lake	belly	pool
/ɹ/	Tongue blade (lip rounding), *Retroflex Alveolar*	liquid, voiced	rake	berry	poor
/j/	— Tongue blade, *Palatal*	glide, voiced	yet	million	—
/w/	— Lips, *Labial*	glide, voiced	wet	power	—

One of the most confusing things about the IPA for English-speaking beginners is that the IPA symbol for the initial sound in "you" (/j/) is the same as the English symbol for the initial sound in "jump." The initial sound in "jump" – a voiced palatal affricate – is written /d͡ʒ/ in IPA. Be careful not to get them mixed up! The "y" symbol stands for a particular kind of vowel in the IPA, but it's a vowel that isn't used in English at all – so there should never be a /y/ in any of the transcriptions you do in this book.

The /l/ sound is called "lateral" because air is allowed to escape around the *sides* of the tongue – say a long /llllllllllllll/ to yourself and you'll see that it's so. The /ɹ/ is called "retroflex" because for many speakers, the tip of the tongue is flexed slightly towards the back of the mouth – again, say a long /ɹɹɹɹɹɹɹɹɹ/ to yourself to feel this. (Some speakers produce the /ɹ/ not by retroflexing their tongue, but just by bunching it up – can you tell which you do?)

All the symbols for the consonants of English organized by manner and place of articulation are given on p. xiii, for quick reference.

2.4 Building Blocks II: Vowels and the IPA

The oral tract is much more open for vowels than for any consonant. Consequently, voiceless vowels are practically non-existent in the languages of the world: there's not enough obstruction in the mouth to make different sounds distinguishable just by using the airstream, as with voiceless consonants. Vowels are more like a vibrating volume of air in a container – a resonating chamber, like an organ pipe. Changing the shape of the container changes the sound produced by the vibrations, just the way a slide trombone player changes the sound of her instrument by pulling the slide in and out. Unlike the trombonist, though, we are able to change not just the size of our resonating chamber, but also its shape, by moving our jaw, tongue and lips into different positions. It is the different shapes of airspace that create the different vowels.

We use our large, muscular tongue to change the shape of our oral cavity and produce many subtly different sounds. The human tongue is a more mobile and precisely controlled one than most tongues in the animal kingdom. The fact that we stand upright, with our heads set squarely on top of our necks, rather than in front of our bodies, plays an important role in speech production as well: it means that our oral tract is a tube with an approximately 90° bend in it, which gives it unique acoustical properties. Animals with a shallower curve to their throats, and without a moldable, mobile tongue, cannot even begin to make the variety of oral sounds that we can, which is one reason why it is impossible to teach chimpanzees or dogs to use spoken human language. Chimps can do better with sign languages, as their hands are almost as mobile and precise as our own. Some animals, like parrots, can make a variety of sounds comparable to ours (though not by using their tongue), and they can be taught to produce good imitations of English words. Whether they can understand and use such sound patterns the way we do is, of course, a separate question.

2.4.1 *Vowel height and backness*

Exercise 2.3 Pronounce *tack, take, tech* and *teak* to yourself several times, and then just the four vowels by themselves. Try to sense the distinct way you position your tongue to produce each isolated vowel.

When you did Exercise 2.3, you may have noticed that your tongue is a little closer to the roof of your mouth for *take* than for *tack*, and a lot closer to the roof of your mouth for *teak* than for *tack*. Once crucial way that vowels can differ is in how *high* the body of the tongue is in the mouth. The vowel in *teak* is a high vowel, while the vowel in *tack* is a low vowel.

Now try it again with *goose* and *geese*, as well as *rote* and *rate*.

Exercise 2.4 Pronounce *goose, geese, rote* and *rate* to yourself several times, and then just the four vowels by themselves. Try to describe, in words, the distinct way you position the various parts of your mouth to produce each vowel.

One thing that you probably noticed is that for *goose* and *rote*, your lips are rounded, while for *geese* and *rate* they are not. That's not the only thing that's different, however. Try leaving your lips in an unrounded position (as for *rate*), and pronounce *rote* like that. Switch back and forth between *rote* (with unrounded lips) and *rate*.

The other thing that's changing in your mouth is how far forward the main body of your tongue is. Besides *height*, and *rounding*, vowels can differ in how far *front* or *back* they are. The vowel in *rate* is a front vowel, while the vowel in *rote* is a back vowel. Figures 2.3a and 2.3b illustrate the positions of the tongue for the front and back vowels of English.

There is one more aspect of vowel pronunciation that we need to note as well. The distinction that your English teacher used to refer to with the terms "short" and "long" – the "short" vowels being those in *bid, bed, but, bought,* and the "long" ones in *bead, bade,* and *boat* – also reflects an articulatory difference.

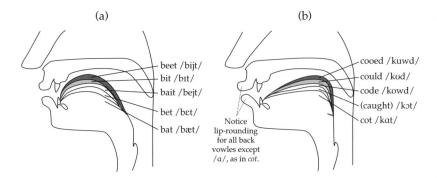

Figure 2.3 (a) Tongue position for the front vowels of American English; (b) Tongue position for the back vowels of American English

---

Exercise 2.5 Say *raid, red, raid, red, raid, red, raid, red* to yourself several times. Draw out the vowels in each word so they're quite long. Put your finger just on the place above your larynx, where your throat takes its 90 percent turn downward. Do you feel a difference there?

Besides the subtle difference in tongue height between the two vowels, they differ in the muscular tension used in the pharynx during their pronunciation – the vowel in *raid* has more tension, and the vowel in *red* has less. Consequently, linguists refer to *tense* ("long") and *lax* ("short") vowels, instead. The short/long distinction has played a very important role in the history of English, as we will see in Chapter 9.

2.4.2 Diphthongs

Some English vowels are made up of two different vowel sounds pronounced in quick succession. The vowel in the word *kite* is like this. Say *kite* very slowly to yourself, lingering over the vowel. You'll find that you start off with your tongue in one place, making a sound rather like the "a" in *father*, and end up with your tongue in another place, making a sound rather like the "i" in *pit* or possibly like the "ee" in *geese*. These "two-vowel" vowels are called *diphthongs*.

In fact, nearly all American English tense vowels (the "long" vowels) end with a little "off-glide" – the sound in *way* is not a single pure vowel, but ends in a little /j/ sound, just as it's spelled. Thus tense vowels are essentially all diphthongs, although for some of them (e.g. the high, front vowel in "free") the off-glide is so minimal that it is difficult to detect. Because the tense vowels all have off-glides at the end, they do also take a bit longer to pronounce than the lax vowels – so calling the tense vowels "long" and the lax ones "short" makes sense.

> **diphthong,** *n.* /dɪfθɑŋ/ Two vowels pronounced in succession within one syllable. From Greek via Latin and French: *di-* "twice" and *-phthong-*, "voice, sound."

The ubiquitous off-glide in English tense vowels can make it difficult for English speakers to accurately produce the vowel sounds in languages like French or Spanish, which have vowels that sound *almost* like our tense vowels, but without the off-glide – their vowels are "pure." For instance, the French word *aller*, "to go," which sounds almost like the English word *allay*, is pronounced without a /j/ ("y"-sound) at the end. Pronouncing such vowels with an off-glide is one of the characteristics of an "English accent" in French.

2.4.3 Reduced vowels

There's another important type of vowel in English, which your English teacher may not have mentioned. These are the *reduced* vowels, which occur only in unstressed syllables. They are shorter even than short vowels, and they are not particularly high, low, back or front – the tongue is in a very neutral position when they are pronounced. We don't have a special symbol in the English alphabet for these, and just about every vowel letter represents a reduced vowel in the spelling of some word. For example, in *banana*, the first and third "a"s are reduced – they're not pronounced like the "a" in *rat*, nor like the "a" in *rate*, nor like the "a" in *father*. In *chicken*, the "e" is reduced; it is not pronounced like the "e" in *pet* or *Pete*. In *tomato*, the first "o" is reduced: it's not pronounced like the "o" in *pot* or *lope* – and so on. Vowel reduction and stress assignment in English words are important topics in the next chapter, when we look at how English suffixes and prefixes affect pronunciation, and in the study of the history of English, in which vowel reduction plays a very big role. To an English speaker, it seems very natural to pronounce unstressed vowels as a kind of quiet "uh" sound, but in many languages, unstressed vowels do not get reduced. French is such a language. Taking our example from above, the first syllable of the French verb *aller*, "to go," is unstressed, and hence quieter and lower in pitch than the second syllable. Nonetheless, the vowel is pronounced with its full value, a sound like the "a" in *cat*. In the English word *allay*, however, the first vowel is both unstressed and reduced, so that it doesn't sound like the vowel in *cat* but more like that quiet "uh."

2.4.4 *IPA transcription of vowels*

The precise transcription of English vowel sounds is a surprisingly complicated task. In the alphabet that we use to write English, there are only five different vowel symbols, "a", "e", "i", "o", and "u". But in my dialect of American English, there are no less than 15 distinct vowels (including diphthongs), each of which must be transcribed differently in a pronunciation-based system like IPA – and 15 is on the low end; many dialects of English make more vowel distinctions than that. (My English is mostly quite similar to that spoken in the (Upper) Midwestern United States, which tends to be the dialect spoken by U.S. news anchors and radio broadcasters, often called Standard American English.)

Further complicating matters, vowels are the most mutable sounds in a language. They are pronounced quite differently in different dialects of English. They're one of the primary components of the "accent" that distinguishes one particular dialect from another. The vowels of Southern American English, for instance, are famously different from those of people with a Midwestern-ish dialect; similarly the vowels of New Jersey English are different from those of California or Canada. Even more radical differences can be heard when comparing North American English speakers to Australian English speakers, or British English to South African English . . . and so on. The vowel symbols I present here are those needed to transcribe my own dialect of Standard American English, and can be used to do a broad transcription of most North American English dialects. You will find that you need to adapt them somewhat if your pronunciation differs significantly. See the official website of the IPA at the University of Glasgow for a thorough discussion: http://www.arts.gla.ac.uk/IPA/ipa.html, and for information on distinctive North American dialects, see the Atlas of North American English at the University of Pennsylvania: http://www.ling.upenn.edu/phono_atlas/home.html.

Because dialects of English differ significantly in details of pronunciation, transcription conventions for different dialects also differ significantly. The transcription system used for the Received Pronunciation (RP) dialect of British English, together with RP transcriptions of all the American English transcriptions presented in the text, are given in the front of the book, organized by page number. If your dialect of English sounds noticeably different from either of these Englishes, you will need to adapt the transcription system here somewhat to represent it.

The vowel symbols are presented in Tables 2.6, 2.7 and 2.8, divided according to whether the tongue starts out positioned in the front, back or center of the mouth.

In some dialects of English, for instance in the northeastern U.S., there are two low back vowels, one unrounded (/ɑ/ as in *father*), and one rounded (/ɔ/ in words like *caught* or *walk*). To decide if you have it, see if you pronounce the vowels in *father, cot, walk*, and *caught* the same or differently. I don't have this distinction in my dialect. I do say this vowel when I'm excited about how cute or lovable something is – I say /ɔɔɔɔɔɔɔ/, (usually written "awwwww!"), not /ɑɑɑɑɑ/. (Most dialects of English do use the low back rounded vowel as part of the diphthong in the word *boy*, even if the vowel doesn't occur by itself, so you will need to use this symbol in your transcription somewhere.)

We will use the symbols for the glides /j/ and /w/ to represent the off-glides in the diphthongs and tense vowels of English, as in the vowel /aj/ in Table 2.6 or /ow/ in Table 2.7.

Unstressed vowels are *central*: the tongue body is neither forward nor back, but in a relaxed, neutral position. The primary unstressed vowel of English, /ə/, is called *schwa*; to hear it, say *banana* to yourself, paying attention to the first and last syllables – they both contain schwa. Sometimes an unstressed vowel is pronounced with the tongue body a little bit higher than the central location of schwa, in which case it can be transcribed as a "barred I": /ɨ/; some students find they prefer to use a barred I for the unstressed vowel in the second syllable of *women*, for instance. When an unstressed syllable ends with a liquid

41

Table 2.6 Front vowels of American English

IPA symbol	Tongue height	Front/back, rounding	Lax or Tense	Examples
/ɪ/	high	front,	Lax	pit, bid, competition
/ɛ/	mid	unrounded		pet, bed, tread
/æ/	low			pat, bad, interact
/ij/	high		Tense	Pete, bead, thief, freed, magazine, bully
/ej/	mid → high			mate, bayed, great, maid participation, weigh
/aj/	low → high	central → front, unrounded		might, tide, by, guy, lie, goodbye

Table 2.7 Back vowels of American English

IPA symbol	Tongue height	Front/back rounding	Lax or Tense	Examples
/ʊ/	high	back, rounded	Lax	put, good, should
/ɑ/	low	back, unrounded		pot, body, father, raw, cough
/ɔ/	low	back, rounded		(only some dialects: caught, talk, walk)
/uw/	high	back, rounded	Tense	toot, booed, rune, flute, lewd, flue, through
/ow/	mid			coat, bode, home, flow, so, sew, though, OK
/aw/	low → high	central, unrounded → back, rounded		pout, bowed, bough, flautist
/ɔj/	mid → high	back, rounded → front, unrounded		boy, oil

Table 2.8 Central vowels of American English

IPA symbol	Tongue height	Front/back rounding	Lax or Tense	Examples
/ʌ/	mid-low	central, unrounded	Lax, **stressed**	putt, bud, flood, what
/ə/	mid		Lax, unstressed	complete, banana, arrest
/ɨ/	mid-high			pitted, chicken, women

or nasal consonant like /l/, or /n/, the vowel can disappear entirely
– the consonant itself becomes the nucleus of the syllable. When this
happens, it can be transcribed with a small vertical stroke underneath
it, to indicate that the consonant forms its own syllable. The word
taken, for instance, could be transcribed /tejkn̩/, as well as /tejkən/,
and the word *little* could be transcribed /lɪtl̩/ or /lɪtəl/.

The only stressed, central vowel in American English is almost
indistinguishable from schwa except in that it's stressed. Many tran-
scribers prefer to use a different symbol, /ʌ/, to transcribe it, since
stress is so important to vowel production in English.

One final note on transcribing vowels: the /ɹ/ sound at the end of a
syllable can strongly affect the vowels which precede it, enough so that
they can sound quite distinct from other vowels. Even when they are
not different vowels entirely, they are sometimes hard to identify; the
tense/lax (short/long) distinction is essentially neutralized before /ɹ/.
Try pronouncing the vowel in *care* to yourself. Is it more like the /ej/
in *wait*, the /ɛ/ in *wet*, or the /æ/ in *wham*? Table 2.9 gives the usual

Table 2.9 Mid and low vowels before "r"

IPA symbol	Tongue height	Front/back, rounding	Examples
/aɹ/	low	central, unrounded	cart, snarl
/ɔɹ/	mid	back, rounded	core, floor
/ʌɹ/	mid	central, unrounded	fur, were
/ɛɹ/	mid	front, unrounded	care, flair
/ɪɹ/	high	front, unrounded	ear, sheer
/ʊɹ/	high	back, rounded	tour, boor

transcription of some easily confused vowels before /ɹ/ in my dialect of American English. Some of you may make a distinction between a mid front vowel before "r" and a low front vowel before "r." To decide, see if you pronounce *marry* and *merry* the same way. If they sound different, you retain a distinction between /æ/ and /ɛ/ before /ɹ/.

Syllable-final /ɹ/ is fairly rare in the languages of the world, and has been lost in several dialects of English, including standard British English, where it has been replaced by either schwa (/ə/) or lengthening the previous vowel, and Boston English, where it has been replaced by lengthening. When you read the RP transcriptions in the *Oxford English Dictionary* or at the front of this book, notice how words like *card* or *hour* are transcribed.

Exercise 2.6 To get started practicing using the IPA, transcribe the underlined words in the following sentences:

a. We must <u>polish</u> the <u>Polish</u> furniture.
   /pɑlɪʃ/, /powlɪʃ/
b. He could <u>lead</u> if he would get the <u>lead</u> out.
c. The farm used to <u>produce</u> <u>produce</u>.
d. The dump was so full that it had to <u>refuse</u> more <u>refuse</u>.
e. The soldier decided to <u>desert</u> in the <u>desert</u>.
f. This was a good time to <u>present</u> the <u>present</u>.
g. The <u>bass</u> player went fishing for <u>bass</u>.
h. When shot at, the <u>dove</u> <u>dove</u> into the bushes.
i. I did not <u>object</u> to the <u>object</u>.
j. The insurance was <u>invalid</u> for the <u>invalid</u>.

Exercise 2.7 To practice reading the IPA, read these IPA transcriptions aloud, and write them down. (Note that because they are trying to make a point about spelling, some of the sentences don't make much sense!)

a. /ðə bændəd͡ʒ wəz wawnd əɹawnd ðə wuwnd/
   "The bandage was wound around the wound."

b. /ðej wɔɹ tuw klows tə ðə dɔɹ tə klowz ɪt/
c. /ðə bʌk dʌz fʌnij θɪŋz wɛn ðə dowz aɹ pɹɛzənt/
d. /tə hɛlp wɪθ plæntɪŋ, ðə faɹməɹ tat hɪz saw tə sow/
e. /ðə wɪnd wəz tuw stɹɑŋ tə wajnd ðə sejl/
f. /æftəɹ ə nʌmbəɹ əv ɪnd͡ʒɛkʃn̩z maj d͡ʒɑ gat nʌməɹ/
g. /əpɑn sijɪŋ ðə tɛɹ ɪn maj klowðz aj ʃɛd ə tijɹ/
h. /aj hæd tuw səbd͡ʒɛkt ðə sʌbd͡ʒɛkt tuw ə sijɹijz əv tɛsts/

Exercise 2.8 Try saying these tongue twisters five times (or more) fast:

a. She sells sea shells by the seashore.
b. The sixth's sheik's sixth sheep is sick
c. Toy boat

Transcribe them in IPA. Which sounds get confused? Which articulators are being used in the places where your pronunciation breaks down? Can you design your own tongue twister?

2.5   Families of Sounds and Grimm's Law: A Case in Point

The primary reason that all the preceding complicated information is important is that English, like all languages, has consistent patterns of organization and pronunciation that apply to *families* of sounds, not just to individual sounds. For example, as we'll see in Chapter 9, in order to understand the changes that English has undergone since the year 1000 AD, for instance, it is crucially important to know that vowels come in low, mid, and high varieties, as well as short (lax) and long (tense). In this section, we look briefly at another interesting example of sound change in the history of English, to do with the consonants.

   In modern English, the sounds /p/, /t/, and /k/ are pronounced in a special way when they occur by themselves at the beginning of a stressed syllable: they come with a little extra puff of air. (Put your hand, or a sheet of paper, about an inch in front of your lips and say *pat, spat, tat, stat, cat, scat*. Feel the difference in each case?) It's not a coincidence that this special pronunciation – called **aspiration** – happens to /p/, /t/, and /k/ but not to any other consonants of English. The extra-puff-of-air pronunciation applies to all (and only) the **voiceless stops** of English in that position. This kind of quirk of pronunciation is the sort of thing that could lead to more significant language change. In another five hundred years, it is possible that syllable-initial /p/, /t/, and /k/ in English will have become fricatives, turning into /f/, /θ/, and /x/, since the extra puff of air is one step towards a more fricative-like quality. (The IPA symbol /x/ represents a sound like that in the German name *Bach*, or the Scottish word *loch*, a velar fricative.) If that happened, we'd be pronouncing the word *pat* as /fæt/, *tat* as /θæt/ and *cat* as /xæt/, while still retaining the present-day pronunciation of *spat*, *stat* and *scat*. (We might still *spell* the words the same way, in this hypothetical future, since spelling is very conservative; in that case, future learners of English would be wondering why the letter "p" sometimes stands for /f/ but other times stands for /p/.)

In fact, this is a type of sound change that has already happened once in the long-ago history of English. This very set of sound changes happened to the ancestral language spoken by the Germanic tribes of Europe, before that ancient language split up into German, Swedish, Dutch, English, and so on. This sound change was one step on the way to the differentiation of the **Germanic** languages from the languages spoken by related peoples in Europe.

There was once a single language spoken by a group of people living somewhere in Central Europe. This language was the ancestor of nearly all the modern European languages, including English, and it was also the ancestor of Hindi and other related languages on the Indian subcontinent. Linguists have named this now-extinct language **Proto-Indo-European**. This tribe split up into several groups, some of which migrated eastwards (spreading their languages all the way to India), some west (bringing their language to Spain, Italy, and France), and some to the far north (the group which came to speak the modern-day Germanic and Scandinavian languages). Northwest, another group went to Eastern Europe and Russia (Figure 2.4).

When two groups of people, originally sharing a common language, are separated for generations, their languages will begin to drift apart, creating, at first, mutually intelligible dialects, but eventually diverging so far that speakers from the different groups can no longer

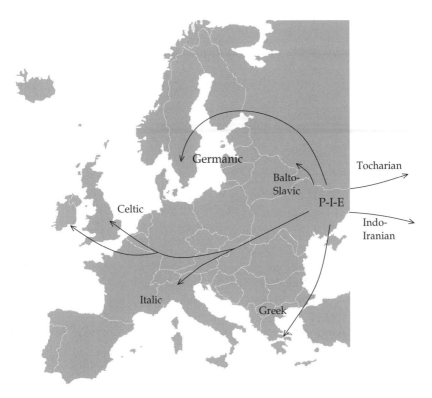

Figure 2.4 A general representation of the spread of some of the western Indo-European language families through Europe as they differentiated from Proto-Indo-European (PIE). Many language families are omitted.

understand each other. This happened between the different groups of Proto-Indo-European speakers. This drift is not simple random alteration of a sound here or there: it occurs quite generally to whole families of sounds and patterns within a language.

English is one of the languages descended from the language of the Germanic group of Proto-Indo-European which traveled to the north; Latin was one of the languages descended from the language of the Italic group of Proto-Indo-European which traveled to the southwestern part of Europe. Proto-Germanic and Proto-Italic were sister languages, both descended from the common mother language, Proto-Indo-European – and, once separated, the sounds of the two languages began to drift apart. Consider the pairs of Latin and English words in (4):

(4) | *Latin* | *English* |
|---------|-----------|
| pater | father |
| pedem | foot |
| penna | feather |
| tri- | three |
| tu | thee |
| cordis | heart |
| octo- | eight |
| quis | who |
| deca- | ten |
| dent- | tooth |
| labia | lip |
| genu- | knee |
| genus | kin |
| granum | corn |
| foro | bore |
| frag- | break |
| haedus | goat |

These words are **cognates** of each other, that is, they are both descended from the same word of Proto-Indo-European. Pairs of cognate words are like two animals of different species which are both descended from a single ancestor species. These words have preserved their core meaning over time, since they are commonly used words which stand for concepts that have remained stable and current over the centuries.

Consider the list carefully. Are there any correspondences between the pronunciation of the consonants in the Latin and English words? It may help you to know that in Latin, the letter "c" is pronounced /k/, and so is the letter "q."

Exercise 2.9 Look at the consonants in the pairs of Latin/English words in (4). Can you detect any regular correspondences between the consonants in the Latin words and the consonants in the English words? State any regularities you see first in terms of individual sounds, and then try to state them in terms of *manner* and *voicing*.

In fact, these correspondences are part of a very general and complete sound change that happened in the ancestral Germanic language. This particular sound change did not happen in the sister language

Proto-Italic or its descendants, so in this respect, Latin remained more similar to Proto-Indo-European, the ancestor of both Latin and English. The change involved stops and fricatives.

In the list, wherever there is a /p/ in a Latin word, there is an /f/ in the corresponding English word. You can see this in *pater/father, pedem/ foot*, and *penna/feather*. In most places, where there is a /t/ in a Latin word, there is a /θ/ in the corresponding English word: *tri/three, tu/ thee, pater/father*, and *dent-/tooth*. (This isn't true in *octo-/eight*, but it is the only exception in the list.) Wherever there is a /k/ (spelled "c") in the Latin word, there is an /h/ in the corresponding English word: *cent-/hundred, cordis/heart*, and *quis/who*. Even in *octo/eight*, although an /h/ isn't pronounced in the English word, there is one present in the spelling. The only case where this correspondence doesn't hold is in *deca-/ten*, but this is because the two-syllable pronunciation with an /h/ in the middle was gradually lost in the English branch of Germanic; the old Gothic word for "ten" was *taihun*. So far, we see that Latin /p/ corresponds to English /f/, Latin /t/ corresponds to English /θ/, and Latin /k/ corresponds to English /h/.

Elsewhere, we see that wherever there is a /d/ in a Latin word, there is a corresponding /t/ in the English word: *dent-/tooth, deca-/ ten, pedem/foot, cordis/heart*, and *haedus/goat*. Latin /g/ corresponds to English /k/ in *genus/kin, granum/corn*, and *frag-/break*; in *genu-/knee* there is a spelled "k" in the English word that is not pronounced. Again, this is a more recent change in English; well into the fifteenth century, *knee* was pronounced with an initial *k* sound in English. So Latin /g/ corresponds to English /k/, and Latin /d/ corresponds to English /t/.

Finally, Latin /f/ corresponds to English /b/, in *frag-/break*, and *foro/bore*, while Latin /h/ corresponds to English /g/ in *haedus/goat*. The nasals and liquids of Latin words generally seem to be the same as the ones in their English counterparts; there's no obvious pattern of change – and the vowels are all over the place. But let's see what we've got among the stops and fricatives:

(5) *Latin*   *English*
  a. p, t, k   f, θ, h
  b. d, g   t, k
  c. f, h   b, g

What is immediately apparent, now that you know about manner of articulation and voicing, is that, at least for the first two groups in this

49

list, the correspondences are not random. In group (a), /p/, /t/, and /k/ are all voiceless stops, and /f/, /θ/, and /h/ are the corresponding voiceless fricatives, produced at pretty much the same place of articulation. In group (b), /d/ and /g/ are voiced stops, and /t/ and /k/ are the corresponding voiceless stops produced at the same place of articulation. In the third group, we can again see a generalization in terms of place of articulation, although they're very different sounds in other regards. /f/ is a voiceless fricative and /b/ is a voiced stop, but they do have the same labial place of articulation. Similarly, /h/ is a voiceless fricative and /g/ is a voiced stop; nonetheless, they do share approximately the same place of articulation in the back of the mouth. In Proto-Germanic, it appears, stops and fricatives changed their manner of articulation and/or their voicing in a consistent way, but retained their place of articulation, or at least as close an approximation of it as possible. We can summarize what we have found in terms of place, manner and voicing in (6):

(6) a. Voiceless stops → Voiceless fricatives
     b. Voiced stops → Voiceless stops   (/b/: unknown)
     c. Voiceless fricatives → Voiced stops   (/θ/: unknown)

At a first glance, it looks like the consonants of the Germanic branch of Proto-Indo-European altered their voicing and manner: voiced stops became voiceless, voiceless stops became fricatives, and voiceless fricatives became voiced stops.

Note that this all had to have happened more or less at the same time. If, for example, the voiced stops had turned into voiceless stops before the voiceless stops became voiceless fricatives, we would expect to see the Latin word *dent-* end up corresponding to an English word *thooth*, since the /d/ would have become /t/, and then that new /t/ would have become /θ/ later, when all the other /t/s did.

Of course, we don't have enough evidence in our list to confirm the complete generality of our correspondences in (b) and especially (c). When looked at in detail, there's an important missing piece of the puzzle: another series of consonants in the ancestral Proto-Indo-European that underwent changes in *both* Proto-Italic and Proto-

Germanic. (These consonants were voiced, aspirated stops – /bʰ/, /dʰ/ , and /gʰ/. In the Italic branch, /dʰ/ disappeared, and was replaced with /bʰ/, eventually becoming /f/, while in the Germanic branch, / dʰ/ just lost the aspiration, becoming /d/ – so several Latin words with "f" in them are cognate with English words with "d": Latin *foris* is cognate with English *door*, for example.) Nonetheless, the overall picture is correct, confirmed by hundreds of cognate words in the various Indo-European languages. This collection of sound changes, part of the development of Germanic as a separate subfamily of Indo-European, is known as *Grimm's Law*, after the linguistic anthropologist who pointed out its importance (and recorded the fairy tales). This work, part of the larger project to reconstruct Proto-Indo-European at the end of the 1800s, constituted a breakthrough in the development of linguistics as a science, and crucially depended on an understanding of the families of sounds we have just learned about. This kind of reconstruction of change through comparison is used by linguists all over the world to investigate the relationships between different languages and language families, and can provide strong evidence about the migration patterns of various groups of people over periods of thousands of years.

More relevant for our immediate concerns, this kind of example makes it clear that knowing about families of sounds is essential if we want to understand the history of English words, a topic we will consider in more detail in Chapter 9.

Study Problems

1. Give the standard English orthography for (one set of) the words below:
   a. pɹɛʃəs, əbɪlətij, wajɹləs, pɪtʃɟ, əntɛlədʒɛnts, pəlajt, kawəɹd, faðɟ, sajkɑlədʒij, əŋkɹɛdəbl̩
   b. nɛkləs, nʌm, kəmpjuwtɟ, ʃæmpejn, nɑlədʒ, æŋzajətij, d͡ʒuwdiʃəs, pɪkpɑkət, sɪzəɹz, jʌŋ
   c. ɹɪstwatʃ, wajnd, fənɑlədʒij, tɹawt, tʃɪlɪŋ, bijɑnd, dəlej, dejlij, θawzənd, fʌd͡ʒ
   d. najf, ɹɛpətɪʃəs, plajəɹz, ɹajð, æŋkɟ, dɪfθɑŋ, kɹʌm, pæθwej, kɑmpləmɛntəɹij, ɛksəɹsajz
2. Transcribe (one or more) of the sets of words below into IPA:
   a. broken, fantastic, psychedelic, ratchet, science, introduction, philosophy, yellow, lamb, rough

    b.   potential, intelligent, condescending, deaden, compliance, telephonic, certain, putrid, further, edition

    c.   jacket, mention, delicious, orange, woman, television, idiom, skiing, excited, inquisition

    d.   wretched, palace, punitive, punish, vexing, portentious, defeat, analogy, bothersome, yucky

3.   Given below is an IPA transcription of a joke. Write it out in standard English orthography.

litl̩ bɪlijz fɪfθ ɡɹejd tijtʃɹ kald hɪz faðɹ wʌn ijvnɪŋ. "ajm saɹij tə tɛl jə ðɪs," ʃij sɛd, "bʌt bɪlij tʃijtəd an əz kwɪz tədej. hij kapijd fɹʌm ðə ɡʌɹl sitɪŋ nɛkst tə hɪm."

"aj down? bəlijv ɪt," həz faðɹ sɛd. "haw də juw now ðə ɡʌɹl dɪdn̩? kapij ðij ænsɹz af əv bɪlijz tɛst?"

"wɛl," sɛd ðə tijtʃɹ, "bowθ sɛts əv ænsɹz wʌɹ ðə sejm al ðə wej dawn ðə pejd͡ʒ, ɛksɛpt fəɹ ðə læst wʌn. fɔɹ ðæt wʌn ʃij ɹowt 'aj down? now,' æn bɪlij ɹowt 'mij nijðɹ'."

4.   Transcribe the following joke into IPA:

A couple in Canada adopted a baby born in Mexico, and enrolled in a Spanish class as soon as they brought him home. When a concerned friend asked the mother how they could find the time for the class with a new baby at home, she said, "Oh, but we have to go! Otherwise, how will we understand him when he starts to talk?"

5.   In many dialects of English, the sounds /θ/ and /ð/ have been lost. In fact, these are rather rare sounds in the languages of the world. In the dialects where they have disappeared, they have merged with other sounds in the language.

    a.   Describe /θ/ and /ð/ in terms of place, manner and voicing.

    b.   In Cockney English, /θ/ became /f/ and /ð/ became /v/, so that speakers of that dialect produce /fɪŋk/ where American English speakers would say /θɪŋk/, and /væt/ where American English speakers would say /ðæt/. Is this a change in place, manner or voicing? What changed, and what did it change to?

    c.   In many other dialects of English, including Newfoundland English, Jamaican English, African American Vernacular English, and Irish English, /θ/ and /ð/ became /t/ and /d/ respectively, so speakers of these dialects produce /tɪŋk/ where American English speakers would say /θɪŋk/ and /dæt/ where American English speakers would say /ðæt/. Is this a change in place, manner or voicing? What changed, and what did it change to?

    d. Many second language speakers of English produce /s/ instead of /θ/ and /z/ instead of /ð/, saying /sink/ for /θɪŋk/ and /zæt/ for /ðæt/. Describe this change in terms of place, manner, and/or voicing.

6. (For discussion) What does it mean to say that someone "has an accent"? Do you think that you have an accent? Who, in your opinion, has one? Does "having an accent" mean "sounds different from me," or does it mean "sounds different from dialect X"?

Further Reading

On dialects of English:
Labov, William (1996) "The organization of dialect diversity in North America." http://www.ling.upenn.edu/phono_atlas/ICSLP4.html.
Trudgill, Peter (1994) *Dialects*. London and New York: Routledge.

On the IPA:
The International Phonetic Association (1999) *Handbook of the International Phonetic Association: A Guide to the Use of the International Phonetic Alphabet*. Cambridge: Cambridge University Press.
Also see their web page: http://www.arts.gla.ac.uk/IPA/ipa.html

On Proto-Indo-European and Grimm's Law:
Fortson, B. (2004) *Indo-European Language and Culture: An Introduction*. Cambridge, MA: Blackwell.
Wikipedia article on Grimm's Law: http://en.wikipedia.org/wiki/Grimm%27s_law

3

Phonological Words: Calling All Scrabble Players!

/fanə'ladʒɪkəl 'wʌɹdz: 'kalɪŋ 'al 'skɹæbəl 'plejəɹz/

In this chapter, we learn about the language-specific restrictions that govern what sound sequences are possible in English phonological words (*phonotactics*), the regular processes that apply to produce different sounds in different contexts (*allophony*), the rules according to which stress is assigned to English words, and how stress affects pronunciation. We'll look at how these three processes intersect to identify phonological words. We also consider all these properties in relation to the problem faced by babies: breaking the speech stream down into smaller parts so they can begin learning *listemes*.

3.1 Guessing at Words: The Scrabble Problem

We are now finally able to consider the central problem of this first part of the book: what is a phonological word? Why do we have intuitions about where we should put spaces in written English text? We saw in the first chapter that our everyday use of the word "word" seems to pick out a kind of a phonological unit. According to our everyday way of thinking, *dogs* is one word, *-s* is not a word, and *works like a dog* is four words. These units that we're counting are not minimal units of meaning, though – they are some sort of unit of *sound*.

Not only do we have firm intuitions about how many of these phonological words are present in a given sentence of English (intuitions that are reflected in, and possibly affected by, the spacing conventions of

English orthography) – we *also* have intuitions about strings of sounds we've never heard before. For instance, consider the following nine strings of sounds, written both in English orthography and in IPA, so you can get a precise idea of what they're intended to sound like:

(1) a. timp   /tɪmp/
     b. rog   /ɹɑg/
     c. mbotto   /mbɑto/
     d. flezk   /flɛzk/
     e. spink   /spɪŋk/
     f. beh   /bɛ/
     g. bod   /bɑd/
     h. psore   /psɔɹ/

It is unlikely you have seen or heard most of these letter sequences before. Now, rate each of these "words" according to how confident you are that they are not English words.

Exercise 3.1   Give each of the strings of sounds in (1) a numerical rating, from 1 to 5, where 1 means the string is definitely *not* an English word, and 5 means that it definitely *is* an English word. Arrange the words in order according to the scores you assign, lowest to highest.

Here is a typical ranking and average score for each of these "words," from a sample of 40 native English speakers:

(2) | Rank | Word | Score |
     |------|--------|-------|
     | 1 | bod | 4.66 |
     | 2 | timp | 4.30 |
     | 3 | rog | 4.2 |
     | 4 | spink | 4.17 |
     | 5 | beh | 2.75 |
     | 6 | psore | 2.02 |
     | 7 | flezk | 1.69 |
     | 8 | mbotto | 1.07 |

It's pretty likely that your ranking comes fairly close to this one. *Bod* gets a high score because it actually is a word of English (short for *body*); *mbotto* gets a low score, and it is clearly not a word of English. But why do *timp, rog,* and *spink* get higher scores than *mbotto*? They are

Figure 3.1 Calvin and Hobbes. © 1990 Watterson. Dist. By Universal Press Syndicate. Reprinted with permission. All rights reserved

not English words either – the people rating the words had probably never seen these strings before! Shouldn't they all seem as unlikely to be English as *mbotto*?

Scrabble players are familiar with this problem. In Scrabble, you get a rack of seven letters, such as, say, IOBUZRP, each worth a certain number of points. Your job is to arrange them in such a way that you can spell an English word with them. You will try to look for the English word that uses the largest possible number of letters, since the longer the word, the more points you will score. Since the "Z" is worth a very large number of points you'll certainly try to use it. Let's imagine the board layout at this point in the game is such that if you can make a four-letter word with the Z at the beginning, you can score double points for the Z! What are the possibilities you consider? You rearrange your letters, hoping to see a word. You might look at the combinations ZOIP, ZURP, ZOUB, ZOIB, ZIRB, ZORB, ZIRP, ZURB, ZUBI, ZOPI, ZORI . . . but you don't recognize any of them as words for sure. (In fact, "zori" is a word in the Scrabble dictionary; it's a name for a type of sandal. If you happen to know this, when you get to "zori," you will say "aha!" and put it down, rejoicing. But if not, you'll just keep scratching your head and rearranging.)

> **zori**, *n*. Japanese thonged sandals with straw (or leather, wood, etc.) soles. From Japanese *so* "grass, (rice) straw" and *ri* "footwear, sole."

The point is, there are hundreds of arrangements of letters that you will never even consider as potential English words: ZPOI, ZROB,

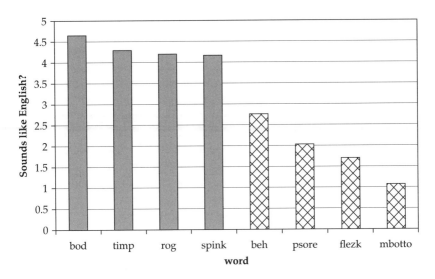

Figure 3.2 Word-like ratings for strings of English sounds

ZIPB, ZBRP, ZIUO, and so on. What is it that you know that makes you pause and wonder whether ZIRP might be a word of English, but makes you pass over ZIPB (unless you're Calvin)?

The answer is that you know English **phonotactics**, or the rules that describe possible sequences of sounds for forming English words. Languages can differ in their phonotactic rules, so that /mbɑto/ might be a possible word of Swahili, or /psɔɹ/ a possible word of Greek. These sequences, however, are not possible words in English.

Notice that a bar chart of the wordhood ratings given in (2) above shows a significant jump between *spink* and *beh* (Figure 3.2).

From *bod* to *spink*, the bars decrease gradually, and similarly from *beh* to *mbotto*. But between *spink* and *beh* there's a big jump. The reason for this is that the four least-wordlike words violate rules of English phonotactics, while the four most-wordlike words do not. That is, these sound sequences fall into two groups: the last four are phonologically impossible words in English, while the first four are phonologically possible words. You might consider playing the first four in an imaginary game of Scrabble, but you wouldn't even wonder about the last four. In this chapter, we're going to look at some of the constraints that determine what sound combinations make for a possible English word.

3.2 Building Blocks III: The Syllable

One condition on a well-formed English word is that it has to be made up of at least one *syllable*. That's one reason why *-s*, as in *dogs*, can't stand on its own as a phonological word, although it has its own meaning. A syllable is, roughly, a phonological unit that contains at least a vowel. Syllables can start or end with one or more consonants, but even without any consonants, a vowel can be a syllable all by itself: the pronoun "I," /aj/, for instance, is a syllable. The first syllable of the word *open*, /ow/, is made up of just one vowel, and so is the first syllable of *apart*, /ə/. Consequently, all English phonological words must contain at least a vowel (as Hobbes, in Figure 3.1, knows very well).

Phonotactic Rule 1: All phonological words must contain at least one syllable, and hence must contain at least one vowel.

How do we know that syllables are important units of speech? We can see that people pay attention to syllables in a number of ways. One very obvious one is in metered poetry. We know, for instance, that two lines of poetry that *scan*, i.e. that fall into a regular rhythmic pattern, usually have the same number of syllables. Consider this famous first verse of the nonsense poem *Jabberwocky*:

(3)   'Twas brillig, and the slithy toves
      Did gyre and gimble in the wabe.
      All mimsy were the borogoves
      And the mome raths outgrabe.

Count the syllables. You should find that the first three lines match, each containing eight syllables, and the last one is shorter, with six syllables. This pattern is repeated throughout the poem:

(4)   One, two! One, two! And through and through
      The vorpal blade went snicker-snack!
      He left it dead, and with its head
      He went galumphing back.

Again, eight, eight, eight and six. Considering that Lewis Carroll made up most of the words in the poem, he must have intended for the syllable counts to turn out this way – it can't just be a coincidence.

Sometimes poets will play with the intuition that syllable counting is an essential ingredient of verse. Consider the first two verses of *Poetical Economy* by Harry Graham:

(5) What hours I spent of precious time
     What pints of ink I used to waste,
     Attempting to secure a rhyme
     To suit the public taste,
     Until I found a simple plan
     Which makes the lamest lyric scan!
     When I've a syllable de trop
     I cut it off, without apol.
     This verbal sacrifice, I know,
     May irritate the schol.;
     But all must praise my dev'lish cunn.
     Who realize that Time is Mon.

In the opposite direction, what about this *Rhyme for Remembering the Date of Easter*, by Justin Richardson?

(6) No need for confusion if we but recall
     That Easter on the first Sunday after the full moon
        following the date of Equinox doth fall.

This particularly unmemorable rhyme fails as a mnemonic (and succeeds as a joke) because it doesn't scan: trying to remember the rhyme is just as hard as trying to remember the plain prose fact. A *good* mnemonic rhyme scans, giving it a rhythm that helps you fit in the right individual words, as in the first two lines of this famous mnemonic for remembering the number of days in a month:

(7) Thirty days hath September
     April, June, and November.

Another place where we see the notion of syllable at work is in hyphenation conventions in written English. When a group of words won't exactly fit into a single line of text, one of the words has to be broken up and part of it placed on the next line, like this:

When an ortho-
graphic word
won't fit onto

a single line of
text, it is hy-
phenated at a
syllable boun-
dary.

> The convention of hyphenating at a syllable boundary can be overridden by other considerations. If putting a hyphen at a syllable boundary would result in there being only one letter on a line, another breaking point is chosen – often an affix boundary. For instance, *unable* is hyphenated as *un-able*, rather than *u-nable* or *unab-le*.

Since phonological words like *can't* and *caboodle* have to be made up of well-formed syllables, understanding what can be a well-formed English syllable will take us a long way towards understanding what is a possible well-formed English phonological word, and hence a long way towards understanding why, in your hypothetical Scrabble game, you wouldn't even consider *zpob* as a possibility.

Syllables can be made up of a simple vowel, even a reduced vowel, such as the intial /ə/ in "attempt," which has two syllables. They can be made up of a consonant and a vowel, such as /hij/, "he." They can be made up of a consonant, a vowel and a consonant, like /sʌn/ in "Sunday." In fact, English syllables can have up to three consonants at the beginning, as in the word /stɹɪŋ/, "string," and up to four consonants at the end, as in the word /tɛksts/, "texts."

Syllables can be divided into three parts: the beginning, or *onset* of the syllable, made up of one to three consonants, the required middle, or *nucleus* of the syllable, made up of the vowel, and the end, or *coda*, of the syllable, again made up of one or more consonants, up to four. The onset and coda are optional, as we saw above; syllables can be made up of just a vowel. Most syllables, though, also have an onset, and many also have a coda. The anatomy of a syllable is shown in (8); "C" stands for "consonant" and "V" for vowel; brackets indicate optionality:

(8)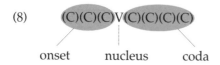
(C)(C)(C)V(C)(C)(C)(C)

onset   nucleus   coda

It's the nucleus plus the coda that make a rhyme. *Coast* and *toast* rhyme, as do *code* and *toad*, but *coast* and *code* don't rhyme, although they have the onset and nucleus in common. (In poetic terms, *coast* and *code* are alliterative and assonant – but they don't rhyme.)

3.3 Phonotactic Restrictions on English Syllables

Now, considering that we earlier identified 24 consonant sounds and 15 vowel sounds in English, and that a syllable can consist of anything from a single vowel to a vowel surrounded by seven consonants, in theory there should be 74,909,241,375 possible syllables in English, i.e., about 75 billion. Obviously, this is far larger than the actual number of possible syllables. For one thing, that figure includes cases where contiguous sequences of the same consonant in onset and coda are considered possible, as in /sssıtttt/. In English, this does not occur.

Phonotactic Rule 2: Sequences of repeated consonants are not possible.

If we incorporate the effects of phonotactic rule 2 into our computation, excluding sequences of identical sounds within an onset or coda, we reduce the number of possible syllables by about 20 percent, to a mere 60,779,920,695 possible syllables. This is still orders of magnitude bigger than the actual number of possible English syllables. It includes such non-starters as /zıpb/ and /msɑl/. What are the underlying principles of English that limit this combinatorial explosion?

Even at first glance, it's clearly wrong to assume that all 24 English consonants can occur freely in all the seven available consonant positions in English syllables. For instance, although the velar nasal sound /ŋ/ frequently occurs at the end of syllables (*sing, jumping, hangman*), it never appears at the beginning of English syllables, and hence never at the beginnings of English words.

Phonotactic Rule 3: The velar nasal /ŋ/ never occurs in the onset of a syllable.

Similarly, although /h/ is a well-formed syllable onset in English (as my own name attests), it is never found at the ends of syllables, and hence never at the ends of words. The symbol "h" is sometimes used at the end of a syllable in English spelling to indicate the pronunciation of a vowel – e.g. *ah* is the usual spelling of the syllable /a/ – but the /h/ sound itself is not pronounced.

Phonotactic Rule 4: The glottal fricative /h/ never occurs in the coda of a syllable.

Taking into account rule 4, the number of possible English syllables is reduced by another 25 percent to 44,881,090,380. Still too much, and we still haven't found out what's wrong with /zɪpb/.

If we look for patterns in the formation of onset consonant *clusters* in English – when there is more than one consonant at the beginning of a syllable – they are easy to find. First, the affricates /t͡ʃ/ and /d͡ʒ/, and the glottal fricative /h/ cannot occur in an onset with any other consonant: there are no English words like /t͡ʃlɪŋk/, "chlink," /d͡ʒlæm/, "jlam" or /khɑt/, "khot," so instead of 23 possible onset consonants, in clusters there are only 20.

> Always keep in mind that we are talking about clusters of consonantal *sounds*, not spellings. Although the *letter* "h" occurs as a letter in the spelling of many simple and complex syllable onsets, because of the English spelling convention of using "h" to indicate certain fricatives and affricates, the *sound* /h/ never occurs in a complex onset. Words like *thin* and *chin* and *through* have more than one orthographic consonant in their spelling, but only *through* is really a complex onset when pronounced, and none of them involve the actual consonant sound /h/. What is the correct IPA transcription of these words?

Phonotactic Rule 5: The affricates /t͡ʃ/ and /d͡ʒ/, and the glottal fricative /h/, do not occur in complex onsets.

Second, when an onset contains a sequence of two consonants, the first consonant of the sequence must be an *obstruent* – an oral stop or fricative. So while we find sequences like /tɹʌk/ "truck," or /dɹɑp/, "drop" we never find sequences like /ɹtʌk/, "rtuck," or /ɹdɑp/, "rdop."

Phonotactic Rule 6: The first consonant in a two-consonant onset must be an obstruent.

Only 14 of the 20 possible onset consonants are obstruents. Between them, generalizations 5 and 6 whittle the number of possibilities down another 35 percent, to 28,956,015,990.

The *second* consonant of a two-consonant onset sequence can be anything except a voiced obstruent – that is, it can be a voiceless stop or fricative, or a nasal, liquid or glide, but not a voiced stop or voiced fricative. So while there are words like /snɪt/, "snit," /swɪl/, "swill," /stɪl/, "still," /spɪl/ "spill," and /sfɪŋks/, "sphinx," in English, there are no words like /sgɪl/ "sgill," /sdɪl/ "sdill" or /svɪŋks/ "svinx." Note that even though the word *svelte* is spelled with the letters "sv," it is pronounced with an /sf/ – /sfɛlt/.

Phonotactic Rule 7: The second consonant in a two-consonant onset must not be a voiced obstruent.

That means that only 13 of the 20 possible syllable-initial English consonants can occur in second position in a two-obstruent consonant cluster in English, bringing our estimate of the number of possible English syllables down a measly 1 percent to 28,578,886,740.

When we consider other combinations of consonants in two-consonant onsets, even more restrictions jump out at us. While it is true that any consonant except a voiced obstruent (13 sounds) can occur in second position, and any obstruent (14 sounds) can occur in first position, they cannot pair up indiscriminately. Rather, when the first consonant is anything besides an /s/, the second consonant has to be a liquid or a glide.[1] So while there are words like /flɪk/ "flick" and /dwɛl/, "dwell," there are no words like /fpɪk/ "fpick" or /dzɛl/, "dzell."[2]

Phonotactic Rule 8: If the first consonant of a two-consonant onset is not an /s/, the second consonant must be a liquid or a glide – it must be /l/, /ɹ/, /w/, or /j/.

The only time the second consonant can be a voiceless obstruent or a nasal is when the first consonant is an /s/: we have words like /snijk/ "sneak," /stejk/ "steak," /skejt/ "skate," /spijk/, "speak" and /sfijɹ/, "sphere." (The only voiceless obstruent that cannot occur after /s/ is /ʃ/, probably because the /sʃ/ sequence is nearly impossible to make distinct.) Taking this two-way restriction into consideration, our syllable possibilities are down another 1 percent to 28,117,067,940.

Here's a summary so far of our observations about onsets in English:

(9) a. /ŋ/ is not a possible onset.
 b. Complex onsets may not contain affricates or /h/.
 c. Two-consonant complex onsets may contain either:
  (i) First consonant: /s/;
   Second consonant: nasal, liquid, glide or voiceless obstruent (except /ʃ/).
  (ii) First consonant: any obstruent other than /s/;
   Second consonant: liquid or glide.

What about three-consonant onsets? Let's consider some examples of words that have three-consonant onsets:

(10) a. /splijn/   spleen
 b. /spɹɪŋ/   spring
 c. /stɹijm/   stream
 d. /skɹijn/   screen
 e. /sklɹoʊsɪs/   sclerosis
 f. /skwijz/   squeeze
 g. /spjuʊ/   spew

One thing that immediately leaps to the eye is that they all begin with /s/. It's also easy to see that they all end in a liquid or glide – that is, the third consonant is always either /l/, /ɹ/, /j/, or /w/. Considered in the light of our previous generalizations about two-consonant clusters, this doesn't seem like a coincidence.

What's going on in three-consonant clusters is that each pair of consonants within the cluster must independently satisfy the restrictions on two-consonant clusters. We can call this the *Substring Rule*:

Phonotactic Rule 9: The Substring Rule: Every subsequence of consonants contained within a bigger sequence must itself obey all the phonotactic rules.

Let's call the three consonants of a three-consonant onset C_1-C_2-C_3. (In the word *string*, /stɹɪŋ/, C_1 = /s/, C_2 = /t/, and C_3 = /ɹ/.) This onset has two subsequences: C_1-C_2 (/st/), and C_2-C_3 (/tɹ/). The Substring Rule says that the C_1-C_2 sequence must obey the two-consonant onset rules, and so must the C_2-C_3 sequence. That places some serious restrictions on what C_2 can be – it has to work as the *first* consonant of

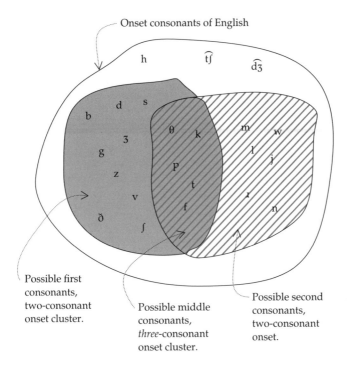

Figure 3.3 The Substring Rule

a two-consonant sequence (considered as part of the C_2-C_3 string), and it *also* has to work as the *second* consonant of a two-consonant sequence (considered as part of the C_1-C_2 string). So, for instance, in our example, the onset of *string*, /stɹ/, contains the two substrings /st/ and /tɹ/, each of which are themselves independently well-formed, as in *stick* /stɪk/ and *try* /tɹaj/. Recall that the first consonant of a two-consonant sequence can be any obstruent, but not a nasal, liquid or glide. The second consonant of a two-consonant sequence can be anything except a voiced obstruent. The consequence is shown in Figure 3.3. The only sounds that can possibly work both as first-consonants and second-consonants in a three-consonant onset are the voiceless obstruents: /p/, /t/, /k/, /f/, and /θ/.

Since the only potential legitimate C_2 in a three-consonant cluster is a voiceless obstruent, it follows from the substring rule that the only possible C_1 in a three-consonant cluster is /s/, since the only well-formed two-consonant onsets with a voiceless obstruent in the second position are ones which begin with /s/. It also follows that the third consonant has to be a glide or a liquid, since the only well-formed two-consonant onsets with a voiceless obstruent in the first position have a glide or liquid in second position. If we include the effects of the Substring Rule on three-consonant onsets in our calculations, our inventory of possible English syllables is reduced by a huge amount – about 96 percent – all the way to 870,327,990. Now we're really starting to help our Scrabble player out.

This number still includes some unlikely onset combinations. Although /sθ/ is a very rare onset in English, it does occur in words like *sthenic*, "producing nervous energy, stimulating"; however, there are no examples of three-consonant onsets that begin with this sequence (a word like *sthrigal* or *sthlinky*), though it's technically possible. Similarly, we don't run into /spw/, /stw/, or /sfl/ onsets, despite the fact that /sp/, /pw/, /st/, /tw/, /sf/ and /fl/ all do occur independently as onsets of at least one or two English words. It's sometimes hard to tell if such gaps are the result of principles of English phonotactics or accidents of history. Try making up some words that begin with such sequences. How do they sound to you, compared to made-up words with other outlawed sequences? Try comparing /spwɛt/ or /sflɪŋ/ to /zbijd/ or /mɹæt/. (There does exist a technical word with an /sfɹ/ onset: *sphragistics*, the study of official seals or signet rings.)

The codas of English syllables are, as you might suspect, subject to similar kinds of restrictions. We've already observed above that you never see /h/ in coda position. Similarly, /w/ and /j/ are not possible English codas. The only places where one might think they occur are in words like *cow*, /kaw̑/, and *lie*, /laj̑/. In such cases, though, they are part of the off-glide of a diphthong. The off-glide counts as part of the vowel in the nucleus of the syllable, not a truly separate and contrastive consonant in the coda.[3]

Phonotactic Rule 10: No glides in syllable codas.

Taking this into consideration, our inventory is reduced about another 44 percent to 490,875,390.

In two-consonant codas, the first consonant can be pretty much anything (except /h/, which doesn't occur in codas at all). This is largely due to the fact that the two most common English suffixes – the past tense, written *-ed*, but often pronounced as just a single consonant /t/ or /d/, and the plural, written *-s*, pronounced as /z/ or /s/, can be suffixed to the end of almost any English noun or verb, creating a complex two-consonant coda.

In the second position in a two-consonant sequence, though, there are a few more restrictions: /ŋ/ doesn't show up as the second consonant in a two-consonant coda, nor does /ɹ/, /ð/ or /ʒ/.

Phonotactic Rule 11: The second consonant in a two-consonant coda cannot be /ŋ/, /ð/, /ɹ/, or /ʒ/.

These four sounds are consequently disallowed in third and fourth positions as well, by the Substring Rule applied to codas. These restrictions get us down another 32 percent to 330,467,370.

For the remaining 21 × 17 possibilities for two-consonant codas, we can't state absolute descriptions of availability in either first or second position, since just about any consonant can occur in either first or second position. Nonetheless, there are significant co-occurrence restrictions between the two. These are summarized in the (fairly complicated!) Figure 3.4. The consonants on the left are 20 of the 21

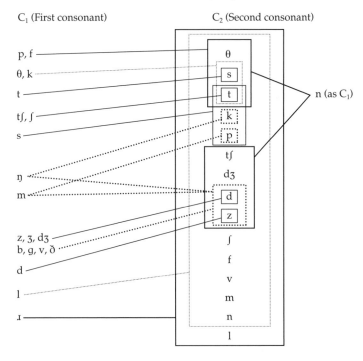

Figure 3.4 Two-consonant coda clusters of American English

possible first consonants (the *n* on the far right is the 21st). The consonants on the right are the 17 possible second consonants. The lines and boxes connecting the two groups indicate which first consonants may co-occur with which second consonants. For instance, /m/ on the left has a line connecting it to a (matching) square containing /p/, and another line connecting it to a (matching) square containing /d/ and /z/. This means that English contains two-consonant codas like /mp/, as in /læmp/, "lamp," /md/, as in /spæmd/, "spammed," and /mz/ as in /dæmz/, "dams." Similarly, the right-hand consonants /z/, /ʒ/ and /dʒ/ have a line connecting them to a square on the left with only a /d/ in it, which means that there are two-consonant codas such as /zd/, as in /bʌzd/, "buzzed," /ʒd/, as in /ɹuwʒd/, "rouged," and /d͡ʒd/ as in /d͡ʒʌd͡ʒd/, "judged." (That lone /n/ on the right, rather than the left, is still intended to be a first consonant. It was just difficult to fit in neatly on the left side where it belonged. It's connected to two boxes, containing /θ/, /t/, /s/ and /d/, /z/, /tʃ/, /dʒ/, showing that it occurs as the first consonant in two-consonant codas like those in *tenth, tent, tense, tend, tens, stench,* and *lunge.*)

Some generalizations are immediately apparent. The only sound in American English which can precede all the other consonants in a two-consonant coda is /ɹ/, in words like *bird, purse, marsh, curl,* etc. The other liquid, /l/, is almost as flexible; it can precede anything except /ɹ/. (Notice that the /l/ and /ɹ/ in the bottom left-hand corner of Figure 3.4 are connected to the biggest squares of any consonants.) Finally, the nasal /n/ can precede any consonant that is pronounced using the tip of the tongue (any **coronal** consonant, which includes all the alveolars and interdentals), except /l/, /ɹ/, and /ʃ/.

> **coronal**, *adj.* From Latin *corōnāl-is*, itself from *corōna*, "crown," via French. Pronounced with the tip of the tongue.

Otherwise, clusters are very restricted. The only sounds that can occur after every consonant are the alveolar stops; any consonant can be followed by an alveolar stop with the same voicing except the alveolar stops themselves. Most consonants can be followed by an alveolar fricative with matching voicing as well, except for other alveolar and palatalalveolar fricatives. The nasals /m/ and /ŋ/, can also be followed by voiceless stops pronounced at the same place of articulation (**homorganic** stops), and /s/ can be followed by any voiceless stop. I won't list all the phonotactic rules summarized by Figure 3.4, but here are a few:

Phonotactic Rule 12: If the second consonant in a complex coda is voiced, the first consonant in the coda must also be voiced.

Phonotactic Rule 13: When a non-alveolar nasal is in a coda together with a non-alveolar obstruent, they must have the same place of articulation, and the obstruent must be a voiceless stop.

Phonotactic Rule 14: Two obstruents in a coda together must have the same voicing.

Taking all these patterns into consideration, we find that there are 74 possible two-consonant codas in English, which reduces our number of possible syllables just a little bit more, to 329,508,000.

> **homorganic,** *adj.* From Greek *homos* "same" + *organikos* "of or pertaining to an organ." Pronounced at the same place of articulation, i.e. pronounced using the same organ (teeth, alveolar ridge, velum, etc.).

Exercise 3.2 Try to think of a phonological word ending in each of the possible two-consonant codas represented in Figure 3.4. Don't forget that consonantal suffixes like *-ed* and *-s* count!

The Substring Rule applies to codas as well as to onsets, as we mentioned earlier in connection with /ŋ/. To see how it affects the possible third consonant in a three-consonant string, examine Figure 3.4 again. In order for a three-consonant cluster to be legitimate, the second consonant in the cluster must be both a legitimate second consonant and a legitimate first consonant. So, for instance, if the first consonant in the cluster is /ɹ/, and the second consonant is /p/, as in *burp*, the only possible third consonant is one that is a legitimate successor to /p/ in a two-consonant coda. The only possible successors to /p/ in a two-consonant coda are /θ/ (as in *depth*), /t/ (as in *clapped*), or /s/ (as in *lapse*). Consequently, they are the only possible extensions of a three-consonant coda cluster that begins with /ɹp/ (as in *burped* /bʌɹpt/ or *burps* /bʌɹps/).

When an obstruent is in *first* position of a two-consonant cluster, it is generally the case that only a coronal obstruent can follow it. Since nearly all the consonants that work in second position are obstruents, we expect third consonants to nearly always be a coronal obstruent. There are only seven cases of three-consonant codas where the Substring Rule predicts that a third consonant could be non-coronal.

Exercise 3.3 (difficult): Looking at Figure 3.4, figure out four of the coda sequences where the Substring Rule predicts that a *non-coronal* third consonant should be possible in a three-consonant cluster.

Here's an example: /ɹm/ is a possible two-consonant cluster (as in *warm*), and /mp/ is also (as in *bump*). The Substring Rule, then, predicts that /ɹmp/ is a possible three-consonant coda. Since /p/ isn't coronal, /ɹmp/ is one of the seven possible cases we're looking for. A made-up word that ends in this cluster might be *termp*.

In fact, despite the fact that the Substring Rule predicts they could exist, none of the seven possibilities ever seem to occur in English codas. All third consonants in English codas are one of five coronal obstruents: /t/, /d/, /s/, /z/, or /θ/. Taking this into account, our possible-syllable count comes down by 93 percent to 22,901,710. Since the only way to get from three to four consonants in a coda is to add the suffix *-ed* (which can be pronounced as /t/ or /d/) or the suffix *-s* (which can be pronounced as /s/ or /z/) to a word, the only possible fourth-consonants are /t/, /d/, /s/, or /z/, which brings the total number of possible syllables down another 70 percent to 6,596,940.

There are many other lesser restrictions on phonotactic patterns in English which we will not consider in detail. For instance, no English syllables begin with a /dl/ or /tl/ onset, although both /dr/ and /tr/ are extremely common. As mentioned in the last chapter, some vowel distinctions are neutralized before certain consonants, like /ɹ/, which reduces the possible inventory of syllables still further. Other restrictions apply only to particular kinds of words. For instance, we'll learn later about stressed, free morphemes in English. Such morphemes, if they are a single syllable, must either contain a coda or they must contain a tense vowel (i.e. a "long" vowel) – if they have no coda, their lonely vowel can't be lax (short). Consequently, for example, *do* is pronounced /duw/, not /dʊ/; *be* is /bij/, not /bɪ/, and *so* is /sow/. (This is why "beh" scored low in our original "Does it sound like an English word?" test.)

In any case, even without taking such subsidiary restrictions into account, our estimate of the possible syllable inventory of English is down to approximately 6,600,000. That's still quite a lot, but keep in mind that it's a *lot* smaller than our first raw calculation based just on the sound inventory of English. In fact, it's four orders of magnitude smaller than our first calculation – we've reduced the total number of syllables by 99.99 percent. The additional constraints which we haven't considered here, of course, mean that the true figure in fact is less than 6,000,000. What we have learned here about English syllable structure, however, should give you a sense of the quantity and complexity of the tacit knowledge that you bring to bear every time you contemplate a Scrabble rack.

> Another game in which your phonotactic instincts are brought to bear is "Ghost," a good car game for spelling geeks. In Ghost, players take turns adding a letter to a string of letters. The letter added must create the beginning of a correctly spelled word, but you don't want to add a letter which will complete the word. If you do complete the word, you are penalized by being assigned the first letter from the word "ghost." The winner begins a new word. Players who lose five rounds become a "g-h-o-s-t" and drop out; the winner is the last player who is not a ghost. The advanced version of the game, where you really see phonotactics in action, is SuperGhost, where players may add letters to either end of a word under construction.

3.4 From a Stream of Sound into Words: Speech Perception

As useful as phonotactic knowledge is in Scrabble, it is far more crucial to the problems faced by people listening to everyday speech. Although there are spaces between the words in the IPA transcriptions of phrases provided at the beginning of every chapter, in the actual speech stream that is heard by speakers of English, and children learning English, there are no breaks, except at the beginnings and ends of phrases. How do we identify the units in the utterance? How do we get from [wʊdʒəlajkfɹajzwɪðæʔ] to understanding the message "Would you like fries with that?"

Phonotactic rules are part of the answer. If you know that the consonant sequence [kf] is not a possible syllable onset or coda, then you know that there must be a syllable break in that spot. From that, you also know it might be a word boundary. Similarly for the sequence [zw]: you know that no English syllable coda can contain that sequence of sounds, so there cannot be a syllable boundary after the [w]. There must be a syllable boundary either before the [w] or before the [z], which again lets you know that there could be a word boundary in one of those places. This is the beginning of a correct segmentation of this stream of sounds.

The process of analyzing the speech stream is called **parsing**, and the first step in parsing is identifying the phonological words in a stream of sound. This is the first problem faced by an infant or toddler trying to learn his parents' language. How can he, not knowing any language at all, take an unbroken string of sound and detect significant sub-units which might have meaning attached to them? For example, in the phrase /ajsijðədɑɡij/, how does the child decide that /sij/ is an individual word with a particular meaning that it contributes to the meaning of the whole? Why not /sijð/? or /ajs/?

Part of the answer lies in the fact that babies are statistical supercomputers. As they hear speech directed to them and around them, their brains are detecting recurring patterns of repetition and tabulating the likelihood that particular sequences of sounds occur together as a unit. Studies have shown that babies can detect repeated sequences that occur in an unbroken string of CV syllables after only two minutes of exposure. To get a feel for what they're accomplishing, try reading the following aloud to yourself in an inflectionless, regular monotone:

bidamodapamopanotabinopatapabinomodadapamobinopapanotadapam
otapabinomodabidamodapamobinopapanotadapamotapabidapamopa
notanomodabidamobinopapanotatapabidapamo . . .

After hearing two minutes of such stimuli, 8-month-old babies have detected that the sequence is made up of six three-syllable "words," repeated in varying orders: *bidamo, panota, dapamo, binopa, nomoda,* and *tapabi.*

How can one tell what an 8-month-old baby has detected? Experimenters have found that they can measure the amount of time a baby pays attention to a sound by how long they keep their head turned toward it. When the baby gets bored, he'll turn his head away. In this experiment, the baby and his mother sit in a booth with speakers in it. At first, they just hear the two-minute string of unbroken syllables given above. (This is the "training" phase.) Later, the babies are presented with just some three-syllable "words" in isolation, e.g. *bidamo, bidamo, bidamo*. When the isolated "word" was one they had heard during the training sequence, babies paid noticeably more attention to it than they did to isolated "words" that hadn't occurred in the original 2-minute stream of syllables – even if the isolated "word" is made up individual syllables that were in the stream, but in a different order. (Although *mobida*, for instance, is made up of individual syllables that appeared in the original string, the syllables in the original string never occurred in that order. Babies would keep their heads turned toward a speaker playing *bidamo, bidamo, bidamo* longer than to one playing *mobida, mobida, mobida*, after hearing the training string given above.) This shows that the babies noticed particular sequences of syllables – the "words" and not just the individual syllables – after just two minutes of exposure. (The real speech that babies hear around them contains thousands of words, of course, not just six – which is why it takes longer than two minutes for them to notice their first words.)

Babies' statistical engines don't just pay attention to syllable sequences. They also detect phonotactic probabilities, and then use these probabilities to help them notice good candidates for "words" from the speech stream. For instance, in English, within many words, the sequence of consonants /ŋg/ appears, as in *finger* /fɪŋgəɹ/, *tingly* /tɪŋglij/, *anger* /æŋgəɹ/, or even *English* /ɪŋglɪʃ/. There are almost no words within which the sequence /ng/ appears, however. The only place where /n/ and /g/ tend to occur next to each other is when the /n/ is at the end of one word and the /g/ is at beginning of the next, as in phrases like "pine grosbeak," /pajngɹowsbijk/ or "I win games" /ajwɪngejmz/ or "thin gruel" /θɪngɹuwl/. Because /ŋg/ is a sequence contained within many words, the likelihood of hearing a /g/ after you hear an /ŋ/ is pretty high. On the other hand, because /ng/ is a sequence that is *not* contained in many words, the probability of hearing a /g/ after you hear an /n/ is quite low – after all, there are usually thousands of words someone could pick to follow a word ending in /n/, and only a few of those words begin with a /g/. Probabilistically speaking, then, it's a good bet if you hear

/n/ and /g/ next to each other in the speech stream, the /g/ marks the beginning of a new word, but if you hear /ŋ/ and /g/ next to each other, the /g/ doesn't begin a new word, but is part of the same word.

To test whether 9-month-old babies had discovered this phonotactic generalization, experimenters chose a CVC word beginning with "g," "gaffe" (/gæf/), that the babies were very unlikely to be familiar with, and embedded it in "sentences" of other CVC words (the sentences didn't mean anything really, they were just strings of nonsense words). In some "sentences," the word immediately before "gaffe" ended in an /n/, as in "... bean gaffe hold ... ,"/bijngæfhowld/. In other "sentences," the word immediately before "gaffe" ended in an /ŋ/, as in "... fang gaffe time ...,"/fæŋgæftajm/. (Of course, there were no pauses in pronunciation between the words that might signal their separation independently.) A group of 9-month-old babies from English-speaking homes was divided into two groups, A and B. Group A was played the sentences where "gaffe" followed a word ending in /ŋ/, (as in "... fang gaffe time ..."), and Group B was played the sentences where "gaffe" followed a word ending in /n/ (as in "... bean gaffe hold ..."). Both groups were then played just the word "gaffe" by itself. The experimenters knew that if the babies had noticed that "gaffe" was a word on its own, then they would pay attention to it significantly longer than to a control "word," like "fooz," that hadn't been in the sentence. Lo and behold, the Group B babies, who heard the sentences where "gaffe" followed a word ending in /n/, paid a lot more attention to the word "gaffe" played alone than they did to "fooz." In contrast, the Group A babies, who heard the sentences where "gaffe" had followed a word ending in /ŋ/, didn't pay any more attention to "gaffe" than to "fooz." This showed that the Group B babies, living around English speakers all the time, already knew that an /ng/ sequence is a pretty improbable sequence, and hence that it's unlikely to be contained in single word. That's why they picked up on the fact that the "gaffe" syllable had to be a word on its own. Similarly, the Group A babies knew that an /ŋg/ sequence is a relatively *probable* sequence, and hence that it's likely to occur within a single word. Those babies assumed that the "gaffe" syllable in the sentences they heard was *not* a word on its own – they probably thought it formed part of a word with the previous syllable ("fanggaffe" in the example above). Consequently, they were as unfamiliar with "gaffe" on its own as they were with "fooz," which they'd never heard.

So phonotactic knowledge is not only very important to the adult listening to the speech stream, but it is one of the first kinds of information acquired by (the brains of) very young children, which are trying to find clues which will enable them to break up the speech stream into smaller segments to which they can attach meaning. The phonotactic rules of English mean that certain kinds of consonant sequences are very likely to occur at the beginnings and ends of words, and hence at the beginnings and ends of utterances. If babies pay attention to the strings of sounds at the beginnings and ends of the utterances they hear, they will notice these high-probability, edge-marking sequences. Then they can use that knowledge to discern the edges of syllables, and hence find potential word boundaries, *within* the speech stream.

3.5 Syllables, Rhythm, and Stress

There is one major segmenting feature of the English speech stream that we haven't yet discussed. Syllables are an important phonological subunit, certainly, as demonstrated by the metered poetry examples given above, but that's not all. Read the limerick below aloud to yourself and count the syllables in each line:

(11) A foolish young hunter named Shepherd
      was eaten for lunch by a leopard.
      Said the leopard, "Egad!
      You'd be tastier, lad,
      If you had been salted and peppered!"

You should have come up with 9 syllables in the first line, 9 syllables in the second, 6 syllables each in the third and fourth lines, and 9 in the last. Indeed, this is a very common syllable pattern for a limerick. But it's not just syllable count that makes for a limerick. Read the following "lame-erick" to yourself, and count the syllables:

(12) A foolish farmer chased elephants.
      Elephants were squashing his best plants.
      The foolish farmer was
      Mad as a bee abuzz.
      His angry hopping seemed like a dance.

75

Correct syllable count, right? And the rhymes are in all the right places. So why doesn't this seem like much of a limerick? The answer is that the *stress* is in all the wrong places.

Exercise 3.4   Go back and read the first limerick to yourself, but don't say the words. Instead, substitute "la" for every syllable, so you can hear where the stress goes.

You should have ended up saying something like this:

(13)   la LA la la LA la la LA la
       la LA la la LA la la LA la
       la la LA la la LA
       la la LA la la LA
       la LA la la LA la la LA la

In the first, second, and fifth lines, there is a regular pattern of weaker and stronger stress:

weak STRONG weak weak STRONG weak weak STRONG weak

and, similarly, there's a particular pattern for the third and fourth lines:

weak weak STRONG weak weak STRONG

Now look at the lame-erick in (12). What is the stress pattern in the first line, if you just read it normally, forgetting that it's trying to be a limerick? It's something like this (There are dots between syllables within a word. "S" and "w" stand for "STRONG" and "weak.")

(14)   A FOO.lish   FAR.mer chased   EL.e.phants
       w S   w   S   w   w   S w w

But of course, we know the first line of a true limerick is supposed to have the rhythm *wSwwSwwSw*, not *wSwSwwSww*. Similarly, the third and fourth lines of the lame-erick, read naturally, have the following rhythm:

(15)   The FOO.lish FAR.mer was   /   MAD as a BEE a.BUZZ.
       w   S   w S   w   w   S   w wS   wS

but the third and fourth lines of the true limerick have this rhythm:

(16)   Said the LEO.pard, "e.GAD!   /   You'd be TAS.ti.er, LAD . . ."
      w   w S   w   wS   w   w S   ww S

Getting the hang of it? Every content word of English (nouns, adjectives, verbs, and adverbs) has its own particular pattern of stress. Less contentful words (prepositions, articles, auxiliary verbs, pronouns) are generally not stressed when they're part of a longer utterance (though they can be stressed for emphasis). To make a good limerick, you have to string together content words and function words so that they add up to the limerick stress pattern, or something fairly close to it.

Exercise 3.5   To practice your ear for stress, sort the 25 words listed below into five groups of five, according to stress pattern. (Hint: start by sorting according to number of syllables, since two words with same stress pattern have to have the same number of syllables.)

arrest, arrogant, atrocious, beautiful, belittle, beware, building, compute, computer, data, defeat, disbelief, donation, hammer, inferno, inspire, intervene, misbehave, national, paragraph, printed, redefine, shadow, telephone, underfed.

In IPA transcription, main stress is indicated by placing a vertical tick (') *before* the syllable that receives stress. So, for instance, the word *mother*, which has stress on the first syllable, is transcribed /ˈmʌðəɹ/, while the word "appear," which has stress on the second syllable, is transcribed /əˈpiɹ/. In transcription, we will use the IPA tick to indicate main stress. However, when indicating main stress in regular English orthography, I'll just write the stressed syllable in capital letters, like this: "MOther," "apPEAR."

The different stress patterns you discovered in Exercise 3.5 have names, which you may be familiar with from English class. A group of syllables containing one strong stress is called a *foot*. Two-syllable feet can have either a Sw pattern, like "MOther," or a wS pattern, like "apPEAR." The Sw pattern is called a **trochee**, or a trochaic foot. The wS pattern is called an **iamb**, or an iambic foot. (Shakespeare wrote in *iambic pentameter* – that is, most of his lines consisted of five iambic feet: "Shall I / comPARE / thee TO / a SUM / mer's DAY?"). Three syllable groups can have a Sww pattern, like "TElephone," a wSw pattern like "comPUter," or a wwS pattern, like "redeFINE." Sww feet are called **dactyls**, and wwS feet are called **anapests**. (Lines 3 and 4 of a good limerick are made up of two anapests.) Feet with wSw stress are called **amphibrachs**.

3.6 Using Stress to Parse the Speech Stream into Words

Because every content word in English has to have a stress on it somewhere, stress is also an important clue for babies trying to parse the speech stream into units. A sequence of unstressed syllables can't contain a content word. So, for instance, in the sentence "John is arrogant," whose transcription is /ˈdʒɑnəzˈæɹəgənt/, we know that the last two syllables of the utterance, /ɹəgənt/, cannot be a content word on their own, or individually, because neither of them bears stress.

We know that babies pay attention to stress as a cue to word boundaries because of another series of "Do they think it's a word?" experiments.

First, it's important to know that stress can be a pretty good indication of a word boundary in English. English has a tendency to initial stress – if a word has two syllables, it's more likely to have a Sw pattern than a wS pattern. Similarly, common trisyllabic words have a Sww pattern, not a wwS pattern. A bar chart showing the number of trochees, iambs, dactyls and "other" patterns among the 1000 most common (printed) English words is given in Figure 3.5. Most of the most frequent multisyllabic words have initial stress. In infant-directed speech, or "motherese," this tendency is even more exaggerated.

Do infants make use of this Sw tendency words have when parsing the speech stream? In an experiment designed to investigate this question, 7.5-month-old infants were divided into two groups. Two trochaic words (e.g. "doctor" and "candle") were played to Group A until they were familiar with them. Two iambic words (e.g. "guitar" and "device") were played to Group B until they were familiar with them. Then, two sentences were played to each group. The first sentence contained the words they'd just heard, while the second reading didn't contain those words. The experimenters hypothesized that if the babies recognized the words they'd just heard, they would listen longer to the sentence that contained them. If the Group A babies recognized their words, but the Group B babies didn't, it would show

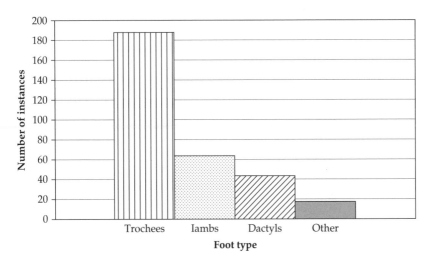

Figure 3.5 Foot types in the 1,000 most common English words

that babies learning English are paying extra attention to trochaic stress as a cue to wordhood.

Sure enough, the Group A babies listened longer to the sentences containing their familiar trochaic words than they did to passages containing unfamiliar words. The Group B babies, however, didn't listen any longer to the passages containing their familiar iambic words than they did to the passages containing words they were unfamiliar with.

The experimenters thought that the Group B babies were having trouble recognizing their iambic words because they were using initial stress as a cue to word boundaries. That is, they thought that babies might be guessing that every stressed syllable began a new word. When they heard a sentence like /ˈbɪlɪzˈbajɪŋəgɪˈtɑɹ/, "Bill is buying a guitar," they (mistakenly) parsed the stressed syllable /ˈtɑɹ/ as the beginning of a new word.

To confirm that that was what was happening, the researchers conducted a second experiment. They familiarized babies with *single*-syllable words that were the same as the stressed syllable in the iambic words from the passage. For instance, instead of playing the babies "guitar" and "device," they played them "tar" and "vice." Then they played the original sentences containing the iambic words "guitar" and "device" to those babies, as well as a control sentence containing other words that they hadn't been familiarized with. Sure enough, this time the babies did listen longer to the sentences containing the iambic words than to the control sentenecs. The babies were using stress as a clue to word boundaries – even though in these cases it was leading them to make a mistake. They thought "tar" was a word in the sentence, even though it was actually a subpart of the bigger word "guitar."

3.7 Misparsing the Speech Stream, Mondegreens, and Allophones

We adults sometimes get a taste of the problem faced by babies when we misparse the speech stream. This kind of mistake is one of the main ingredients of a particular type of joke, usually a pun.

Bart Simpson of the TV show *The Simpsons* specializes in this type of joke. He phones Moe, the dimwitted barman, and asks to speak to someone with an improbable name, which Bart gives in the order last name, first name. Moe shouts out the requested name, in the right order, to the assembled barflies, who respond with hoots of laughter, to Moe's consternation. Here are some typical exchanges:

Bart: I want to talk to a guy there named Coholic, first name Al.
Moe: Phone call for Al . . . Al Coholic . . . is there an Al Coholic here?

Bart: I want to talk to a guy there named Butz, first name Seymour.
Moe: Hey, is there a Butz here? Seymour Butz? Hey, everybody, I wanna Seymour Butz!

Bart: I'm looking for a Miss Huggenkiss, first name Amanda.
Moe: Uh, Amanda Huggenkiss? Hey, I'm looking for Amanda Huggenkiss! Ah, why can't I find Amanda Huggenkiss?

Another place where this phenomenon can inspire a few chuckles is in "Mondegreens." A mondegreen is a misheard song lyric. One famous one comes from the Jimi Hendrix song *Purple Haze*. He sings, "Excuse me, while I kiss the sky," but many people hear "Excuse me, while I kiss this guy." Children are particularly susceptible to this problem: they sing about "Olive, the other reindeer" (from the line "All of the other reindeer," in "Rudolph the red-nosed reindeer"), say prayers to "Our father, who art in Heaven, Howard be thy name" (from the line ". . . hallowed be thy name" in the Lord's Prayer) and think "Donuts make my brown eyes blue" (from "Don't it make my brown eyes blue," a Crystal Gale song).

> Mondegreens are named after a mondegreen that arose when people mis-heard the lyric of an old English ballad: "They had slain the Earl of Moray, and laid him on the green," heard as ". . . the Earl of Moray, and Lady Mondegreen."

This doesn't just happen with song lyrics or set phrases; it often happens in speech too, and is only revealed when the misparser writes down what she *thought* she heard, for example, *old wise tale* for "old wives' tale," or *take for granite* for "take for granted." (These are often called *eggcorns* – from someone who misunderstood "acorn". A collection of eggcorns can be found at http://eggcorns.lascribe.net/.)

What happens when we misparse speech in this way? Obviously our phonotactic system is fooled by such examples. How does this happen? Sometimes it's just that one phrase is homophonous with another phrase, and the only way to detect which parse is the correct one is by context. This is true of "Olive, the other reindeer," and "All of the other reindeer." For most people, "Olive" and "All of" are just homophonous, and context is the only thing which will allow you to figure out which is intended.

In other contexts, more complicated phenomena come into play. Sounds often vary a little bit in pronunciation, depending on what other sounds precede or follow them. For instance, when the alveolar stop /t/ is followed by the palatal glide /j/, the stop quality of the /t/ is softened, and the combination is pronounced more like the in-between alveopalatal affricate /t͡ʃ/ (for some speakers of English, this happens within words like "Tuesday" and "tune"). When you're speaking precisely, the phrases "Wouldn't you?" and "wooden shoe" sound quite distinct: /ˈwʊdənt'juw/ vs. /ˈwʊdən'ʃuw/. However, when you're speaking quickly, the /t/ at the end of "Wouldn't" and the /j/ at the beginning of "you" get smeared together into the alveopalatal affricate, and you end up saying /ˈwʊdən'tʃuw/ – which is essentially indistinguishable from "wooden shoe." Normally you'd never confuse a /t/ and a /ʃ/ – but if the /t/ is followed by a /j/, it can happen easily.

Expectations about stress assignment can facilitate misparses as well. In a song by Queen, *Bohemian Rhapsody*, one lyric goes,

/be'jɛlzəbʌbhæzə'dɛvəlpʊtə'sajdfɔɹ'mij/, "Beelzebub has a devil put aside for me." This line has a very odd, but nonetheless common, mondegreen: "Beelzebub has a devil for a sideboard. Eeeeee . . ." Consider the word boundaries and stress assignments in the last phrase of the correct parse and also in the mondegreen:

(17) a. . . . a DEvil put aSIDE for . . .
     b. . . . a DEvil for a SIDEboard

In the correct lyric, there's an iambic word – a word whose main stress does *not* fall on the first syllable. The mondegreen doesn't contain an iamb – it only contains single-syllable words and trochees. The person hearing this mondegreen has reanalyzed the phrase so that it conforms to the normal English expectation that a stressed syllable begins a new word. They're falling prey to the same expectation that the babies in the stress experiment did when they behaved as if the phrase /'bɪləz'bajɪŋəgɪ'taɹ/ contained the word /'taɹ/.

Here's a slightly more complicated example. Consider the transcriptions of the last part of the Hendrix line that we started with and its mondegreen:

(18) Excuse me while I . . .
      a. /kɪsðiskaj/
      b. /kɪsðisgaj/

Evidently, people hearing the mondegreen mishear the /k/ as a /g/. This doesn't happen most of the time. Is anyone likely to mishear the phrase "the coat" as "the goat"? Try saying them aloud to yourself, and comparing them to "the sky" and "this guy."

It turns out that the difference in syllabification is playing a role here. In "the sky," the /k/ is the *second* sound in a syllable, following an /s/ in the same syllable – *sky* is a syllable with a complex onset, made up of two consonants. By contrast, in "the coat," the /k/ is a syllable onset all by itself. Is there anything about the pronunciation of /k/ that is different when it occurs as a syllable onset by itself vs. when it occurs as the second consonant in an onset? It turns out there is.

Remember, early in the last chapter (pp. 45–6), we observed that voiceless stops were often *aspirated* in English. Words like *pot*, *tab*, and *kill* are pronounced with an extra puff of air right after the consonants /p/, /t/, and /k/. If you compare these words with *bought, dab* and *gill*, by placing your hand close to your mouth, you will detect that voiced stops are not pronounced with aspiration – no extra puff of air. But remember, in some cases, we noticed that the voiceless stops are *not* aspirated. When they're part of a complex onset in words like *spot*, *stab*, and *skill*, the voiceless stops lose that extra aspiration.

It is this difference in pronunciation of /k/ which makes it easy to mistakenly hear *the sky* as *this guy*: the /k/ in *sky* is unaspirated, because it's the second element in a complex onset, which makes it sound much more like /g/ than a /k/ in a simple onset does.

3.8 Allophony

We've just seen that the same basic sound – /k/ – has two slightly different pronunciations, depending on where in the syllable it is. This is an example of a phenomenon called *allophony*. **Allophones** are different pronunciations of the same sound that arise in different phonological environments. Compare your pronunciation of the vowels in the following two lists of words:

(19) | | |
|---|---|
| write | ride |
| trite | tried |
| height | hide |
| tripe | tribe |
| rice | rise |
| trice | tries |
| lice | lies |
| lout | loud |
| bout | bowed |
| house (*n.*) | house (*v.*) |
| mouth (*n.*) | mouth (*v.*) |
| sat | sad |
| bat | bad |
| cat | cad |

You perhaps have noticed that the vowels in the column on the left sound different than the vowels in the column on the right. This is again allophony in action. There are two different pronunciations of each of these vowels, a shorter one, and a longer one. (In some dialects of English, the difference is just in the length of the vowels. For others, there's also a difference in the way some of the vowels are pronounced.) Which column has the longer vowels in it, and which has the shorter ones? What aspect of the surrounding phonological environment seems to determine whether the vowel is long or short?

Exercise 3.6   What is the conditioning environment which dictates when to produce a longer vowel and when to produce a shorter vowel in the words listed above?

In modern English, certain vowels are longer when they appear before voiced consonants, and shorter when they appear before voiceless consonants. These different pronunciations are allophones of the same basic vowel sound, in the same way that aspirated and unaspirated /k/ are allophones of the same basic consonant.

In the two cases of allophony we have so far considered, the difference in pronunciation usually helps the listener to distinguish an otherwise potentially difficult-to-hear contrast. Aspirating voiceless stops at the beginnings of stressed syllables heightens the difference between them and voiced stops – it makes the difference between "pat" and "bat" easier to detect. Changing the vowel length before voiceless stops at the *end* of the syllable does the same thing. The length of the vowel is a clue that helps the listener to tell the difference between voiced and voiceless stops, this time in an environment – the end of the syllable – where aspiration does not provide the extra hint.

The differences in pronunciation make the distinction easier for listeners to hear, and makes misparses less likely to occur. Only in rare cases, like *Excuse me while I kiss the sky*, do they have the opposite effect. Allophony, then, is another tool that is useful to the parser in dividing the speech stream into discrete phonological words.

3.9   What We Know about Phonological Words

We've covered a broad range of material in this section on phonological words, and assimilated a lot of new information. In Chapter 2, we learned a precise system for representing actual pronunciation, the International Phonetic Alphabet. The architecture of the vocal apparatus provides the means to produce families of sounds that differ by only one feature: Place, Manner, and Voicing, in the case of consonants;

Height, Tenseness, and Backness in the case of vowels. These families of sounds tend to behave alike with respect to particular phonological patterns.

We then moved on to consider what kinds of patterns of sounds define a possible phonological word in English. Words are divided into syllables, which have very significant restrictions on the ordering of the elements that make them up. These restrictions constitute the *phonotactics* of English words. Understanding phonotactic patterns enables us to understand what kinds of sound sequences can be legitimate phonological words of English, and also how we can parse the speech stream into discrete units. We saw evidence that babies use phonotactic probabilities to identify the strings of sounds that are potential words of their language. Next, we learned about the requirement in English that content words receive stress, and saw that the most common pattern in English words is for stress to fall on the first syllable of the word. Finally, we considered cases where misparses of speech strings arise, even in adult speech, and saw how allophony can help speakers avoid misparses, providing additional clues to speakers about how to divide up the speech stream into phonological words.

Having identified some of the factors at work in creating the English phonological word – the factors that our orthographic spacing conventions are based on – we'll now move on to think about the relationship between phonological words and listemes. (Remember listemes? They are the *minimal meaningful* units of sound.) First, we'll consider where new listemes come from. We've already seen one mechanism that can generate new listemes – misparses of the speech string by learners of the language. In the next chapter, we'll think about that some more, and also look at other ways that new words can enter the language. We'll gradually move into the wild world of word-formation, full of prefixes and suffixes and other exotic beasts: **morphology**.

Study Problems

1. In the text, phonotactic rules are given describing possible combinations of sounds in the onsets of English syllables. Here are some generalizations about possible combinations of sounds in the codas of English syllables. (These generalizations only apply in words with no suffixes attached.)

a. If a syllable ends in two consonants:
  (i) If one of the last two consonants is a *nasal*, then
    (a) both the consonants have the same place of articulation;
    (b) the non-nasal consonant always comes second;
    (c) the non-nasal consonant is always either a stop or a fricative;
    (d) if the non-nasal consonant is bilabial or velar, it must be voiceless;
  (ii) If the first of the last two consonants is /s/, the second consonant must be a voiceless stop.
  (iii) If the first of the last two consonants is an obstruent, then both consonants must have the same voicing.
b. If a syllable ends in *three* consonants:
  (i) The last consonant must be dental, alveolar, or palatal.

Below are some invented "words" written in IPA, each of which violates one of the above generalizations, and hence are not actual or possible words of English. For each of the words below, try pronouncing it, and then state which of the generalizations above it violates:

a. kɪɹlf
b. pɛðəsθ
c. zeibk
d. flɔjsh
e. slʌgθb
f. ʃɹænk
g. sɪŋg
h. əlajsz

2. Using a dictionary that gives information about word origins, e.g. the Oxford English Dictionary, Merriam-Webster's, etc., look up the following words:

a. psychiatry
b. psilocybin
c. psoriasis

  (i) What language do these words trace their origins to?
  (ii) Transcribe each word in IPA as it is pronounced in your dialect of English. Indicate main stress with a tick before

the stressed syllable, and indicate syllable boundaries by placing a dot between syllables.

(iii) How is the spelling of these words misleading? Given their spelling, how do you suppose the onset of the first syllable of each of these words was pronounced in the original language (show it in IPA)? What phonotactic rule of English did these words most likely violate?

3. In several dialects of English, including American English, there are subtle variations in the pronunciation of the /l/ sound. It occurs in two variants, one that is transcribed as [l] and the other as [ɫ]. Here is a list of words containing /l/, with transcriptions showing its varying pronunciation in these dialects of English.

leaf	[lijf]	filter	[fɪɫtɹ]
feel	[fijɫ]	sold	[soɫd]
collect	[kəlɛkt]	lap	[læp]
inhale	[ənhejɫ]	milking	[mɪɫkɪŋ]
police	[pəlijs]	letter	[lɛtɹ]

a. Some of these words have more than one syllable in them. Which ones are they? Re-transcribe them showing where the syllable boundary is by placing a dot between the two syllables, and indicate which syllable receives main stress by putting a tick before it, as described in the chapter.

b. The two different kinds of /l/ are allophones. Which one you get depends on where in the word the /l/ appears. Describe where each variant of /l/ occurs in terms of syllable structure by filling in the blanks:

(i) /l/ is pronounced as [l] when it occurs in the _____ of a syllable.

(ii) /l/ is pronounced as [ɫ] when it occurs in the _____ of a syllable.

c. The [ɫ] sound is often called a "dark l," while the [l] sound is called "clear l." Dark l is produced by pulling the body of the tongue back toward the velum while making the /l/ sound; in the clear l, the tongue body is more towards the front of the mouth. In some dialects of English, particularly in Southeastern Britain, the dark l allophone has altered still further, becoming the glide [w] or the vowel [u]. In these dialects, "feel" is pronounced [fijw], "table" is pronounced [tejbu], and so on. Why do you think this sound change happens to the dark l allophone but not to the clear l allophone? (Consult the vowel diagrams given in Chapter 2. Your answer should mention the position of the tongue.)

4. We have seen that /t/ has an aspirated allophone [tʰ] and an unaspirated allophone [t]. We learned that the aspirated one occurs when the /t/ is by itself at the beginning of a stressed syllable. In American English /t/ also has other allophones. One of them is written [tˀ]; this allophone is called "unreleased t," and involves a glottal stop. Another allophone of /t/ is written [ɾ]; this one is called a **flap**, and involves quickly touching the tongue to the alveolar ridge without creating a full closure like a regular stop. Below, some words containing these other two allophones of /t/ are given, with transcriptions showing which allophone of /t/ occurs in each:

pat	[pʰætˀ]	patted	[pʰæɾəd]
repeating	[ɹəpʰijɾɪŋ]	Batman	[bætˀmæn]
repeat	[ɹəpʰijtˀ]	bucket	[bʌkətˀ]
atom	[æɾəm]	analytic	[ænəlɪɾək]
quiet	[kwajətˀ]	quietly	[kwajətˀlij]
quieted	[kwajəɾəd]	footman	[futˀmən]

a. Seven of these words are multisyllabic. Retranscribe them, showing where the main stress is with a tick in front of the stressed syllable. The first one is done for you:

['pæɾəd]

b. Describe the distribution of the [ɾ] allophone of /t/ by filling in the blank:

The [ɾ] allophone of /t/ is produced when the syllable before the /t/ is _____ , the sound immediately following the /t/ is _____ and that following syllable is _____ .

c. Describe the distribution of the [tˀ] allophone by filling in the blank:

The [tˀ] allophone of /t/ is produced when the /t/ occurs in the _____ of a syllable.

Further Reading

On English phonotactics (technical!):
Hammond, M. (1999) *The Phonology of English*. Oxford: Oxford University Press.

On child language acquisition and speech perception:
Golinkoff, Roberta M. and Hirsh-Pasek, Kathy (1999) *How Babies Talk*. New York: Penguin.
Werker, Janet F. (1995) "Exploring developmental changes in cross-language speech perception," in L. Gleitman (ed.), *An Invitation to Cognitive Science*, Vol. 1: *Language*. Cambridge, MA: The MIT Press.

On poetry and meter:
Attridge, Derek (1995) *Poetic Rhythm: An Introduction*. Cambridge: Cambridge University Press.

Notes

1   In a few words borrowed from German or Yiddish, there can be a /ʃ/ instead of an /s/ before non-liquids, as in *shtick*.
2   Again, in a few borrowed words, we see the /ts/ sequence: *tsunami, tsetse*. It is arguable, however, that this is not a sequence of two phonemes (a complex onset), but a new affricate.
3   Of course, as noted in Chapter 2, many dialects of English do not allow the /ɹ/ sound to occur in coda position at all. In such dialects, including RP, the number of available syllable codas is consequently somewhat different than in the American English dialect we are examining here.

4

Where Do Words
Come From?

/'wɛɹ 'duw 'wəɹdz 'kʌm 'fɹʌm/

> In this chapter, we look at some of the ways words come into a
> language, and how old words can change into new words. We'll
> learn about *back-formation, compounding, clipping, semantic drift,
> register change, jargon,* and *slang*. We then go on in subsequent
> chapters to discuss two of the most important word-creation
> methods, affixation and borrowing, in greater detail.

4.1   Getting New Listemes

We now have the beginnings of a grasp on how children can go from
an unparsed speech stream to a string of phonological words. In Chapter 8, we'll look at how they go from phonological words to listemes,
eventually learning a complete inventory of function and content
listemes, each with their own meaning attached. Every child discovers
their own set of listemes, each one potentially a little bit different. But
they have to have a speech stream to work with! The speech stream, of
course, comes from the adults and older children around the child,
who have already accomplished this feat for themselves. So the listemes
a child identifies in the speech stream will depend entirely on the
listemes produced by adults and older children ... whose listemes
depended on the speech of the people around them when they were
learning language ... and of course *that* community's listemes would
depend on the listemes of the older people around *them* when they
were children ... and so on, back to the beginnings of speech itself.
Shouldn't every generation's listemes match the ones of the generation
before?

Of course, they don't. The listeme inventory of any language changes from year to year. Each year, the American Dialect Society awards select new words a variety of titles from a list of relatively new words and phrases that have become popular in the previous twelve months. In 2002, they voted *blog* the Most Likely To Succeed; in 2004 *carb-friendly* won the Most Unnecessary category; in 2003 the Word of the Year was *metrosexual*. Who decides what words become popular, what ones fall out of fashion, which stay and which go? (It's not the American Dialect Society; they're just observing what *has* happened, not deciding what *will* happen.) And where do new words come from? We turn to these questions next.

4.2 When Do We Have a New Word?

It's actually only very rarely that anyone sits down and deliberately coins an entirely new word, and it's even rarer for such a deliberately coined word to actually become common currency among many speakers of the language. Most "new" words are created by some innovative manipulation of an already existing word or words.

One problem we face in discussing how words appear and disappear in a language is deciding what counts as a genuinely new word. The meaning of a particular word can change gradually over time, until the connection between the original and the modern meaning is so remote that one feels justified in saying it's not the same word anymore. The language has a "new" listeme, but it would be hard to say exactly when the new word appeared. The word *bully* used to mean "lover, sweetheart," and gradually came to have its current, almost opposite meaning over a long period of time. Does the language have a new listeme? Or is it the same listeme with a changed meaning?

Let's say for the purposes of this discussion that a new sound–meaning connection – a new listeme – is what we mean by a new word. If a change in meaning is radical enough, as in the case of *bully*, an old, familiar sound sequence counts as a new word.

Now, let's look at some of the things English speakers do to create new listemes.

4.3 New Words by "Mistake": Back-Formations and Folk Etymologies

Particular listemes – particular sound-meaning connections – are re-created anew in the mind of every new child that learns them. This learning process, although amazingly accurate for the most part (accurate enough to allow the learner to communicate effectively with his or her speech community), allows for some slippage. A child can acquire a listeme that was never in the vocabulary of the person he or she learned to speak from, given the right circumstances.

One common way in which new listemes can get pulled out of a speech stream that never contained them is via the same process that gives us mondegreens, eggcorns, and the game Telephone: misparsing a word or phrase. If the misparse has legs – if it makes enough sense – it may well enter the language as a new listeme. In this way, words that were originally single listemes in the mind of an adult speaker can come to be complex words containing two or more listemes in the mind of the learner. Similarly, complex words made up of multiple listemes in an adult's mind may be learned as a single unit, or divided into different units, by a misparse. Listemes that never existed before can spring into existence as a result.

Misparses come in two main varieties: **back-formations** and **folk etymologies**. Eggcorns and mondegreens are produced by folk etymology, where someone doing their best to make sense of an unfamiliar word or expression matches it as closely as possible to listemes already in their vocabulary. Some examples: There's an expression, *(waiting) with bated breath*, which uses an old verb *bate*, related to *abate* – it means "(waiting while) holding one's breath," and is supposed to connote anticipation or apprehension. Many people write that expression now *(waiting) with baited breath*, misparsing the unfamiliar word *bate* as the homophonous, more familiar word *bait*. Some folk etymologies almost completely replace their original word; a recent example of this type is *straightjacket* and *straight-laced*, which have replaced *straitjacket* and *straitlaced*; these contained the word *strait*, meaning "narrow" (often used to denote nautical tight spots, as in "the Straits of Gibraltar"). That word has fallen out of common usage, and people unfamiliar with it have re-parsed the word as containing the more familiar homophonous word *straight*. For a long time while I was a teenager, I thought the word *facetious* was related to the word *feces* – during that time, for me, *facetious* was a fancy way of saying "full of shit." I had created a folk etymology.

> **fog,** *n.* Back-formation from *foggy,* "thick, murky" (of air); "boggy" (of land); derived from *fog,* "coarse grass, moss" + *-y.* Thick mist or water vapor suspended in the air at or near the earth's surface.

A back-formation is a subspecies of a folk etymology that results in a totally new listeme entering the language. This occurs when a learner encounters a word that contains a sound sequence that sounds like a particular suffix. The word doesn't in fact contain that suffix, in the minds of the other people using it, but the learner doesn't know that. Consequently, the learner's word-analysis machinery strips off the apparent suffix, and invents a meaning for the leftover part by subtracting the apparent suffix's meaning. Some words that entered English this way are *juggle, burgle, televise* and *fluoresce.* The word *burglar,* referring to someone who enters a house to commit *burglary,* was in common use in English in the 1500s. Sometime around 1870, the word *burgle* first appeared. Where did it come from? Evidently, seduced by pairs like *write–writer, fiddle–fiddler, meddle–meddler,* and *wrangle–wrangler,* some enterprising person assumed that *burglar* was made up of a verb *burgle* plus the *-er* suffix present in those words. Just as a writer is someone who writes, and a meddler is someone who meddles, this learner thought, a burglar must be someone who "burgles." That is, the new verb *burgle,* by the logic of word-formation, must mean whatever it is a burglar does; burglars steal, so *burgling* must mean something like "stealing." The hypothetical learner would have started using *burgle* as a verb meaning "steal" – "Joe, I heard your house was burgled last night!" Because the *burgle* + *-er* derivation seems so plausible as analysis for *burglar,* the newly back-formed word caught on, and now is used widely in British English, though not so widely in American English. The same thing happened to *juggler. Televise* is back-formed from *television* (originally *tele+vision*); *fluoresce* from *fluorescent.* The same logic underlies the recent introduction of the verb *to lase,* from *laser. Laser* was originally an acronym for *Light Amplification by the Stimulated Emission of Radiation* – no *-er* suffix involved.

A very popular postcard from the early 1900s had a joke on it that relied on a back-formation. It shows a young man and woman seated under a tree; he's holding a book. He asks her, "Do you like Kipling?" She says, "I don't know, you naughty boy, I've never kippled!" The idea is that she had never heard of the author, Rudyard Kipling, who he was really asking about, and assumed that *-ing* was a suffix on a mysterious verb *kipple* that he was asking whether she liked. She was doing back-formation. One wonders what she thought *to kipple* might mean.

This process is going on all the time, as learners are constantly encountering new phonological words and doing their best to parse them. The creation of the word *monokini*, from an imaginary swimwear-related root listeme *-kini*, is apparently motivated by a back-formation of *bikini*. The two-piece swimsuit originally got its name from a South Pacific island, Bikini, which was one single listeme with no subparts. but it came to be analyzed as the prefix *bi-*, meaning "two" in words like *bicycle, biweekly, bivalent*, etc., plus a stem *-kini*. The stem *-kini* must obviously refer to a swimsuit piece, as *bi-kini* is a two-piece swimsuit; hence half a bikini must be a *monokini*. (One wonders why not a *unikini*, like *unicycle*?) The OED even lists the word *trikini*, built on the same principle.

Similarly, the use of *ology* to mean "advanced study of some topic" is a folk etymology. In words like *psychology, criminology, immunology*, etc, the listemes originally involved were *psych-* (as in *psychiatry*), *crimin-* (as in *criminal*), *immun-* (as in *immune*) and *-log-* (as in *logic*). The *-ology* part wasn't a listeme at all. The *-o-* represents a "theme vowel," a meaningless vowel inserted into the middle of Greek and Latin compounds to help them conform to the phonotactic rules of the language: you couldn't have an /kl/ or /nl/ consonant sequence in the middle of words, so *psych+logy* or *immun+logy* would have made an illegal sound sequence. (When a *-logy* form was created in which the first root ended in a vowel, no additional *-o-* was inserted: *geo-logy, eco-logy*.) So the *-o-* in *-ology* didn't originally belong with the *-logy* at all.

Two things conspired to make the *-o-* become a part of the *-logy* in the minds of English speakers. From other words containing the first part of the compound, it was clear that the *-o-* wasn't part of that root: *psych-* appears in *psychiatry, psychic*, etc.; *crimin-* appears in *criminal, immun-* appears as a word on its own, *immune*. Second, the stress rules of English resulted in main stress falling on the third-to-last syllable in *-logy* words, which nine times out of ten was the *-o-* syllable. The inclination of English speakers was to assume that the *-o-* syllable must be part of some meaningful root. Consequently, all these words came to be reanalyzed as *psych+ology, immun+ology,* etc, and the *-ology* part was understood as a listeme meaning "study of X." Since /ˈɑlədzij/ is a perfectly well-formed English word, phonotactically, now *ology* is an independent word of English.

4.4   New Words by Economizing: Clippings

A somewhat related way in which new words can be formed is *clipping*. In clippings, a multisyllabic word is reduced in size, usually to one or two syllables. It's often the case that a word is clipped because it comes into more common usage – its frequency count increases – and speakers find that they don't need to use the full sesquipedalian version to identify the concept. They prefer a more quickly and easily pronounced version. Some words that have come into the language this way are *fridge* (from *refrigerator*), *fan* (from *fanatic*), *mike* (from *microphone*), *fax* (from *facsimile*), *ammo* (from *ammunition*), *flu* (from *influenza*), *plane* (from *aeroplane*), and many more. Recently, *carb* has come into general use – a clipped form of *carbohydrates*. Some of these clippings may also qualify as back-formations: *refrigerator* contains several subparts that look like English affixes: *re-, -er, -at(e)* and *-or*; perhaps the *fridge* part is just the part that speakers assume is the unaffixed central listeme of the word. *Burger* is a clipping from *hamburger*, but it probably also qualifies as a folk-etymology, since *ham* is a meat-related listeme of English, although that word isn't a listeme in the original word *hamburger*. Burgers are made of beef, not ham, and the original item was named after the German town Hamburg. Indeed, *burger* often occurs in a compound with other words that specify what kind of burger it is: *buffalo burger, veggie burger, beefburger* – or what's on it: *cheeseburger* – which perhaps supports the idea that *burger* itself is understood to refer to a generic grilled-patty sandwich, and a compounded element is required to indicate what the content of the sandwich is.

Most clippings follow specific, phonologically determined patterns, though, and don't pay attention to morpheme boundaries. Clippings tend to retain the syllable of the word that bears main stress. In clipping the word *raccoon* to *coon*, or *opossum* to *possum*, the initial unstressed syllable is dropped. When the result of a clipping has two syllables, it nearly always is an "ideal" word of English, stress-wise – it's nearly always a trochee. as in *burger* or *possum*.

Nicknames are created by clipping: *Pete* from *Peter*, *Sue* from *Susan*, *Jeff* from *Jeffrey*, *Chris* from *Christopher*, etc. My own name, *Heidi*, was originally formed by clipping an old German name, *Adelheid* and adding the Germanic diminutive suffix -*i*, used in many English nicknames (*Jimmy*, *Betty*, *Archie*). The connection to *Adelheid* is largely lost, now, however, and *Heidi* is usually not recognized to be a nickname at all; it has entered the language as an independent name in its own right. The name *Elizabeth* has both primary and secondary stressed syllables, /əˈlɪzəˌbɛθ/, and the many nicknames formed on this long name use one of these two syllables as the intial stressed syllable in the trochaic ones: *Lizzie, Lizbeth, Liza, Lisa, Betty, Libby*, and *Bessie*, as well as *Liz, Beth, Bess*, and *Bets* are all versions of *Elizabeth*, some of which, like *Heidi*, have entered the language as independent names. The phonology of nicknames and clippings is a topic of considerable study.

4.5 *Extreme* Economizing: Acronyms and Abbreviations

A relatively new source of new words and listemes that is becoming increasingly important, especially in English, is a kind of extreme clipping: using the initial letters of the content word in a phrase to stand in for the whole phrase. This process has been around in English for a relatively long time (*C.O.D.* and *P.D.Q.* originated in the 1800s, for example), but it really took off as a new means of word-formation in the second half of the 1900s.

The whole family of inventions is called *initialisms*, and it has two main subgroups: *acronyms*, which are a collection of initials that are pronounced as a single phonological word according to the spelling conventions of English, and *abbreviations*, where the letters are read out one at a time. *AIDS* /ejdz/, from Acquired Immune Deficiency Syndrome, and *SARS* /saɹz/, from Severe Acute Respiratory Syndrome, are acronyms; *MS* /ɛmɛs/, from Multiple Sclerosis, and *DOA* /dijowej/, from Dead On Arrival, are abbreviations.

The proliferation of initialisms was a natural outgrowth of a proliferation of bureaucratic institutions named with long, unwieldly compounds and phrases, in particular in the US Army. Franklin Roosevelt (who is often referred to as FDR, rather appropriately), initiated many programs in the 1930s with such names, which commonly came to be referred to by their initials: the CCC, the WPA, the CWA, PWAP, FERA. These programs and their initialisms are long gone, but the floodgates were opened. The tendency of the American armed forces to initialize everything in sight also had a big impact on common usage around this time, since such a large percentage of the population was involved one way or another with the military in the 1940s. Initialisms like *GI, AWOL, snafu,* and *radar* entered the language during this period.

> **Humvee,** *n.* From the acronym HMMWV, for High-Mobility Multi-purpose Wheeled Vehicle. A proprietary name for a type of four-wheel drive diesel-powered vehicle, which replaced the jeep in the US military.
>
> **jeep,** *n.* From the initials G.P., for General Purpose. A small, four-wheel drive, general purpose vehicle used by the US military.

Since then, initialisms have become a completely accepted way of referring to organizations in American English. Very often an organization or group will pick a phrase for their name based entirely on the word that will result when it's initialized. One of the many on-line initialism lists, for instance, is *Ben's Incredible Big List of Initialisms and Acronyms* – BIBLIA for short. It's actually one of the smaller such lists; many acronym dictionaries for institutional and scientific use contain tens of thousands of entries. It's likely that you can think of several local acronyms that are familiar in your own school, workplace or town, but which would be mysterious to anyone outside your own community.

Ben's BIBLIA list is actually a list of a specialized and relatively new type of initialisms: initialisms that have come into use primarily in electronic communications of one kind or another: email, instant messaging, and chatrooms. People who are typing, rather than talking, have a particular impetus to economize on frequently used phrases, or phrases that are inserted to maximize communicative flow rather than convey actual information. Consequently, a barrage of new initialisms have appeared, some more familiar, some less: *imho* (In My Humble (or Honest) Opinion), *lol* (Laughing Out Loud), *motos* (Member Of The

Opposite Sex), *rotfl* (Rolling On The Floor Laughing), *rtfm* (Read The Fucking Manual), *ykwim* (You Know What I Mean), and many, many others. Some are specialized to a particular group or chatroom; for example, Dave Barry's blog uses *wbagnfarb* for "Would Be A Good Name For A Rock Band," an in-group catchphrase. Others are a private joke between just two or three people. The main thing of note for us is that abbreviations and acronyms are now being formed on a daily basis by millions of Internet users. Most will die the day they're coined, but a few will persist, and the net effect will be that new listemes enter the language.

In one way, initialisms and acronyms are an extreme form of clipping. Especially in military-speak, acronyms and clipping cohabit comfortably in several listemes. Clipped words can be compounded, as in *CENTCOM*, from CENTral COMmand, or a phrase can undergo a combination of clipping and initializing, as in *UNSCOM*, the United Nations Special COMission, or *COMDEX*, the COMputer Dealers' EXposition. These initialisms blend clipping and initializing freely, partly to create a final form that will be easily pronounceable as an English word.

4.6   Building New Words by Putting Listemes Together: Affixation and Compounding

We've already seen that phonological words can be made up of more than one listeme, as in *walk-s* or *dog-s* or *un-happy*. The affix listemes can usually mix and match with the listemes they attach to (called **stems**). If you put together an affix and a stem in a new way, you've created a new word.

People make new words like this all the time, of course. Very often, though, the newly formed words don't survive very long. In most cases, someone has "made a new word" in the sense that they've created a new *phonological* word. If a complex word's meaning is clearly derived from the meanings of its parts, as in *chair+s*, it doesn't seem accurate to say that we're looking at a new *listeme* – this phonological word is made up out of existing listemes and their meanings, and the meaning of the whole is entirely predictable. It's only when a new combination of affix + stem comes to be slightly idiomatic, with a meaning that you couldn't really guess from the meanings of its parts, that we really have a new listeme. At *that* point, it's fair to say a new word has entered the language. *Awe+some* and *terr+if+ic* used to have predictable meanings when they were first formed – "inspiring awe" and "inspiring terror," respectively – but after a while, they became idiomatized. At that point, the language had two new listemes, whose meanings weren't connected to the meanings of their component parts.

Affixation is one of the two main ways new words enter the language, and we will spend a considerable amount of time studying it in the next two chapters. There is another process for putting listemes together, though, that's not quite affixation, which we won't touch on in later chapters. This process is responsible for many of the listemes in modern English. It's called **compounding**.

Compounding occurs when two independently meaningful roots are directly combined to form a new, complex word, usually a noun or adjective. Examples of each are given below:

(1) | *Adjective* | *Noun* |
|---|---|
| headstrong | high school |
| skin-deep | rattlesnake |
| easygoing | sunshine |
| white-hot | hubcap |
| outspoken | afterthought |

In fact, noun-noun compounding is completely **productive** in English; new compound noun phrases are made up every day. If you know what a *scandal*, an *investigation*, and a *committee* are, you know what a *scandal investigation committee* is, even if you haven't ever heard the compound before. And if you know *chairperson* (itself a compound), you know what a *scandal investigation committee chairperson* is. And you probably know what a *scandal investigation committee chairperson appointment meeting* would be ... and what a *scandal investigation committee chairperson appointment meeting ruckus* would be ... and what a *scandal investigation committee chairperson appointment meeting ruckus investigation* would be ... and just imagine if they formed a committee to investigate *that*, it would be ...

Compounding creates a new, multiword item that behaves like a single part of speech. In the case of noun–noun compounding, the result behaves like another noun. Consequently, it's often considered part of the domain of morphology and word-formation, even though it often involves clearly separate phonological words. You can tell that a noun–noun compound behaves like a simple noun because it's not possible to insert an adjective in between the nouns of a compound: we have to say *the long$_A$ committee$_N$ meeting$_N$*, not **the committee$_N$ long$_A$ meeting$_N$*.)

The thing of particular interest to us here is that compounding frequently results in a new listeme, because the meaning of the whole often cannot be computed from the meaning of its parts. The intended meaning relationship between two nouns in any given compound can vary unpredictably from one to another: *alligator shoes* are shoes made *from* alligators (skin), but *nurse shoes* are not shoes made from nurses. Rather, they're shoes made *for* nurses. A *newspaper* is a paper with news printed on it, but *wallpaper* is paper that goes on walls. As has been remarked many times, we oddly *drive* on a *parkway* but *park* on a *driveway*.

In order to interpret a compound correctly, speakers often have to understand quite a lot about the way the two elements in the compound are connected, which can often lead quickly to the whole thing becoming idiomatic, and hence a listeme. It's not impossible to use the compound *alligator shoes* to refer to shoes made *for* alligators, rather than *from* them, but you'd have a lot of explaining to do to people who have memorized the compound as a listeme, with a fixed meaning.

> **goodbye,** *excl.* From Early Modern English, a contraction of *God be with you*. An exclamation of farewell.

In any case, compounding with idiomatization, like other kinds of productive morphological processes, is a major source of new listemes. If a compound is used frequently enough, parts of it may get phonologically reduced, even to the point where it's no longer recognizable as a compound at all. The word *breakfast* is like this. The names of the days of the week are like this, too.

Exercise 4.1 Look up the words *lord, hussy, woman,* and *gospel* in the OED or other dictionary with etymological information. What were the root words in each of these former compounds?

So far, the examples of compounding we've seen have all used listemes that are themselves complete phonological words. In fact, some of the most lasting compounds made in modern English are made from listemes that never occur by themselves. Scientific and technical vocabulary is almost entirely created out of listemes borrowed from Greek and Latin (we'll discuss why that is in Chapter 9). Greek and Latin listemes are mostly **bound** – they can't stand on their own as phonological words – but that doesn't stop them from being independently meaningful listemes in modern English. (We'll learn more about "bound" and "free" listemes in the next chapter.) *Psych-* is a subpart in *psychology, psychiatry, psychedelic, psychic,* and *psychoanalytic* – and none of these words existed before English speakers created them using the Greek root. Similarly, *tele-* is an element of the modern compounds *television, telephone, telekinesis, telegraph,* and *telecast*. Because these listemes always occur attached to other elements, it's more difficult to detect their meaning contribution in a given compound – you can't usually look at their meaning by itself – but in principle, the complex listemes they are a part of are formed according to the same process of composition + idiomatization that applied to all the other listemes formed by compounding.

4.7   Compounding Clips and Mixing It up: Blends

Some new words are created by a sort of combination of all of the above processes. If you clip a couple of words and smoosh them together to make a new word whose meaning is connected to the meanings of the originals, you've made a *blend*. Blends are some of the new words that we're most conscious of, probably because someone usually made them on purpose. Some famous examples are *motel (**mo**tor **hotel**), smog (**sm**oke and f**og**), brunch (**br**eakfast and l**unch**), chunnel (**Chunnel** tunnel), napalm (**na**phthenate and **palm**itate), guestimate (**guess** and **estimate**).* Humpty Dumpty described several blends to Alice in *Through the Looking Glass* (he called them *portmanteau* words): *slithy* from **lithe** and **slimy**, *mimsy* from **miserable** and *flimsy*, and *wabe* from **way before/way behind/way beyond**. The *Washington Post* Style Invitational often pits readers against one another in creating the funniest new blend, where the challenge is to do it by adding, deleting, or changing only one letter of an existing word. Here are some examples from the 2003 contest:

Sarchasm: the gulf between the author of sarcastic wit and the person who doesn't get it.

Osteopornosis: a degenerate disease.

Beelzebug: Satan in the form of a mosquito which gets into your bedroom at 3 a.m. and cannot be cast out.

Ignoranus: A person who's both stupid and an asshole.

Sometimes it's difficult to decide if a word is a blend or a compound of a folk-etymologized root with another root. A good example of this is *infotainment*, which seems like a classic blend, meaning something like **info**rmation enter**tainment**. There's a possible break in *entertainment*, though, right after an independently recognizable listeme *enter-* in English, and *info* is a free listeme on its own now, resulting from a clipping of *information*, so it might be that *infotainment* is really a case of folk-etymology (*-tainment* from *enter+tainment*) + compounding (*info+tainment*). It has a sister blend *edutainment*, that might support the independent-listeme status of *-tainment*. In any case, blends show us that people generally feel quite free in manipulating subparts of words to form new words, whether there's historical justification for the decomposition into subparts or not.

4.8 New Listemes via Meaning Change

As we noted in the introduction to this chapter, if a listeme changes its meaning enough, it can earn itself a new dictionary entry. Our example word *nice* from Chapter 1 is certainly like that, as it has gone from meaning "stupid" to meaning "pleasant" in the past few hundred years. As meanings change, of course, the connection of a word with its original use becomes more obscure, which can lead to a pleasant feeling of surprise and discovery when one looks at the original interpretation. Looking at how the meaning of a word changes over time can give us a little window on how the surrounding culture has changed over time, and hence often enhances historical understanding, not just lexical understanding. Why do we *dial* a phone number? Where does the word *car* come from? Why is gossip sometimes called *scuttlebutt*? How is the word *surly* related to the word *sir*, and how is *sir* connected to *senator*? (These three are certainly all separate listemes in modern English!) The history of the meaning of nearly every word is a little cultural story, if one pursues it, and it's an endlessly fascinating topic.

Meaning change is by nature a flexible process, but there are a few recognized paths of change that words can take.

4.8.1 Widening and narrowing

A word's meaning *widens* when it was formerly used to describe a more specific concept, and over time comes to refer to a more inclusive concept. The word *bird*, for instance, used to mean just "young fowl," but it gradually came to have its broader, modern meaning, which includes all fowl both young and old. Similarly, *manage* used to mean specifically "handle a horse," but now it means handling anything difficult successfully. Widening often happens as a result of metaphorical or fanciful application of a term. When a learner hears such a use and doesn't recognize that it's metaphorical, they simply conclude that the word has a more inclusive basic meaning, one that covers a broader range of situations. Children are very literal-minded; mastery of metaphor, humor and meaning extension is a linguistic skill that is fairly late to develop, and so the metaphorical or humorous nature of a particular usage can easily be lost on them.

Similarly, *narrowing* happens when a word with a formerly broad application is reanalyzed by learners as having a more narrow application. Sometimes this happens when another word with a similar meaning comes along and takes over the meaning of the original. This is the case of the word *deer*, which in Old English meant "animal." In the Middle English period, though, the French borrowing *beast* came to be commonly used for the meaning "animal," and *deer* came to be restricted to its current meaning, describing a common kind of wild, herbivorous quadruped ungulate. (Later on, the word *animal* was borrowed from Latin, with its modern meaning, and pushed *beast* into a narrower meaning as well.) Other examples of narrowing include a shift in the meaning of *accident*, from simply "a happening" to today's meaning, "unplanned unfortunate event," and *ledger*, which used to be the unmarked word for "book" but now refers specifically to a book of financial records.

---

knight, *n.* From Old English *cniht, cneoht,* "boy, lad." A mounted man-at-arms serving a feudal ruler. (Formerly: a youth in service, a gofer.)

4.8.2   *Social climbing:* amelioration *and* pejoration

Part of the information connected to a listeme is a note about its *register*. Words can be polite, rude, or neutral, suitable for high society or the neighborhood bar. Using a word from a particular register in the wrong context can lead to negative social consequences, whether it's using a slang term in a formal situation or using a high-falutin' term in a casual situation. A given listeme's annotation for register can change over time, often from high to low, and sometimes from low to high. A word that used to be polite might now be rude; similarly, sometimes a word that used to be casual or slangy might now represent the height of sophistication.

When a word moves from a lower register to a higher register, or from having negative connotations to having positive connotations, we can say that it has undergone **amelioration**. Our example word *nice* from Chapter 1 has undergone amelioration; it used to have the negative meaning "stupid, simple," and now, of course, it means "nice." *Fond* underwent a similar change: in Shakespeare's time it meant "foolish, crazy, dazed"; over time it came to mean "over-infatuated, dazed with love." From there it just came to mean "in love with" and then "affectionate towards," losing the negative sense entirely.

Pejoration is what happens when a word moves downward, socially or emotionally. We saw that *bully* used to have a positive meaning, "sweetheart, lover," and we know that it now means "abusive person." It got there via a meaning extension from "lover" to "pimp"; from "pimp," the meaning widened to include not just men who control women's sexual behavior for their own profit, but all stronger people who impose their will on weaker people, particularly for petty reasons.

Pejoration is the constant fate of euphemistic words. The word *retarded* was first applied to developmentally delayed children as a nicer way to describe their condition than the former technical term, borrowed from Greek, *moron*, which had become cruel – *moron* had gone through pejoration. Then the same thing happened to *retarded*. A new set of technical terms – *special needs, developmentally disabled* – has begun to replace *retarded* now, again with the intention of allowing a purely medical diagnosis to be made without an implication of social stigma. Changing the word may mask the underlying problem of social prejudice in a superficial way, temporarily, but it can't help for long without a corresponding change in the underlying cultural attitudes towards the people referred to by the term. If there is no such change, then *special needs* will ultimately suffer the same fate that *moron* and *retarded* have. Perhaps you have noticed the term "special" being used in a derogatory way already.

> **toilet**, *n.* From French *toilette*, "a small piece of cloth," a diminutive of *toile*, "cloth." A porcelain fixture with a seat and a water-flushed bowl used for excretion. (Formerly, a towel or cloth placed on the shoulders during hair-dressing or shaving; also, the table at which one dressed or shaved; also, the process of washing and grooming.)

Pejoration is therefore particularly revealing about the underlying attitudes of a given culture. Sociolinguists of English have long noted that terms that were originally neutral ways of referring to the female equivalents of male roles or entities acquired a negative spin that their masculine counterparts lacked. Consider the pairs *mistress/master*, *spinster/bachelor*, *bitch/dog*, and *princess/prince*. In each case, there's at least one use of the feminine term that has negative overtones – overtones that the masculine term lacks. The feminine term has undergone pejoration, while the masculine term hasn't. It has been argued that this is symptomatic of society's underlying negative attitude towards women: negative attitudes towards a group result in negative connotations attached to the words referring to the group. As attitudes change with the change in the status of women in English-speaking countries in the past 50 years, we may see fewer such pairs in the language.

4.8.3 Conversion

There are a few other sources of new words in the language. One, rather like affixation or compounding, occurs when a word of one part of speech is converted into another part of speech. This is a very productive process in English, which people regularly perform on the fly. The sentence "Babe Ruth homered his way into the hearts of America" involves conversion of *homer* (a noun describing a type of excellent hit in baseball) into *to homer* (verb). This particular conversion hasn't resulted in a new listeme, however, since it hasn't caught on as a verb on its own. Conversions do sometimes give new listemes, however: *to impact* is now a verb with a life of its own, independent of the conversion that originally produced it from the noun *an impact*; similarly *throw-up* is now a noun with a life of its own, independently of the conversion that produced it from the particle verb *to throw up*.

One kind of conversion that frequently results in a new listeme is the conversion of a proper name, like *Watt* (James Watt, inventor of the steam engine), to a common noun, in this case *watt*, a unit of power, particularly electric power. This kind of conversion is often used to refer to an invention or discovery of the person whose name it is, or sometimes as a verb or adjective describing a characteristic way of behaving or speaking that is associated with the person named. Some words derived in this way are *galvanize, mach (speed), teddy bear, Kafkaesque, Darwinian*, and *sandwich*.

> **byzantine**, *a*. From Latin *Bȳzantīnus*, f. *Bȳzantium*, "Constantinople, Istanbul." 1. Belonging to Byzantium or Constantinople. 2. Reminiscent of the manner, style, or spirit of Byzantine politics. Hence, intricate, complicated; inflexible, rigid, unyielding.

Another instance of this type of conversion is the use of the official trademark proper name of a company or their product as a common noun or regular verb referring to all products of that type. Companies hate this tendency – they want their name to be associated with their own product, not just any old knock-off – but it is, to a certain extent, inexorable. Some famous cases are *Kleenex* for facial tissue, *Xerox* for photocopying, *Lycra* and *Spandex* for stretch fabric, and *Frisbee* for flying discs. A recent one is the verb *to google*, meaning to execute an Internet search on a term, from the name of the dominant search engine, Google.

4.9 But Are These Words Really *New*?

Still, though, we haven't really seen any cases where the word has really been created out of nothing. Doesn't anybody actually sit down and make up a completely new word, ever?

In fact, the answer is generally "No." People don't make up new words deliberately very often. There are only a few real cases of words being made up out of whole cloth. For instance, the inventor of a new photographic process, Mr Eastman, invented *Kodak* out of nothing in 1888 to serve as a trade name for his product and company. The internet search engine Google derived its name from another word made up out of nowhere: the word for the number 10^{100}, *googol*. *Googol* (also *googolplex*) was invented on the spot by a mathematician's nephew, when he was asked what he thought a one with a hundred zeroes should be called. Generally, though, this kind of event is the exception rather than the rule. People usually get new words by modifying old words.

Throughout this discussion, though, we have only lightly touched on the *primary* source of genuinely new words in English, which is **borrowing**. Borrowing occurs when a community that speaks one language comes into contact with a community that speaks another language, and adopts a word from that community, as English borrowed *spaghetti* from Italian, or *karate* from Japanese. Depending on the history of a given language, borrowing can be a very important or almost negligible source of new listemes. It so happens that the number of new words introduced to English by borrowing makes the combined number of new words added to English via all of the above methods look truly titchy, like 10 next to a googol. To understand borrowing properly, and the remarkable effect it has had on the English vocabulary, we really have to look at the history of English in some detail. We will do that in Chapter 9.

4.10   What Makes a New Word Stick?

The forces which drive both the creation and the loss of listemes are cultural. Most new listemes come into common use because of a sudden general need to refer to the concept which they name. In the year 2000, the word *chad*, previously known to nearly no one, suddenly became a term familiar in American mass culture, when the presidential election seemed to depend on hanging ones. With the election, and the need to refer to them, past, *chad* receded into the background. In the late 1990s, weblogs gradually became more and more common; in the early years of the new millennium, the clipped word *blog*, for referring to them, became broadly known and used, and will likely remain around as long as weblogs are a central feature of Internet life. You likely don't know what kind of animal a *gilt* is, but if you had lived in a farming community which raised pigs, you'd be much more likely to have encountered it. People have words for the concepts they need or want to talk about; words for concepts that they don't need or want to talk about much gradually become less and less frequent, sometimes disappearing from the language entirely.

The real question, then, is what is it that makes people need or want to talk about something? This is part of the field of study of *socio-linguistics*, and deserves a whole book of its own.

The "need" part of the question is fairly easy to identify. A group of people will need to talk about something if they are thinking about or using that something on a regular basis. In such a situation, the word for that concept will gain common currency in that group.

> **bellwether,** *n.* From Old English *belle,* "bell" + Old English *weðer,* "a castrated ram." A leader of a movement or activity; also, a leading indicator of future trends. (Formerly referred to the leading ram in the flock, around whose neck a bell was hung.)

When a "needed" word remains specialized to one particular group, it becomes part of the *jargon* of that group. *Gilt* is pig-breeding jargon; *allophone* is linguistic jargon, *tranny* is snowboarding jargon, *red-shift* is astronomy jargon, *biner* (/bijnɟ/) is rock-climbing jargon, and so on. Jargon is just specialized terminology used by a particular group to serve its everyday communicative needs. It is special to that particular group because other groups aren't thinking about or working with the same concepts on a daily basis.

The harder question has to do with what makes people *want* to talk about a certain concept, or to use a new word for a concept that they already had a different word for. Why have certain kinds of flashy jewelry come to be called *bling-bling* in recent years? Why did people stop using the exclamation *rad!* ? Who first called someone they disliked a *douche bag* – and how did the expression catch on? The infinite mutability of **slang** has to do with the dynamics of fashion and status, in-group and out-group, what's hot and what's not. You can probably come up with 20 slang expressions that have appeared (and perhaps disappeared) in your generation. Because the negotiation of in-group status is a constant, ongoing process, slang tends to be very transient – new words and expressions come into fashion every day, and drop out just as fast.

Some slang expressions become more widely used, and hang on longer than average, or enter the language and culture more broadly and permanently. *Jazz* was originally a slang term; going back a little farther, so were *banter*, *filch* and *scamper*.

Exercise 4.2 Visit the website of the American Dialect Society, http://www.americandialect.org/, and go to their "Word of the Year" section. Look at the words and phrases that they discuss for the most recent year, and try to predict which ones will quickly be forgotten, and which will last a little longer. Are any of them associated with a specific, widely discussed event that happened that year? Do any seem like they might become widely used, long-lasting words? Now have a look at the words and phrases that they picked out from some year five or more years ago. Have any of those remained in common use? Do any of them seem completely unfamiliar to you?

One has to be a particular kind of cultural leader to introduce a new slang term and have it picked up on by the rest of the group. But there is a kind of new-word-creation that's available to anyone. We all engage in it every day, when we put affixes and stems together to create new phonological words. This is what we're going to look at next: we turn to the study of English *morphology*.

Study Problems

1. Begin to explore the *Oxford English Dictionary*.
   a. Look up the word *fool*. How many separate entries have *fool* as their headword?
   b. Look at the entry for *fool, n.*[1] and *a*. Find the *Etymology* portion of the entry, in square brackets (after the *Spellings* portion).
      (i) What do the abbreviations "*ME.*" and "*OF.*" stand for? What about the abbreviation "*ad.*"? (Consult the "Abbreviations List." If you are using the OED online, click on "Help," then "Abbreviations Used in Definitions and Etymologies.")
      (ii) What is the modern French form of the old French word that is the source of English *fool*? What is the feminine form of that modern French word?
      (iii) What are the Latin forms that correspond to the old French word that is the source of English *fool*? What did these forms originally mean in Latin?

      (iv)   What is the date of the earliest example given of the word *fool* in a written English text?

      (v)   There is a note in definition A.I.1.a. about a difference between earlier uses and modern uses of the word *fool*. What does it say?

   c. Look up the word *town*, entry 1: *town, n.*

      (i)   Is this word of Germanic or Latinate origin?

      (ii)   What general principle determines the order in which the different definitions are given?

      (iii)   What does *Obs.* stand for? What does it mean?

      (iv)   What is the earliest date that some form of the word *town* appeared in a written English text? What was the meaning of the word in that appearance?

      (v)   Which definition (number and letter) is the one that best captures the everyday modern English use of the word?

2.   Look up the following words in the OED or other dictionary with etymological information. What type of word-formation does each exemplify?

prom
pasteurize
gas/petrol (in the sense "fuel for a car")
sonar
scuttlebutt

Further Reading

Nash, Walter (1993) *Jargon*. Oxford: Blackwell.
Michael Quinion's World Wide Words website:
http://www.worldwidewords.org/

A bibliography of etymological dictionaries and books:
http://www.takeourword.com/bibliography.html

Neologisms:
Algeo, John (1991) *Fifty Years Among the New Words: A Dictionary of Neologisms 1941–1991*. Cambridge: Cambridge University Press.

5

Pre- and Suf-fix-es: Engl-ish Morph-o-log-y

/ˈpɹij ən ˈsʌfɪksəz ˈɪŋglɪʃ ˌmɔɪˈfalədʒij/

In Chapter 1 we saw that there was a significant mismatch between independently meaningful units (*listemes*) and phonological words. One of the main reasons for this mismatch is that there are meaningful elements contained *within* phonological words. There are even some elements that are obviously regular subparts of words even though they *aren't* independently meaningful. These subparts, whether independently meaningful or not, are called *morphemes*. We will look at the morphemes which make up English words in some detail in this chapter, learning about the processes of *derivation* and *inflection*. We will also learn about the ways affixation interacts with stress assignment and part of speech.

5.1 Listemes

In Chapter 1, we arrived at a distinction between **listemes** and **phonological words**. Phonological words are a unit of speech that may be made up of one (*dog*) or several (*dogs*) or no (*caboodle*) listemes. Listemes are the units that encode a sound-meaning connection – they are the things that are *listed* in the mind of a speaker of English.

In the next three chapters, we're going to try and discover something about what those listings must be like. If they encode a sound–meaning connection, they at least must include information about sound – how the listeme is pronounced – and information about meaning. Our first idea of a listeme, then, will be something like a dictionary entry. Here's some first attempts at representations of listemes:

Phonology		*Semantics*
/ˈkæt/	↔	CAT, i.e. "four-legged animal, pointy upstanding ears, carnivore, domestic, furry, 'meow' noise"
/ˈkɪkðəˈbʌkət/	↔	"die"
/əd/	↔	"past tense"

(Of course, the semantics part here is only approximate; we'll refine it more in Chapter 7.) So this is the minimal amount of information that we have to know about listemes.

But of course we need to say more. Even though /əd/ means "past tense" in a verb like *patt-ed*, it can't mean past tense by itself – it has to have a verb to attach to. We'll have to include that information somewhere. In this chapter, we'll look at what else we need to add to these representations so that they can show all the information that is listed in a listeme. First, though, we need to look a little more closely at the kinds of listemes that are smaller than phonological words – we need to look at the prefixes and suffixes and roots that words are made of.

5.2 Making up Words

The 43rd President of the United States, George W. Bush, is (in)famous for his tendency to coin words on the fly. Here are some examples:

(1) The war on terrorism has *transformationed* the US–Russia relationship. (Nov. 14, 2001)

We're working with Chancellor Schröder . . . to help Russia *securitize* . . . the dismantled nuclear warheads. (Berlin, Germany, May 23, 2002)

Thirdly, the *explorationists* are willing to only move equipment during the winter . . . (Conestoga, PA, May 18, 2001)

The results . . . will make America what we want it to be – a literate country and a *hopefuller* country. (Washington, DC, Jan. 11, 2001)

This case has had full *analyzation* and has been looked at a lot. (June 23, 2000)

When your economy is kind of *ooching* along, it's important to let people have more of their own money. (Boston, Oct. 4, 2002)

Setting aside the question of whether you think these new words reflect poorly on Bush's vocabulary, there's no question that he knows his morphology. And so do you: if you're a native speaker of English, you likely understand very precisely what he meant by each of his **neologisms**. Take a moment and try to define each of the italicized words from the list above.

Exercise 5.1 Define each of Bush's neologisms from the list in (1).

It's not too challenging a job. You've seen words like *partitioned*, *positioned*, and *conditioned*, which are formed on the same principle as *transformationed*; you've seen *fossilize*, *nationalize*, and *customize*, which are formed in the same way as *securitize*; *artist*, *cyclist*, and *receptionist*, for *explorationist*; *smarter*, *prettier*, and *harder* for *hopefuller*; *civilization*, *naturalization*, and *immunization* for *analyzation*, and *scream*, *whistle*, and *rattle (along)* for *ooch (along)*. Chances are you came up with something like the following:

(2) a. *transformationed*: transformed, caused a transformation of
    b. *securitize*: to secure, cause the security of
    c. *explorationists*: explorers, those who conduct explorations
    d. *hopefuller*: more hopeful
    e. *analyzation*: analysis, "had full analyzation" = "been fully analyzed"
    f. *ooching*: limping painfully, moving while going "ooch"

In fact, it's pretty clear that you yourself could have made up any of these words with exactly these meanings if you'd wanted to. These words, though, sound a bit funnier than some other possible neologisms. Another new coinage, associated with the above, is *Bushisms*, a word made up to describe the funny-sounding expressions of George W. Bush – but the word *Bushism* itself isn't particularly odd-sounding.

In this chapter and the next, one of the topics we'll investigate is why these Bushisms "sound funny".

Securitize is actually an accepted English word, of recent vintage – the OED lists the first use in print as 1981 – but it doesn't have the meaning that Bush seems to intend in the quote given here. To *securitize* a financial asset, e.g. a loan, is to convert it into the financial instruments called *securities* – an unlikely thing to do to nuclear warheads.

One reason Bushisms are funny is that many of them are redundant – there are other, simpler words that express the intended meaning: *transform, secure, explorer* and *analysis. Hopefuller* is funny for reasons we'll explore later in this chapter. *Ooching along* is an example of a word-formation strategy which is very common in English (but uncommon in many other languages). In English, we can name a verb that describes movement after the sound that is made while the movement is happening. Hence we have sentences like *Sue whistled to work, The train rumbled into the station,* and *The door creaked shut.* Bush's verb *ooching* is notable in that the sound–word he chose to form it from is rather uncommon and evocative. We'll look at all these examples in more depth as we go on. But first, let's consider how you knew what all of Bush's neologisms meant!

5.2.1 Compositionality within words

Bush's word-analyzation machinery, like yours, can compute the meanings of novel words from the meanings of their parts, if each part has an independent meaning. Take *explorationists*. How many parts does it have? At least *explore, -ation, -ist,* and *-s,* right? The meaning of each of these parts is part of the knowledge of most adult speakers of English. Let's take each in turn:

(3)   *explore*: to conduct a systematic search (this is the sense of *explore* Bush was using in his quote above)
   -ation: the action or process of Xing
   -ist: one that performs an action Y
   -s: more than one Z

Splitting the word into its components, our grammar deduces that:

explorationists means "more than one *explorationist*"
  explorationist means "one that performs the action of *exploration*"
    exploration means "the action or process of *exploring*"
      exploring means "conducting a systematic search."

Putting it all together, we can say that:

explorationists means "more than one person performing the action of conducting a systematic search."

The meaning of each subpart fits together with the meanings of the others to give the meaning of the whole.

In many cases, however, there are subparts of words which don't seem to have independent meanings – they're the equivalent of our *caboodle* example from Chapter 1, except at a sub-phonological-word level. Consider the words *cranberry, loganberry* and *raspberry*. They're all types of *berries*, and the word *berry* seems to be a subpart of each – but what does the other part mean? In *blueberry* and *blackberry*, the first half of the word describes the color of the fruit, but that's not the case with *cranberry* or *loganberry*. Can you come up with a meaning for *cran-, logan-*, or *rasp-*, as used in these words, off the top of your head? Similarly, *deflect, inflect,* and *reflect* each seem to have an element *-flect* in them – but can you define a uniform meaning for *-flect* that is part of the meanings of these verbs? (I can't.) Finally, *unkempt* and *disheveled* seem to be made up of *un+kempt* and *dis+sheveled* – but *-kempt* and *-sheveled* aren't words of English by themselves. (They could become words, though, through the process of back-formation, that we discussed in the previous chapter – if someone back-formed them and then they caught on.)

In these words, there are structural subparts that seem to be linguistic units of some kind, but they don't have their own meaning. In our example from Chapter 1, *kit and caboodle*, we had a phonological word, *caboodle*, that didn't have its own meaning. Here, we have a piece of a phonological word that doesn't have its own meaning.

Word-pieces are called **morphemes**. **Prefixes** and **suffixes** are morphemes, and so are the things they attach to. Morphemes can be identified in a number of ways. In the easiest cases, morphemes are also listemes, so that when they show up as part of a phonological word, they bring along their own meaning to that word. The word *dogs* is made up of two pieces, both of which are listemes, and the meaning of the whole word is made up of the meaning of the pieces. Each of those pieces is a morpheme.

As we've just seen, however, words sometimes seem to be made up of independent pieces that don't have their own independent meaning. How can we identify those morphemes? For example, just now I asserted that the string *cran*, in *cranberry*, was a morpheme, but that it is not a listeme – it doesn't have a meaning of its own. But in a word like, say, *Scranton* (a town in Pennsylvania), the same sound sequence is not a morpheme – *Scranton* is not made up of *s+cran+ton*.[1] How can we tell the difference?

In *cranberry*, it's easy: *berry* is obviously both a morpheme and a listeme; we know that because it can occur as a word on its own and also because it's familiar from all the other names of berries. If the listeme *berry* is a piece of *cranberry*, then the part that's not *berry* must be another piece. We'll see other ways to detect the presence of a morpheme without meaning later in the chapter. Meaningless morphemes are often called **cran-morphs**, after the *cranberry* example.

> Ironically, after linguists had come to use *cran-morph* to name a particular kind of unproductive morpheme, marketers started using it productively to form juice names: *cranapple, cranpassion*, etc. – to indicate a blend of cranberry + X juices. At least the marketers' innovation does make the point that *cran-* is a morpheme, although now it's a more independently meaningful and productive one than it used to be!

Morphemes, then, are subunits of phonological words. They are usually, but not always, also listemes. In order for Bush to use *-ize* or *-ist* in a novel word, he had to have an idea of the meaning he'd get by using them. When morphemes are also listemes, and the meaning of the whole word is created from meanings of its morphemes, as in *securitize*, we say the word is **compositional** – the meanings of the morphemes *compose* the meaning of the entire word.

Non-compositional words include those which contain cran-morphs, of course. However, there are also non-compositional words which are made up of morphemes which do have their own meanings, but where the meaning of the whole word doesn't seem to be related in a regular way to the meanings of its parts. For example, *terrific* is made up of *terrify* + *-ic*, but the meaning of *terrify* doesn't seem to be part of the meaning of *terrific*. (If something terrifies, it causes terror, but if something is terrific, it doesn't usually cause terror!)

Words like *terrific* with multiple morphemes that don't semantically compose are exactly like idioms – they're word-sized equivalents of a phrase like *kick the bucket* when it's used to mean "die." Compositional words, on the other hand, are like the literal interpretation of a phrase like *kick the bucket* when it's used to mean "kick the bucket." The phrase *kick the bucket* has both a compositional and a non-compositional meaning. So does the word *transmission*, which can mean, compositionally, "the action or object of transmitting," or, non-compositionally, "a piece of machinery in a car which shifts gears."[2]

A phonological word with only one morpheme in it, like *cat*, is **monomorphemic**. One with two morphemes in it is **bimorphemic**. Phonological words with two or more morphemes in them are **multimorphemic**.

5.2.2 Function vs. content listemes

Now that we've got a handle on the difference between listemes and morphemes, we need to learn to distinguish two subtypes of listemes, and two subtypes of morphemes.

Consider the following two groups of monomorphemic phonological words.

(4) that   monkey
     an   squint
     did   wriggle
     but   bright
     of   massage
     the   carpet
     to   sad

Do you notice anything different? One obvious difference is that the words on the right are mostly longer than the ones on the left. The ones on the left are all just one syllable, but many of the ones on the right contain two.

Another difference is one we touched on briefly in the previous chapter: the listemes on the right all contain a necessarily stressed syllable, and consequently have to be pronounced with at least one full vowel. The ones on the left, on the other hand, can all be pronounced with no stress and just a reduced vowel: /ən'æpl̩/ "an apple," /ə'lɛtəɹtə'dʒɑn/ "a letter to John," /'sɪksəv'wʌn/ "six of one," etc.

A third difference has to do with the relative "meaningfulness" of the two sets. The words on the left convey mostly grammatical information – they only do any real work when they're actually in a sentence. It would be difficult to write a conventional definition for these words.

The ones on the right, on the other hand, convey more of a real message. If you were pretending to be Tarzan, or sending a telegram, you'd be likely to leave out the words on the left: Tarzan might say "Monkey sad" for "The monkey is sad," or "Tarzan want banana" for "Tarzan wants a banana."

The words on the left are examples of the **function** words we learned about in Chapter 3 (p. 77). The richly meaningful words on the right, on the other hand, are **content** words.

Function words are an integral component of grammar – knowing how to use *the* or *of* is part of knowing how to speak English. They are the glue that binds phrases together. If you don't know a content word, you can always get around it, with a filler word like *thingy* or *whatchamacallit*. There's no getting around function words, though – there's nothing you can say instead if you suddenly forget the word *if*, for example.

The function words of a language are part of a fairly fixed list, which doesn't vary much from speaker to speaker, or even from dialect to dialect. Consequently it's very difficult to introduce a new function word, or change an old one. A few years ago there was a determined effort to introduce a new, gender-neutral singular pronoun *sie* into English, which just never caught on, despite its obvious usefulness when you don't know someone's gender (as in *A doctor was called to the scene, but sie arrived too late*). The problem was that the pronouns of a language are function words, not content words, and consequently very difficult to change, since they are a part of the grammar.

Because it's difficult to introduce new ones, function words are called *closed-class* words. Content words, on the other hand, are *open-class*, because it's extremely easy to invent or borrow new ones. Nearly every new word in any language is like the words on the right – contentful, descriptive – and it's almost impossible to introduce a new word into the list on the left. Any language can borrow a word from any other language in the open-class category – in fact, this is how modern English got much of its vocabulary, by borrowing open-class words from various languages, mostly French and Latin (see Chapter 9).

This distinction between more and less contentful elements can be seen below the level of the phonological word, too. Every word that is made up of more than one morpheme has a central element – a **root** – that usually contributes the meaty part of the word's meaning. Roots are open-class morphemes. So in *dog-s*, the root is *dog* and *-s* is just a function affix indicating plurality. Similarly, in *unhappiness*, the main "dictionary" meaning comes from the root *happy*, and *un-* and *-ness* just indicate negation and nounhood, respectively.

This can lead to the frustrating serial look-up effect, where the information you really need is what the meaning of the *root* morpheme is, but the dictionary entry just tells you the meaning of an affix, which you already know, and leaves the mysterious root in the definition. Let's say you've just read the sentence, "I remember a fashionable perruquier being tried for treason many years ago" in your nineteenth-century novel, and naturally you want to know what a *perruquier* is. You get out your dictionary, which tells you that it's "One who makes, dresses or deals in perruques" – but you could have guessed that much, because you know *-ier* from *furrier, chocolatier, hosier, clothier, farrier, courtier*, etc. The real problem is that you don't know what the meaning of the root is – you don't know what a *perruque* is. Only when you look up the root *perruque* do you finally find out that a *perruquier* is someone who makes, dresses or deals in *wigs*.

5.2.3   Free vs. bound morphemes

It's important to notice that not all root morphemes are independent phonological words. In the words *electric, toxic* or *emphatic* (all of which contain the adjectival suffix *-ic* that we know from *photograph-ic* or *prophet-ic*) the roots are *electr-* /əlɛktr/, *tox-* /tɑks/ and *emphat-* /əmfæt/ – none of which are independent phonological words on their own.

Any morpheme which can be an independent word on its own – including many roots, like *happy* or *dog* – is called a *free* morpheme. Morphemes which cannot be independent words on their own – often affixes, like *-ed* or *-ness*, but sometimes also roots like *electr-* – are called *bound* morphemes.

Exercise 5.2   Try to think of five other bound roots in English. How many different words do they occur in? Hint: most bound roots in English are Latinate in origin. There are many bound roots in scientific and scholarly words.

5.2.4   Roots vs. stems

There's one more piece of terminology we need before we move on. The **root** of a word is its central, contentful morpheme. But it's possible to add an affix to a word that already has an affix on it. When you do that, you're not adding the affix to the root directly. The unit that you add an affix to is called the *stem*. In *childishness*, the suffix *-ness* has been added to the stem *childish*, which has been formed by combining *child* with the adjectival suffix *-ish*. *Child* is both the root of the whole word, and the stem to which *-ish* attaches. The difference between roots and stems is illustrated in (5).

(5)

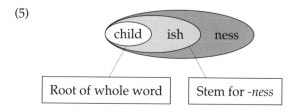

Words like *competitive* provide clear illustration of the need to differentiate between roots and stems. In *competitive*, an adjective, we clearly see the presence of the adjective-forming suffix *-ive*, as in *act-ive* or *impress-ive*. This suffix looks like the same suffix *-ive* that turns verbs (*act*, *impress*) into adjectives. But what is the verb from which *competitive* is formed? We want to say *compete*, but the stem – the bit to which the affix *-ive* attaches – is actually not *compete*, but *competit-*. *Competit* is not a verb! The *-it-* part is a meaningless morpheme (a cran-morph) that attaches to *compet-* to produce a stem that allows other affixes to attach. We also see the *-it-* in *competition* and *competitor*. The root of all these words, including the verb *to compete*, as well as *compet-it-ive*, *compet-it-ion* and *compet-it-or*, is *compet-*. In these cases, the stem has to be different from the root. (We'll talk about the variation in the pronunciation of the "e" in words like these in the next chapter.)

5.2.5 *Inflection and derivation*

Even among the less-contentful bound morphemes of English – affixes like *-ive* or *-ed* – there are some that seem more contentful than others. The change in meaning from *intend* to *intends* or *intended* seems less significant than the meaning change from *intend* to *intention*. Similarly, the change from *intention* to *intentions* feels like it has less effect on meaning than the change from *intention* to *intentional*.

Sometimes this distinction can be very dramatic. The change from *terrify* to *terrifies* is considerably less significant than the change from *terrify* to *terrific*. Similarly it's much less of a step to go from *arrest* to *arrests* than it is to go from *arrest* to the adjective *arresting* (as in "He had an arresting voice").

Endings like *-s* and *-ed* don't seem to have much effect on "diction-ary" meaning, but they are essential elements of the grammar of English. If you are a native speaker of standard American or British English, you will immediately know what's wrong with the following sentences:

(6) a. *Two crows lands on my porch every morning.
  b. *Two crows have land on my porch.
  c. *Two crow land on my porch every morning.
  d. *Two crow have landed on my porch.

The problem in every case is a suffix. The meanings of all four utter-ances are perfectly clear; (a) and (c) are saying "Two crows land on my porch every morning," while (b) and (d) are saying "Two crows have landed on my porch." The only thing wrong with (a) is that the verb form should be *land* and not *lands*; the only thing wrong with (b) is that the verb should be *landed*, not *land*; in (c) and (d) *crow* should be *crows*. These suffixes carry a little information – that the verb has a third person singular subject, for instance, or that the noun is plural – but the dictionary meaning of the root is preserved exactly in every case. Further, the addition of the suffix is *required* by the grammar. *Any* regular verb in a sentence like (b) above would have to have the *-ed* suffix, and *any* regular noun in the position of *crow* in sentence (a) above would have to have an *-s* suffix. Even if I make up a noun or a verb that you've never heard before, you can still tell me that there's something wrong with these sentences:

(7) a. I heard some yelping outside, and when I went out to look, I saw that two crows had caloop the dog.
    b. Two bondle bought all the duct tape in the store.

Standard American English speakers know it should be *had calooped* and *two bondles* – whatever *caloop* and *bondle* mean. Knowing these suffixes is part of what it means to know Standard American English. These affixes are like function words.

In contrast, it's possible to imagine that some English speakers might never learn to use a suffix like *-ize* or *-er*. The grammar of English doesn't force these suffixes on anyone; they're voluntary. If you wanted to say sentence (8)a without using *-ize*, you could say something like sentence (8)b; essentially the same message would be conveyed. Similarly, if you wanted to say (8)c without using *-er*, you could say (8)d:

(8) a. Congress criminalized flag-burning today.
    b. Congress made flag-burning a criminal act today.
    c. Mary is a writer.
    d. Mary writes for a living.

The grammar doesn't require you to use *-er* or *-ize* – or *-ion* or *-ish* or *-ness*, for that matter. You could go through your entire life without using a single word containing one of those suffixes and yet still be considered a speaker of Standard English (albeit one with a fairly limited vocabulary).

The fact that affixes like *-ize*, *-ish*, or *-ion* are not required is also reflected in the fact that sometimes it doesn't seem possible to add them to a word – even when it seems like it should be possible. If you *reserve* something, you make a *reservation*. If you *conserve* something, you are doing *conservation*. If you *preserve* something, you are engaging in *preservation*. So if you *deserve* something, why aren't you involved in **deservation*?

Functional affixes like *-ed* or *-s*, which the grammar requires, are called **inflectional** affixes. The meaning of the root to which they are attached always remains the same – inflectional affixes always form completely compositional words. Affixes like *un-*, *-ize* or *-er* which the grammar doesn't pay such strict attention to are called **derivational** affixes.

The key point is that words containing derivational affixes are sometimes compositional (like *writer*) and sometimes not (like *terrific*). Words containing inflectional affixes, however, are nearly always compositional.

Inflectional affixes just "inflect" a stem to satisfy the grammar, leaving its core meaning essentially unchanged. Words formed with derivational affixes, however, sometimes gradually take on their own, unique meaning over time, in the same way that an oft-repeated metaphor can become an idiom. Such meaning drift is called **idiomatization**.

Exercise 5.3   The suffix *-ion* is usually added to some verb X, to derive a noun meaning "the act of Xing" or "the result of Xing." What are the verbs that correspond to *conception*, *reception*, *deception* and *inception*? Notice anything strange? Which of these *-ion* words have undergone idiomatization?

5.2.6   Dual-use affixes: both *inflectional* and *derivational?*

There are a few suffixes that seem to be on the border between inflection and derivation. The verbal suffix *-ing* is one such. One of its functions is to produce the progressive participle – the form of the verb you use when you want to talk about something that is in progress right when you're speaking: *Sue is walking, Bill is calling Joe, I'm thinking out loud.* That use is clearly inflectional: it is required by the grammar. (You can't say **Bill is call.*) It has another function, too, however – it turns verbs into nouns: *The singing woke me up, I really don't like all the word-processing I have to do in this job, Jane made $10 baby-sitting.* This category-changing function seems more derivational.

The dual nature of this suffix can be pretty funny. The headline *Police Stop Slaying Suspect Look-Alikes* is amusing because *slaying* is intended to be read as a noun, forming part of a bigger compound noun describing a group of people – *slaying suspect look-alikes* – but in this headline, *slaying* can also be interpreted as the progressive participle of the verb *to slay*, which results in the idea that the police have been killing people who look like their suspect (though the headline informs us that fortunately they've stopped doing this).

In this case, it looks like there are actually two distinct suffixal listemes, *-ing₁* and *-ing₂*: an inflectional *-ing* which forms the progressive participle, and a derivational *-ing* which changes the category of the word. These listemes are distinct in our mental lexicons, because they mean different things, but they are **homophonous**: they sound the same. In that way, they're similar to words like *bank* "a financial institution" and *bank* "a sloped incline of earth, esp. by the side of a river": same sound, different meaning. There are other affixes that are homophones, like the *-s* in *two dogs* and the *-s* in *John knows French*. The *-s* in *two dog-s* signals plurality, and the *-s* in *know-s* signals that the verb is in the present tense with a singular, third-person subject. They sound the same, but they have two different meanings. They must be two distinct listemes.

5.3   Affixal Syntax: Who's My Neighbor? Part I

We have seen that derivational morphology can change the part of speech of the stem it attaches to. So for instance, *nation* is a noun, but when the suffix *-al* is added, the resulting word *national* is an adjective. You might have noticed that the suffix *-ness* attaches to adjectives to form nouns: *sick–sickness, weird–weirdness, silly–silliness*.

Derivational suffixes don't *always* change the part of speech of the stem they attach to, but they do always specify the part of speech of the words they produce. The suffix *-ness*, for example, always produces nouns, no matter whether it's attached to an adjective or to a word that's already a noun. (Although a prescriptive English grammar wouldn't recommend attaching *-ness* to nouns, it often is attached to them in less formal contexts. A website about caring for basset hounds, for instance, includes the opinion that "The one thing I believe everyone who deals with these problems will agree on is that many owners aren't paying enough attention to their dog's 'dogness'.") When it attaches to nouns, of course, the new word ends up being the same part of speech as the stem.

Affixes (both inflectional and derivational) also care about the category of the thing they're attaching to. The suffix *-ness* really doesn't like to go on verbs, for instance: **effectness, *competeness, *repelness* sound very bad, compared to *effectiveness, competitiveness,* and *repulsiveness*, where we've added the adjective-forming suffix *-ive* before attaching *-ness*.

Similarly, you might have noticed that *un-* attaches to adjectives and verbs – *unwilling, unafraid, undo, unwrap, un-American* – to produce more adjectives and verbs. Even though it doesn't *change* the category of the stem, it still cares what the category of the stem *is*: it doesn't much like to go on nouns, for instance: **unfear, *unAmerica.*[3]

Exercise 5.4 In the word *unhappiness*, which affix was combined with the root first? Is *unhappiness* built out of *un-* combined with the stem *happiness*, or is it built out of *-ness* combined with the stem *unhappy*? Or does it matter? Why?

Besides information about its pronunciation and its meaning, then, our mental dictionary entry for *-ness* has to include a note about what it can combine with. That is, it contains information about the *syntax* of *-ness*. We saw above that *-ness* likes to attach to adjectives or nouns. Our listeme for *-ness*, then, must look something like this:

(9) *Phonology Syntax   Semantics*
     /nɛs/   [[____]$_{A \text{ or } N}$ -ness]$_N$ "the quality of being [___]$_{A \text{ or } N}$"

In (9), the blank space in the syntax and the semantics entries is intended to represent the stem to which *-ness* is attached. The subscript labels outside the brackets show what the part of speech of the whole thing inside those brackets is.

Syntactic structures like the one in the entry for *-ness* above can be drawn with upside-down trees, rather than brackets. In syntactic tree drawings, the root of the tree represents the whole word, and its branches represent the subparts. The labels show what the category of each subtree and branch is, and the morphemes themselves are the leaves at the end of each branch. We could represent the bracketed structure that represents the requirements for *-ness* in (9) as the tree in (10)a, and the structure of a word like *happiness* as in (10)b:

(10) a.

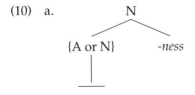

b. [[happi]_A-ness]_N

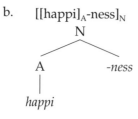

A word like *powerlessness*, which has a more complicated structure than *happiness*, would look like this, in bracketing and tree-drawing:

(11) a. [[[power]_N -less]_A -ness]_N

b.

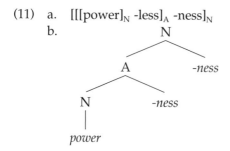

Now that we know that an affix specifies what category of word it wants to attach to, we can see the answer to the question posed in Exercise 5.4. Consider the derivation of the word *unhappiness*. The root is *happy*, an adjective. Let's try putting the *-ness* on first. The suffix *-ness* can go on adjectives just fine, so *happy* can combine with *-ness* to form the noun *happiness* (which is indeed a fine English word).

However, can we add *un-* to the noun *happiness* to get *unhappiness*? No! We saw above that that *un-* doesn't like to go on nouns. (You can say *un-American* but you can't say *un-America*.) Consequently, we know we can't make *unhappiness* by combining *un-* with *happiness*. But *un-* is perfectly happy to go on adjectives. It must be the case, then, that, *un-* is prefixed to *happy* first, to form the adjective *unhappy*; then *-ness* can combine with *unhappy* to form the noun *unhappiness*. In other words, the operations which form *unhappiness* happen in the order illustrated in (12)a, with the structure illustrated by bracketing in (12)b and by a tree in (12)c:

(12) a.   Adj   +   Adj
          <u>un-   +   happy</u>
        = Adj
          unhappy

Adj + N
<u>unhappy</u>   <u>-ness</u>
= N
unhappiness

b. [[un- [happy]_A]_A-ness]_N

c.

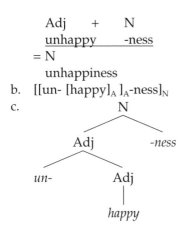

Exercise 5.5 *Un-* goes on verbs as well as adjectives: *undo, unbutton, unlock.* It has a slightly different meaning on verbs than it does on adjectives, however. How would you describe *un-*'s meaning when it attaches to verbs? What does it mean when it attaches to adjectives?

5.4 Affixal Phonology: Who's My Neighbor? Part II

Above, we saw that affixes must be memorized complete with syntactic information about what kind of stem they can attach to. Affixes care about the part of speech of their stem.

Some affixes also care about phonological properties of their stem. In some cases, everything else seems right – the meanings of the stem and affix are compatible, and the part-of-speech requirements of the affix are compatible with the category of the stem – but it still seems wrong to put them together into one word. Look at the following pairs:

(13)

	Adjective	*Comparative*	
		Suffixed	*Periphrastic*
a.	smart	smarter	?more smart
	intelligent	*intelligenter	more intelligent
b.	pretty	prettier	?more pretty
	attractive	*attractiver	more attractive

c.	dark	darker	?more dark
	opaque	*opaquer	more opaque
d.	quick	quicker	?more quick
	rapid	*rapider	more rapid

> **periphrastic**, *adj.* From Latin via Greek *peri-*, "around, round-about," Greek *-phrast*, "one who declares," and Greek *-ic* "in the manner of." A construction which uses multiple words to express a meaning which is elsewhere expressed in a single word.

The (inflectional) suffix *-er* creates the **comparative** form of an adjective. (Don't get it mixed up with the homophonous derivational suffix *-er* which forms a noun from a verb, as in *writer* and *driver*!) But comparative *-er* doesn't seem to be happy going on all adjectives, even when they have a meaning that is very similar to that of other adjectives that *-er* attaches to perfectly well. For comparatives of adjectives like *intelligent*, you can't attach *-er* – you have to use the **periphrastic** form, with the separate phonological word *more*. What's wrong with the *-er* forms in these cases?

The problem is that this suffix places restrictions on the phonology of the things it can attach to, just as we saw that *-ness* places a syntactic part-of-speech restriction on the things it can attach to.

Exercise 5.6 Figure out what the phonological restrictions are on the suffix *-er*. Feel free to consider any extra examples you can think of, though be sure that they're examples of a comparative adjective with *-er*, not an agentive noun decoy with *-er*!

One difference in the list above between the phonology of the things that *-er* attaches to easily and the things it doesn't attach to is that the former are all one syllable long, while the ones it refuses to attach to are more than one syllable long. From the list above, you might conclude that that's the restriction: *-er* only attaches to monosyllabic words. It turns out that that's only part of the story.

In fact, there are a few multi-syllable adjectives that comparative *-er* attaches to perfectly happily. Let's compare some ones it can go on with some ones it can't:

(14)   Bisyllabic adjectives and comparatives in *-er*

Good comparatives		*Bad comparatives*	
happy	happier	pallid	*pallider
tiny	tinier	afraid	*afraider
shallow	shallower	naked	*nakeder
brainy	brainier	active	*activer
mighty	mightier	verdant	*verdanter

Notice anything different about these two sets? What do the good comparative adjectives on the left have in common? What do the bad ones on the right have in common?

The second syllable of the words on the left all end in just a vowel. The ones on the right all have a second syllable whose vowel is followed by at least one consonant. That is, the second syllable of the words on the right all have a coda, while the second syllable of the words on the left are codaless. Codeless syllables are called **open syllables**; syllables with a coda – with one or more consonants on the end – are called **closed syllables**. (We'll see in Chapter 9 that the distinction between open and closed syllables has played an important role in the history of English. Don't get this mixed up with the difference between open (contentful) and closed (functional) classes of words that we introduced earlier!)

The open/closed distinction only matters to *-er* when it's attaching to a word that has more than one syllable. Any one-syllable adjective is fair game for *-er*, no matter whether its single syllable is open or closed. (Think about words like *slower*, where it's attaching to a single, open syllable, and *faster*, where it's attaching to a single closed syllable.) But when there's more than one syllable in the stem, it can only attach to an open syllable, not a closed one.

So, the comparative suffix *-er* cares (1) whether the stem it's attaching to has one or more syllables; and, (2) if it has more than one syllable, whether the last syllable is open or closed. (Notice that the noun-forming suffix *-er* has no such restrictions – *receiver*, *compiler* and *interpreter* are all fine, though their stems are multisyllabic verbs whose last syllable has a coda.) We have to find room in the listeme entry for comparative *-er* for this information.

The way we'll represent it is like this. In the syntactic part of the entry, that shows what the affix can attach to, instead of having a simple blank space representing the stem that the affix attaches to, we'll include symbols that stand for the syllable structure of the stem. We'll specify one, or optionally two syllables, and indicate that the second syllable must be open.

We'll use the linguist's standard symbol for syllable, the lower-case Greek letter sigma (σ), and subscript it with the letter "o" to indicate "must be open." Regular round brackets around the second syllable symbol indicate that it's optional, as usual:[4]

(15)   *Phonology*   *Syntax*   *Semantics*

    /əɹ/ $[[\sigma \ (\sigma_o)]_A$ -er$]_{Comp}$ "more [____]$_A$"

Now we can see what's so odd-sounding about George Bush's neologism *hopefuller*. He put the comparative suffix *-er* on a two-syllable adjective whose second syllable has a consonant on the end – he ignored the open-second-syllable restriction on *-er*.

5.5   Allomorphy

In the previous chapter, we learned that sometimes the same underlying sound, or *phoneme,* could be pronounced in different ways, depending on the context; for instance, /p/ is pronounced with aspiration – as /pʰ/ – when it occurs alone as the onset of a stressed syllable (compare *pit* and *spit*). We called these different pronunciations of the same sound *allophones.*

The same sort of thing happens with morphemes, both inflectional and derivational. Try pronouncing the following phrases aloud to yourself:

(16)   a.   The dog wagged his tail.
      b.   The dog smelled the food.
      c.   The cat cleaned out his bowl.
      d.   The dog barked.
      e.   The dog lapped up some water.
      f.   The cat hissed at the dog.
      g.   The cat trotted out the door.
      h.   The dog padded down the street.
      i.   The dog wounded the cat.

Exercise 5.7 Carefully transcribe the verbs from the phrases in (16). What do you notice about the pronunciation of the past tense morpheme?

If you did your pronunciation and transcription carefully, you should have noticed that the pronunciation of the past tense morpheme varies quite a lot, even though we consistently spell it "-ed." In *wagged*, it's pronounced /d/, in *lapped* it's pronounced /t/, and in *wounded* it's pronounced as a separate syllable: /əd/ or /ɨd/. These different pronunciations of the same morpheme are called **allomorphs**, in the same way that different pronunciations of the same sound are called *allophones*.

> In words like *patted*, *wadded*, or *fitted*, you may find that you hear the unstressed vowel in the *-ed* suffix sometimes as /ə/, sometimes as /ɨ/, and sometimes even as /ɪ/ or /ʌ/, if you're pronouncing it very slowly and carefully. Following the convention established in Chapter 2, though, we will transcribe all these unstressed vowels as /ə/ here and in the discussion that follows. The precise quality of the vowel isn't as important here as the presence of a vowel at all!

Even though these are three quite distinct pronunciations, we *spell* the suffix exactly the same way in all cases – it's always spelled "ed." We don't need to indicate in the spelling when it's pronounced one way or when it's pronounced another way. We don't need to because this variation in pronunciation is 100 percent predictable: it's determined by the pronunciation of the last sound in the stem that the past tense suffix attaches to. What characteristics of the preceding phoneme is the past-tense morpheme sensitive to?

Exercise 5.8 What aspects of the preceding sound in the stem determine the pronunciation of the plural morpheme?

You probably noticed that you get the /əd/ pronunciation when the verb stem ends in a /t/ or a /d/, i.e. when it ends in an alveolar stop, as in *patted* or *waded*. When you don't have the /əd/ pronunciation, the voicing of the preceding sound determines the pronunciation of the past tense – it's /t/ when the preceding sound is voiceless, as in *barked* or *hissed*, and /d/ when the preceding sound is voiced, as in *raised* or *smelled*.

Intuitively speaking, this variation in pronunciation makes the stem-suffix sequence easier to pronounce. Imagine trying to pronounce /sd/ at the end of a word like *hissed*, keeping the -*s* clearly voiceless and the -*d* clearly voiced! Or trying to pronounce /dd/ at the end of a word like *waded*, making it clear that the extra-long /d/ is different from the single /d/ in the unsuffixed word /wejd/. These changes in pronunciation of -*ed* help out both the speaker and the hearer We could describe distribution of each allomorph of -*ed* as follows, where "P" stands for the last phoneme in the stem:

(17)   *Semantics:*   *Pronunciations:*
       [+Past]   /əd/, /t/, or /d/

      When you get each pronunciation
      a.   [. . . P]$_V$-/əd/   when P is an alveolar stop
      b.   [. . . P]$_V$-/t/   when P is voiceless
                         (but not an alveolar stop)
      c.   [. . . P]$_V$-/d/   when P is voiced
                         (but not an alveolar stop)

5.5.1   Which one is the listeme?

If these are "variations" in pronunciation of -*ed*, though, what are they varying from? We shouldn't need to include all this information in our listeme for -*ed* – it is completely predictable, after all, which pronunciation shows up where. It seems like it would be better to make one of these pronunciations the "real" one – the one listed in the listeme – and then let the rules of English phonotactics decide when the pronunciation has to vary. After all, we know from our discussion of phonotactics that two obstruents in the coda of a syllable have to match in voicing (remember Study Problem 1 from Chapter 3?). Thinking about the phonotactic rules of English, then, will let us figure out which of these pronunciations of the past tense morpheme is the *real* one, the one we should include in our listeme for the past tense.

Let's assume that the pronunciation of the suffix changes only if adding the "real" suffix would result in a sound sequence that violates

English phonotactic rules. Let's take each of our three pronunciations in turn, and consider the possibility that it is the real one.

First, let's consider the possibility that the "basic" pronunciation is the syllabic one, /əd/. If the past tense morpheme is /əd/, would there be any phonotactic reason to change the pronunciation to /t/ or /d/ in some circumstances? That is, would adding /əd/ to a word ever produce an unpronounceable string of phonemes? Take the verb /wæg/, *wag*, for example. If the "basic" pronunciation of the past tense suffix is /əd/, adding the past tense to "wag" would produce the form /wægəd/. Is that a possible phonological word of English? The answer, of course, is yes. There's nothing about the sequence /wægəd/, or /snɪfəd/, that violates the phonotactic rules of English. After all, words like *pallid* or *wicked*, with this very phonological structure, are perfectly good English words. If the "real" morpheme was pronounced /əd/, it would be perfectly easy to retain that pronunciation in all circumstances – there'd be no phonotactic reason to change the pronunciation to /wægd/ and /snɪft/. So we can conclude that /əd/ isn't the basic form. It must be a variation on one of the other forms.

What about /t/? Can we explain the other two forms as variants of /t/? We know that there are constraints on what sounds can co-occur in a syllable coda together, so it's likely that a morpheme that was a single consonant like /t/ could get pushed around by those restrictions. For instance, if the listed pronunciation of the past tense suffix were /t/, it would be easy to understand why the /t/ would change to a /d/ after a voiced consonant, as in /wægd/. The phonotactic rules of English forbid two obstruents in the same coda to have different voicing (Rule 14 from Chapter 3). While there are syllables that end in two voiceless obstruents, like *box* /bɑks/, and syllables that end in two voiced obstruents, like *wagged* /wægd/, there are no syllables that end in a voiced obstruent followed by a voiceless one. So if the suffix was /t/, the voicing change to /d/ after voiced consonants could be explained as a change in pronunciation that helps the newly formed syllable to conform to the phonotactic rules of English, making the voicing match.

Similarly, if the basic form is /t/, the phonotactics of English would require a change in the pronunciation of the morpheme when it was suffixed to another word ending in /t/ or /d/. The phonotactic rules of English forbid two alveolar stops together in a coda. It would be very hard to say a sequence like /pætt/ "pat-t" or /wejdt/ "wade-t" so that it was distinguishable from /pæt/ or /wejd/. Changing to the

/əd/ pronunciation when the verb ends in an alveolar stop would fix that problem.

There are two problems with the idea that /t/ is basic, however. First, if the basic suffix is /t/, why does the pronunciation change to /d/ when it is suffixed to words that end in vowels? (Try pronouncing *cooed*, *played*, and *treed* to yourself. Definitely different from words ending in /t/, right? Compare them to *coot*, *plate*, and *treat*.) In these verbs, the past tense suffix is pronounced /d/, not /t/. But this can't be due to a phonotactic requirement, because lots of English syllables end in a vowel followed by /t/: *coot*, *plate*, *treat* are just three of the many words that illustrate this.

Second, in the case where the suffix is added to a word that ends in /d/ or /t/, why do we change the suffix to /əd/ rather than to /ət/? If the suffix were /t/, there would be no explanation for the change in voicing quality of the final consonant after a vowel in these cases, either. (There are lots of English words that end in /ət/: *muppet*, *puppet*, *gullet*, *parrot*, *wallet*; it's a perfectly legitimate syllable, phonotactically speaking.) So /t/ can't be the basic pronunciation either. It also must be a variant of the basic form.

The best explanation is to assume that the underlying pronunciation of the past tense suffix is just /d/. The change from /d/ to /t/ after voiceless consonants, as in /snɪft/ *sniffed*, is still easily understood as an effect of Phonotactic Rule 14 (p. 69). And best of all, we can understand why and how the pronunciation changes to /əd/. It's just as phonotactically bad to add /d/ to verbs ending in an alveolar stop as it would be to add /t/ – try saying /pætd/ "pat-d" or /wejdd/ "wade-d" to confirm this. If the basic suffix is /d/, all one has to do to account for the change to /əd/ in these cases, is assume that an extra ("epenthetic") vowel is inserted between the suffix and the stem to make the suffix audible. And finally, if the morpheme is really /d/, there's no reason to change it to anything else when it's suffixed to any other voiced consonant or a vowel, so it remains the same, giving /cuwd/ *cooed*, /plejd/ *played*, and /wejvd/ *waved*.

Our listeme for *-ed*, then, will look like this:

(18) *Phonology*   *Syntax*   *Semantics*
      /d/   [[____]ᵥ -ed]ᵥ   "past tense of [____]ᵥ"

This kind of variation in pronunciation is called *phonologically conditioned allomorphy*. Its effects on a given morpheme are 100 percent regular and predictable, according to the phonological environment. It happens for the various suffixes spelled -*s* too, in all of their many functions: the 3rd person present tense verbal suffix, the plural suffix, the possessive suffix (spelled -'*s*), or the reduced forms of *is* or *has* (also spelled -'*s*). The pronunciation of these suffixes varies considerably, just as the pronunciation of -*ed* does, but as with -*ed*, we don't need to vary the spelling of -*s* to show the different pronunciations, because they're predictable.

Exercise 5.9 Try and determine what the underlying phonological form of the plural suffix -*s* is, using the same type of reasoning as we used for the past tense suffix above. Start by carefully transcribing the words *caps, picks, wrists, dogs, heads, buns, roses, dresses, hazes, bees, fries,* and *shoes.*

5.5.2 Phonologically conditioned allomorphy in derivational morphemes

Phonologically conditioned allomorphy is not restricted to inflectional morphology, either. Consider the derivational prefixes in the following groups of words:

(19) a. impossible   intangible   inconsiderate
       imperfect   intractable   incorrigible
       impenetrable   insoluble   incorruptible

    b. empower   ensure   enclose
       embitter   entrain   enquire
       embroil   encircle   encapsulate

    c. compare   consolidate   concur
       combine   contain   concatenate
       compatible   conceal   concoct

Again, be very careful that you're considering the pronunciation of these forms, not the spelling, which can be misleading. Transcribe one or more rows from each group. Do you notice anything about the pronunciation of these prefixes that depends on the pronunciation of the stems they're attached to?

Exercise 5.10 What determines the variation in form of *in-* ("not"), *con-* ("together") and/or *en-* ("in") illustrated in (19)? Can you think of three words which would have to show the true underlying form of these prefixes with no possibility of influence from neighboring consonants?

Remember from Chapter 3 that English words almost never contain a nasal followed by a stop pronounced at a different place of articulation. So, for instance, the sequence /ɪŋglɪʃ/ is a likely word of English, but a sequence like /ɪngrijn/ is likely to be two words, *in* plus *green*. Similarly, /ɪmprɪnt/ is a good English word, because both /m/ and /p/ are labial, but /ɪnprɪnt/ is likely to be two words, *in print*, with the alveolar /n/ being the end of one word and the labial /p/ being the beginning of another. That is, there's a phonotactic rule of English that says that in nasal-plus-stop sequences within the same phonological word, the nasal has to be pronounced at the same place of articulation as the stop – the nasal has to be **homorganic** with the stop, even across syllables. This phonotactic rule is the reason for the changes in pronunciation of the derivational prefix *in-*, meaning "not," above.

> **concatenate**, *v.* to connect like the links of a chain, to link together. From Latin *concatēnāre* "to link together," made up of *con-* "together" + *catēnāre* "to chain," itself from *catēna* "chain."

5.6 Closed-Class and Open-Class Morphemes: Reprise

One final note concerning derivation and inflection. Above, we saw that certain kinds of function words and inflectional morphemes were similar in that they are part of the grammar of English: if you don't know the use of the suffix *-ed* or the definite determiner *the*, you're not a speaker of English. We contrasted these elements with open-class root morphemes like *cake*, *amuse*, *cold*, *fun*, *qual-*, *cred-*, and *necess-* – a speaker of English could go through their entire life without knowing the meanings of these particular roots, if they never happened to come across them.

Are derivational affixes more like open-class or closed-class morphemes? Above, we argued that they're not a necessary part of the grammar of English – you could speak English and still never use a single derivational morpheme. In that regard, they're more like open-class morphemes: while you certainly need *some* open-class morphemes in order to say anything at all, you don't need any *particular* ones – if I know an open-class morpheme that you don't, that doesn't mean that you don't speak English. Similarly, if you know and use a particular derivational morpheme that I don't know, that doesn't mean that I don't speak English either.

Another respect in which derivational morphemes are more like open-class words is that, in all cases, they produce words that are either nouns, verbs, adjectives or adverbs. Free open-class roots all belong to one of these four syntactic categories as well. Closed-class words, on the other hand, tend to be things like determiner articles and auxiliary verbs – they're grammatical in nature. So derivational morphemes are more like open-class words in that they belong to one of the four part-of-speech categories that content words may have.[5]

One final way in which derivational affixes are like open-class morphemes is that we can borrow or create new ones. English is still borrowing derivational affixes; one recent one is *-nik*, from Slavic via Yiddish, which shows up in *refusenik, beatnik, peacenik,* and *no-goodnik*, and whose earliest attestation in the OED is in 1945. We also create new affixes on a regular basis. After the Watergate scandal in 1972, *-gate* was detached from the compound *Watergate* and became a derivational suffix used to mean "a political scandal involving X," e.g. *Hollywoodgate, Irangate, Monicagate.* People suffering from various addictions or compulsive behaviors now have names formed with a new suffix *-(a)holic*, extracted from the word *alcoholic* (which itself is formed, of course, from *alcohol+ic*, not from *alc+oholic*), so now there are *chocoholics, shopaholics, workaholics,* etc. (There could even be *alcoholoholics,* now that *-aholic* has a life of its own!) Recently, young speakers have added a bound morpheme *-licious* to the language, meaning essentially the same thing as "delicious because of X" – *applelicious* would mean something like "full of apple-y goodness." The hit single by Destiny's Child called "Bootylicious" discusses the extremely delicious qualities of the singer's body, specifically those associated with her booty.

Alcohol, *n.* The intoxicating component of fermented drinks such as wine, beer, or vodka. From Arabic *al-kohl* "the eyeshadow," *circa* 1500. "Alcohol" originally referred to a dark metallic powder which was used for cosmetic purposes in the East, also known simply as *kohl*. The Arabic definite determiner article, *al*, was borrowed together with the noun, giving *al-kohl* (the Arabic borrowings *algorithm*, *alchemy* and *alkaline*, among others, also contain the determiner). *Alcohol* came to refer to any metallic powder produced by sublimation, and consequently to the concentrated distillate of any liquid. The phrase *alcohol of wine* came into common use to refer to concentrated spirits made from wine, and was then shortened to *alcohol*, from which our present meanings for the word arose.

Other recently coined or borrowed affixes include *-(a)rama* and *-meister*, as well as *-erific*, and *-tacular* as used in the following affixally extravagant sentence by *Tucson Weekly* movie critic James DiGiovanna in February 2003: "Then, right after that, [you'll see] the trailer for the nerd-a-licious *League of Extraordinary Gentlemen*, the trailer for the geek-a-riffic *Hulk* movie, and then, if you're lucky, the grosstacular trailer for the upcoming *Willard* remake starring Crispin Glover." In this regard, derivational affixes seem more like open-class than closed-class morphemes. In the next chapter, we'll consider how this can help us to shed some light on a peculiar distributional fact about derivational morphology: derivational *pre*fixes almost never change the part of speech of the word they attach to, while derivational *suf*fixes often do.

Study Problems

1. Consider the following limerick:

    > There was an old man with a beard
    > Who said, "It is just as I feared!
    > Two owls and a hen
    > Four larks and a wren
    > Have all built their nests in my beard!"

    Using the data above, show how *morphemes* are different from *syllables*. Hint: What do the rules for constructing limericks care about?
2. Practice turning bracketed words, representing the order of combination of prefixes and suffixes, into syntactic trees, and vice versa.

a. For each bracketed word below, first, transcribe it in IPA, then draw the corresponding syntactic tree.

   (i)   *institutionalization*   [[[[[institut]$_V$-ion]$_N$-al]$_A$-iz]$_V$-ation]$_N$

   (ii)   *unhappiness*   [[un-[happy]$_A$]$_A$-ness]$_N$

   (iii) *wirelessly*   [[[wire]$_N$-less]$_A$-ly]$_{Adv}$

   (iv) *redecorating*   [[re-[[decor]$_N$-at]$_V$]$_V$-ing]$_V$

   (v)   *disapproval*   [[dis-[approv]$_V$]$_V$-al]$_{Adj}$

b. For each word in a syntactic tree below, first, transcribe it in IPA, then write the tree out as the corresponding bracketed structure.

   (i)   *defibrillator*

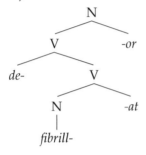

   (ii)   *fictionalization*

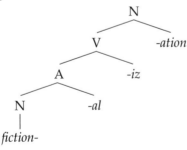

   (iii) *unjustified*

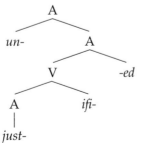

(iv)   *repopularize*

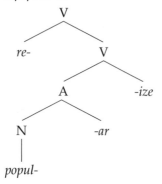

(v)   *antidisestablishmentarianism*

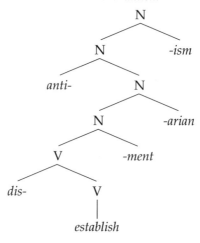

3. *-Able* goes on verbs and produces adjectives: *doable, buttonable, lockable. Un-* goes on both adjectives and verbs: *unhappy, unaware* and *unwrap, unfold*. As a result, words like *unlockable* have two different potential derivations. Each derivation has a different meaning, illustrated in the following sentences:
    (i)   The door was unlockable, so I had to leave it open.
    (ii) The door was unlockable, so I got it open without trouble.
    Explain the ambiguity of *unlockable* by describing the two different affixation sequences that can create it. Draw two trees like the ones above, one representing each affixation sequence, and indicate which tree represents which meaning.
4. Here is a set of words with derivational suffixes on them, some of them with bound roots and some with free roots.

baptize	military
bluntness	carnage
glorious	reference
amplify	childish
eventual	ironic

For each word:

a. Identify its part of speech.

b. Identify what the derivational suffix on it is and what the root is. (You can look them up in a dictionary if you're not sure).

c. Is the root free or bound?

d. For each word, give another word with a different root that uses the same derivational affix.

e. For each word with a bound root, think of (or look up) at least one other word which is formed from the same root but has a different suffix.

f. For the words with free roots, decide whether you think the word is semantically *compositional* or not. Explain why or why not. (Hint: is the meaning of the free root clearly part of the meaning of the whole word?)

5. Consider the list of 20 words ending in *-al* below.

dismissal	betrayal	surreal	annual
natural	gradual	reversal	referral
survival	federal	floral	rebuttal
typical	renewal	denial	cerebral
appraisal	recital	legal	trivial

a. They are all either nouns or adjectives. Identify the 10 nouns and the 10 adjectives in the list.

b. Identify the form to which *-al* attaches of the words in each list. Which are bound, and which are free?

c. The noun-forming suffix *-al* imposes a syntactic and a phonological requirement on the stems to which it attaches:

   (i) What is the syntactic requirement that noun-forming *-al* impose on its stems? (I.e., what part of speech does noun-forming *-al* attach to?)

   (ii) Here are some non-existent nouns in *-al*: **abandonal, *promisal, *fidgetal, *investigatal, *qualifial.*

      1. What is the stress pattern of all the stems to which noun-forming *-al* has attached in your list of 10 from

above? Transcribe those stems in IPA, indicating where main stress is with a tick before the stressed syllable.
2. What are the stress patterns of the stems in the non-existent nouns in *-al* in the ill-formed examples above?
3. Describe, in words, the stress-based phonological restriction on noun-forming *-al* that is illustrated by the contrast between the grammatical nouns you have identified above, and the ungrammatical made-up nouns above.

Further Reading

On *un-* and nouns:
Horn, Laurence R. (2002) Uncovering the un-word: a study in lexical pragmatics. *Sophia linguistica* 48:1–64.

On Latinate roots in English:
Ayers, Donald (1986) *English Words from Latin and Greek Elements*. Tucson, AZ: University of Arizona Press.
Stockwell, Robert and Minkova, Donka (2001) *English Words: History and Structure*. Cambridge: Cambridge University Press.

On morphology generally:
Bauer, Laurie (1990) *Introducing Linguistic Morphology*. Edinburgh: Edinburgh University Press.
Payne, Thomas (2005) *Exploring Language Structure*. Cambridge: Cambridge University Press.

Notes

1 Actually, *-ton* probably is a morpheme in Scranton; it's a reduced form of 'town'. But *-cran* definitely isn't!
2 A car's transmission actually does have something to do with transmitting – it transmits power to the drivetrain. However, as an instrument, rather than an action, a truly compositional name for the thing would be formed with the instrumental *-er* suffix. It should be *transmitter*, as in *screwdriver*, rather than *transmission*, which contains the action-suffix *-ion*.
3 Sometimes people do put *un-* on nouns, as in the old ads for 7-UP, the *unCola*, or as Humpty Dumpty did when he was talking about his cravat being an un-birthday present. It doesn't happen too often, though, so for

the moment we'll just ignore these occasional formations and say *un-* doesn't go on nouns. When you do problem 2 in the study problems for this chapter, though, you might think about the special meaning that *un-* gets when it DOES attach to nouns.

4   To be completely descriptively correct, we'd have to include the information that the last syllable in a multisyllabic adjective has to be unstressed for it to take -*er*, which is why we say *more astray*, not **astrayer*. Also, we'd need a notation that allowed for more than two syllables in the stem, as long as the last one is unstressed and open (*shadowy–shadowier, persnickety– persnicketier*). The following notation would do the job: $[\sigma\ (\sigma^n\ {}^u\sigma_0)]_A$, where $n \geq 0$, and the prefixed superscript "u" indicates "unstressed." Finally, as we saw in the last section, liquids and nasals can sometimes form the nucleus of an unstressed open syllable by themselves, in words like *little*, *common*, and *clever* (transcribed as /lɪtl̩/, /kɑmn̩/, and /klɛvɹ̩/), which is why we get *littler, commoner*, and *cleverer*. (Even this extension won't cover certain just plain irregular cases: What's the stress pattern of *polite*? And yet, *politer* is a well-formed -*er* comparative, unlike the -*er* comparatives of other wS adjectives: **astrayer, *afraider, *erecter*.)

5   It's a harder question to decide what part-of-speech category inflectional morphemes belong to. The traditional approach says that they belong to the same category as the word they attach to, so plural -*s* makes Nouns, past-tense -*ed* makes Verbs, etc. We will adopt this practice here. However, linguistic analysis suggests that this approach may be too simpleminded. The past-tense morpheme -*ed* alternates with the auxiliary verb *did* in sentences like *John walked to school*/*John **didn't** walk to school* and *Mary passed the butter*/***Did** Mary pass the butter?* This distribution suggests that -*ed* should also itself be considered to be some kind of "auxiliary." Similar arguments suggest that plural -*s* belongs to a functional category Number, etc.

6

Morphological Idiosyncrasies

/ˌmɔɹfəˈlɑdʒɪkəl ˌɪdijowˈsɪŋkɹəsijz/

> In the previous chapter, we saw that affixes could be picky about
> what kind of stem they attach to. In this chapter, we'll look
> at ways that stems can be picky about their affixes – at *stem-
> conditioned, homosemous*, morphemes. Inflectional alternations of
> this type are sometimes also called *irregulars*. Sometimes they
> involve totally arbitrary connections between morphemes –
> *suppletion*. We'll see how these phenomena can tell us a lot about
> the history of English. We'll also see that they can tell us a lot
> about the way we store and produce words as we speak, and
> learn how *blocking* works.

In the last chapter, we saw that phonological words often can be broken
down into bits – morphemes. Morphemes usually have their own
meanings, and usually the meaning of the whole phonological word is
composed out of the meanings of individual morphemes.

We also saw that affixes usually have particular requirements about
what kind of item their stem can be. These requirements can be
phonological (e.g. having a particular stress pattern), or syntactic (e.g.
being a noun or a verb).

In this chapter we'll examine some more complicated interactions
between stems and their affixes. Not only can affixes choose a particular
kind of stem to attach to, they can sometimes actually change the
phonology of the stems they attach to. In addition, we'll find that
affixes can be even more picky about their stems than we've seen up
to this point. We've seen that affixes can systematically demand stems
of a certain category, or a certain phonological shape – but they can
also demand arbitrary kinds of stems, not identifiable by any category
or phonology. This kind of arbitrary selection is called *irregularity*, and
it can reveal interesting facts about the history of English.

6.1 Different Listemes, Same Meaning: Irregular Suffixes

So far, all the affixes we've considered have had distinct meanings, so it's been clear that they've been distinct listemes. We have the *-ed* affix for the past tense (phonologically /d/), the *-s* affix for the plural (phonologically /z/), etc. We've seen a couple of cases where we have homophonous affixes: the *-s* affix for forming the plural of nouns is homophonous with the *-s* affix for forming the third person singular of verbs, for example. They have the same phonology, but different semantics. These don't pose any special problems for us: it seems clear that they're distinct listemes that happen to have the same phonological representation.

There are other cases, however, where it seems like we have two clearly distinct affixes – they're phonologically completely dissimilar – but the different pronunciations don't correlate with different meanings! That is, they have different phonology but the same semantics. Consider, for instance, the following sets of singular/plural pairs:

(1)   *Singular*   *Plural*
   a.   dog   dogs
        cat   cats
        witch   witches

   b.   alumnus   alumni
        focus   foci
        cactus   cacti
        radius   radii

   c.   sheep   sheep
        fish   fish
        quail   quail
        shrimp   shrimp
        bison   bison

   d.   addendum   addenda
        curriculum   curricula
        bacterium   bacteria
        millennium   millennia
        ovum   ova
        symposium   symposia

e.	analysis	analyses
	thesis	theses
	axis	axes
	diagnosis	diagnoses
	ellipsis	ellipses
f.	child	children
	ox	oxen

All of the above nouns have singular and plural forms, but the plural suffix is different from group to group. The first group is the regular English plural in -s. The second group is the Latin plural -i, which applies to some singular words ending in -us. The third group doesn't seem to make a distinction between singular and plural – they have the same form. The fourth group is another Latin plural, -a, which applies to some words ending in -um. The fifth group is a Greek plural, -es, which applies to some words ending in -is. Last, I've given an Old English plural, -en, which applies to only three roots in modern English. (Can you think of the third?)

These suffixes are all synonymous – they all mean *plural* – but they are pronounced significantly differently. They certainly meet our criteria for a defined "listeme" – each one is an arbitrary sound–meaning pair – so we can definitely say that they are listemes. It's only when taken as a group that they seem somewhat odd. If listemes with the same pronunciation but different meanings are *homophones* ("same-sound"), we could call these listemes **homosemes** ("same-meaning") – listemes with different pronunciations but the same meaning.

Why don't we use the more usual term "synonym" here, rather than this technical term "homoseme"? The everyday use of "synonym" is not precise enough. Synonyms are generally very similar in meaning, but are not completely interchangeable. For instance, Merriam-Webster's online thesaurus gives *inscribe* as a synonym for *write*, but it's clear that the two have quite different ranges of use and connotations. For example, it'd be very odd to talk about *inscribing a novel*, though it's perfectly natural to *write a novel*. These plural markers, however, which are function listemes, are crucially *not* interchangeable (it's "incorrect" to say *childs* rather than *children*), and *do* mean exactly the same thing, namely just [+ plural]. This difference between homosemy and synonymy reflects a deep distinction between the meanings of content listemes and those of function listemes, which we discuss more in Chapter 7, on acquisition.

The choice of affix for indicating the notion *plural* in these cases cannot be ascribed to the phonology of the stems to which they attach – there's nothing phonotactically wrong with putting the regular plural suffix -*s* on these words. Rather, these idiosyncratic plurals depend on the identity of the stem to which they attach. If a noun stem belongs to a particular class, it takes a different plural suffix than normal English nouns.

When you learned the root *bison*, you memorized the fact that for this particular root, the plural is not *bisons* but simply *bison*. Other words like this include *deer*, *sheep*, and *antelope*. One thing that makes this slightly easier to remember is that this particular group of null plurals all have a similar meaning: they're all words referring to herd animals that people raise or hunt. One might be tempted to say that the null plural on these words is conditioned by the meaning of the word, rather than by the phonology – but this meaning doesn't have the same effect everywhere. The plural of *cow* is *cows*, not *cow*, even though cows are herd animals; similarly for *goat–goats*, *horse–horses*, etc. So the correlation must be memorized one root at a time, although the tendency for this type of plural to apply to nouns of a certain semantic class probably helps as a mnemonic.

Similarly, the Latin and Greek plurals must be learned one at a time. Take *focus/foci*: There's no perfectly general rule that produces plurals of stems ending in -*us* by deleting -*us* and adding -*i*, otherwise *walrus* and *circus* and *bus* would have plurals *walri*, *circi*, and *bi*. With these, there's no semantic mnemonic to help you remember which ones it applies to. The fact that the singulars are all -*us* forms can help, but, since it's not perfectly general, relying too heavily on the -*us* clue can lead you into error. *Octopus* sounds like it ought perhaps to have a plural *octopi*, but classical scholars among you will know it's not so. *Octopus* is based on Greek roots, not Latin, *octo-* "eight" and *"pod-"* "foot" (as in *podiatrist*). Greek didn't use -*i* to mark plurals: the historically "proper" plural is *octopodes*, or the regularized English plural *octopuses*.[1] It's interesting to note that enough people have made this "mistake" that it has made it into the Merriam-Webster dictionary as a legitimate plural of *octopus*, though the more historically oriented OED omits mention of *octopi* altogether, insisting on *octopodes* or *octopuses*. (Mistakes of this type are called *back-formations,* remember?)

In any case, it's clear that the choice between -*s*, on the one hand, and -*i*, -*es*, -*a* or nothing at all, on the other, is determined by the particular stem one is trying to pluralize. These suffixes are different listemes, clearly, but they have the same semantics. All these suffixes – -*s*, -*i*, -*es*, etc. – have the same meaning: [+Plural]. The appearance of each one is determined by the identity of the stem the speaker is applying the [+Plural] meaning to.

Our lexical entries for these suffixes will mention each of the stems that they can attach to. The crucial difference between the -*s* plural suffix and all the other plural suffixes is that there *are* no particular stems in the listeme for -*s* – -*s* is completely free in its application. All plural -*s* cares about is that it attaches to nouns. That's what makes -*s* the *regular* plural marker. All the other plural suffixes are irregular.

We'll introduce a new kind of brackets to represent the idea "one of the following": curly brackets, like this {}. A list of information inside curly brackets in the syntactic section of a lexical entry indicates that the affix can apply to any one of the stems in the curly brackets I've also included ellipses, . . . , to show that there are other roots in the list of items that are not included for space reasons. The set of listemes with the meaning [+Plural] will look like this:

(2)　　　*Phonology*　　*Syntax*　　　　　　　　　*Semantics*

　a.　/aj/　　　[{[alumn], [radi], ...} -i]$_{+Pl}$　　+ Plural

　b.　/ijz/　　　[{[thes], [analys], [ax], ...} -es]$_{+Pl}$　　+ Plural

　c.　/Ø/　　　[{[sheep]$_N$, [deer]$_N$, [bison]$_N$, ...} -Ø]$_{+Pl}$　　+ Plural

　d.　/ə/　　　[{[addend], [symposi], [bacteri], ...} -a]$_{+Pl}$　　+ Plural

e. /ən/ $[\ \left\{\begin{array}{l} [\text{child}]^2_N \\ [\text{ox}]_N \\ [\text{brother}]^3_N \end{array}\right\}\ \text{-en}\ ]_{+Pl}$ + Plural

f. /z/ $[[\underline{}]_N\ \text{-s}\ ]_{+Pl}$ + Plural

> The symbol "∅," the mathematical symbol for a null set, is used by linguists to indicate the pronunciation of a morpheme that has a meaning but no phonological form – a null morpheme, like the plural of *sheep* or the past tense of *hit*.

Of course, the particular stems in an individual English speaker's lists can vary, depending on which ones the speaker is familiar with. If it so happens that you've never heard or read the word *ox* in the plural, then *ox* won't be in your list of *-en* plurals. If you need to talk about more than one *ox*, you'll make it's plural with the unspecified plural affix *-s*: *oxes*. Similarly, if you think *octopus* has the *-us* singular suffix on it, like *alumnus* or *cactus*, you might have a root *octop-* in your list for the *-i* plural, and produce the plural form *octopi*.

Knowledge of some of these irregular plurals are still considered marks of education, since they're part of the learned lexicon borrowed from Latin and Greek, and only educated people are likely to run into them often enough to learn them. It used to be that any educated person would have some grounding in classical languages, so they could be expected to know, for instance, the difference in plural form between a Latin second-declension stem and a Latin fourth-declension stem. That is no longer so, and back-formed plurals like *octopi* no longer mark their user as inexperienced in academe.

> Although knowledge of Greek and Latin is no longer an in-group badge of the college-educated, there are plenty of other such markers. Mastery of apostrophe use in the pair *it's/its*, and of the spelling of homophones like *they're*, *their* and *there*, or *reign* and *rein*, are some of the current flags indicating membership in the well-educated classes.

There are also sets of derivational-morpheme listemes that are homosemes in a similar way. One set of examples is given in (3):

(3) *Derivational homosemes: Irregular nominalizers*

	Verb	Noun
a.	correspond	correspondence
	appear	appearance
	repent	repentance
	accept	acceptance
b.	reply	reply
	run	run
	cough	cough
	hit	hit
c.	condemn	condemnation
	realize	realization
	converse	conversation
	determine	determination
d.	qualify	qualification
	beautify	beautification
	apply	application
	publish	publication
e.	propel	propelling
	eat	eating
	write	writing
	mix	mixing

These suffixes – *-ance, -Ø, -ation, -cation, -ing* – are all listemes sharing a meaning like [+NounOfAction], just as *-s, -i*, etc. are listemes that share the meaning [+Plural]. Their lexical entries would look something like this:

(4)

	Phonology	*Syntax*	*Semantics*
a.	/əns/	$[\{ \begin{smallmatrix} [\text{govern}]_V \\ [\text{appear}]_V \\ \dots \end{smallmatrix} \}$ -ance $]_N$	+NounOfAction
b.	/Ø/	$[\{ \begin{smallmatrix} [\text{reply}]_V \\ [\text{run}]_V \\ \dots \end{smallmatrix} \}$ -Ø $]_N$	+NounOfAction

c. /'ejʃən/ $\left[\begin{cases} [\text{condemn}]_V \\ [\text{converse}]_V \\ [[\underline{\quad}]\text{-ize}]_V \\ \dots \end{cases}\text{-ation}\right]_N$ +NounOfAction

d. /'kejʃən/ $\left[\begin{cases} [\text{apply}]_V \\ [[\underline{\quad}]\text{-ify}]_V \\ \dots \end{cases}\text{-cation}\right]_N$ +NounOfAction

e. /ɪŋ/ $[[\underline{\qquad}]_V \text{-ing}]_N$ +NounOfAction

There are many more examples of homosemy in English, and indeed in any language. This is the essence of irregularity: one functional meaning is realized by several different suffixes, depending on the stem in question. In English, nouns meaning *"one who Xes/the agent of Xing"* can be formed with *-ant* (*assistant, contestant*) as well as the default *-er* (*writer, producer*). Adjectives meaning *"full of X/characterized by X"* are formed from *-ous* (*venomous, envious*), *-ful* (*hopeful, fearful*) and the default *-y* (*dusty, hairy*). Verbal participles are formed with the suffixes *-en* as in *(had) driven, (had) written* and *-Ø*, as in *(had) put, (had) hit* as well as the default *-ed*, as in *(had) played, (had) added*. Examples can be multiplied *ad nauseum*. Clearly, our mental lexicon is full of sets of listemes of this kind: a single meaning, but multiple, arbitrarily varying pronunciations. All this irregularity is not tremendously efficient at first glance – when one invents a computer language, for instance, one usually designs it so that a single meaning is invariably represented by a single form. We'll examine the source of all this variation in English, and why it doesn't just all go away, as we continue.

It is important to realize the deep difference between phonologically conditioned allomorphy, which messes with the final pronunciation of a particular suffix, like the participial listeme /d/, and these stem-conditioned homosemous listemes with identical meanings. For the [+Participle] meaning, for example we've got the different listemes *-Ø*, *-en*, and *-ed* (/d/). The *-ed* one undergoes phonologically conditioned allomorphy, and ends up pronounced as /t/ (as in *walked*), /d/ (as in *calmed*) or /əd/ (as in *shouted*), according to the phonology of its stem. Phonologically conditioned allomorphy is quite general, applies indiscriminately to every phonological word produced by affixation of a particular listeme, and is motivated by the phonotactic rules of the language. No one has to memorize which particular stems that each phonological allomorph of the participle suffix *-ed* attaches to, because which allomorph you get is entirely determined by the pronunciation of the final sound of the stem. On the other hand, *everyone* has to memorize which particular stems the listeme *-en* goes with.

One way to think about it is that when you want to say something, you pick out particular listemes on the way from an abstract meaning to the base phonological form. Then, phonologically conditioned allomorphy happens on the way from the base phonological form to the actual pronounceable form which emerges from your lips. You could think of the whole process of producing a word like this:

(5) a. Arrive at a meaning you wish to convey. For example, in answer to the question, "Who arranges the President's schedule?", you might want to convey a meaning like the following:

[[ASSIST]+ AgentOfAction]+Plural]

b. Go to your lexicon and look up the listemes for each of these meanings in turn:

(i) Look up ASSIST. You get this listeme:

[ə'sɪst]$_V$

(ii) With [ə'sɪst]$_V$ in mind, look up NounOfAction. You will get the *-ant* listeme, rather than the default *-er* listeme, because *-ant* has ASSIST on its list:

[[ə'sɪst]$_V$ ənt]$_N$

(iii) With [[ə'sɪst]$_V$ ənt]$_N$ in mind, look up Plural. This will give you the default Plural affix /z/, since no homoseme of Plural specifies [[ə'sɪst]$_V$ ənt]$_N$ in its list:

[[[ə'sɪst]$_V$ ənt]$_N$z]$_{Pl}$

c. Send this off for preliminary pronunciation arrangements. Here, you will detect that the phonological word /ə'sɪstəntz/ ends in a voiceless stop followed by a voiced fricative, violating the phonotactic rules of English. Consequently, phonologically conditioned allomorphy is triggered, applying to the final /z/ to produce:

[ə'sɪstənts]

> d. Do final fine-tuning of the pronunciation – find the right allophone for all the phonemes in the form, give it the correct intonation for the meaning you desire (assertive or questioning), and send the instructions off to your articulatory system.

We'll see some psycholinguistic evidence for this general picture of word production in Chapter 8.

6.2 Root Irregulars

We see a phenomenon that looks like homosemy in root morphemes, too. Consider the following lists:

(6) *Root homosemy*

	Present Tense	*Past Tense*
a.	sink	sank
	eat	ate
	feel	felt
	sleep	slept
	make	made
	keep	kept
	write	wrote

	Verb	*Noun*
b.	induce	induction
	produce	production
	reduce	reduction
	deduce	deduction
	produce	production
	seduce	seduction
	(*conduce)	conduction
	(*subduce)	subduction
	(*abduce)	abduction

In (6), the morpheme which is pronounced differently depending on context is not the suffix, but rather the root itself. In (6)a, we see that some verb roots in English have different forms in the past tense – instead of just adding a past tense suffix, they use a form of the root with a different vowel or consonant in it. (Sometimes they also seem to add a suffix, as with *sleep–slept*; other times there is no suffix.) Similarly, a number of bound Latinate root morphemes, including *-duce*, the root of all the words in (6)b, have distinct allomorphs for use when they're nominalized; in this case, /duws/ becomes /dʌkt/. There are several other Latinate root morphemes of this type; *-ceive/-cept-* and *-volve/-volu-* are two of them. The lexical entries for *eat/ ate* and *-duce/-duct* will look like this:

(7)   *Phonology*   *Syntax*   *Semantics*

     a.   /ejt/   [ate]$_V$ [[EAT]Past]

         /ijt/   [eat]$_V$ EAT

     b.   /dʌkt/   [[___$_{Prefix}$] duct]$_V$ [[DUCE]NounOfAction]

         /duws/   [[___$_{Prefix}$] duce]$_V$ DUCE

Now, *-duce/-duct* (and *-ceive/-cept*, *-volve/volu*, etc.) don't have a meaning on their own. They are *cran-morphs*, like the morphemes we saw in the last chapter. But now we see that they have to be listemes after all, because there is *some* kind of individually listed information about them. An underlying form DUCE has two homosemous surface forms, /dʌkt/ and /duws/ (in some dialects, /djuws/). It doesn't matter what else it goes with (*reduce, induce, deduce* . . .), they all have that listeme DUCE in them, and they all get the homoseme *-duct-* when they show up in a noun of action (*reduction, induction, deduction* . . .).

So what happens when one tries to interpret the meaning of a listeme like *-duce* when one is putting together all the parts of a word and trying to figure out its meaning? It doesn't have a meaning on its own, as we've seen. It must be the case that it *does* have meaning, but its meanings are restricted to only certain contexts. When you get to DUCE in your semantic analysis, you'll find a series of interpretations like this: "DUCE: 'make smaller' when attached to RE"; "DUCE: 'figure out' when attached to DE"; etc. The same kind of thing is going to be true of *caboodle* in *kit and caboodle*, and of *rasp-* in *raspberry*. What we said before about cran-morphs was that they had no meaning, so they weren't listemes. Now we see that what really makes cran-morphs special is that they have no meaning that doesn't depend on something else. And they are listemes, after all. They're just a very, very specialized kind of listeme.

The main point for us here, though, is that DUCE, like EAT, WRITE, KEEP, MADE, etc, are listemes with two homosemous phonological forms – roots that exhibit root irregularity, conditioned when a certain kind of affix is attached to it.

6.3 Linguistic Paleontology: Fossils of Older Forms

Homosemes come in families, grouped according to the meaning that they share. Most of them are restricted to appear only in certain circumstances, but in each family, there's one listeme that can apply pretty much everywhere – one that has no restrictions on its appearance at all. As we saw above, among the [+Plural] homosemes, -*s* is the everywhere form. Among the action-noun-forming homosemes, -*ing* is the everywhere form. Among the doer-of-action-noun-forming homosemes, -*er* is the everywhere form. Among the adjective-forming homosemes, -*y* is the elsewhere form.

Why doesn't the regular listeme just take over completely, displacing its irregular sibling affixes? Wouldn't it be much more economical to just have one form for each meaning? Everyone would know what I meant if I said I was feeling very *hope-y*, rather than *hopeful*. It's clear what a child means when they say they liked what they *eated* yesterday, rather than what they *ate*. Everyone knew what Bush meant when he was talking about an *analyzation*, rather than an *analysis*. Where did the irregular listemes come from? And why do they persist?

In general, the unpredictable forms of English have four kinds of sources: incomplete application of some historical change (a) in an English morpheme or (b) in a sound pattern, or borrowing of (c) a set of morphemes or (d) set of sound patterns from another language. In this section, we'll look at examples of all four kinds. Irregulars are kind of like linguistic fossils, the last remnants of formerly productive structure in some earlier stage of development, or productive structure borrowed from some other language entirely.

6.3.1 Fossils of older forms I: Incomplete change in morpheme: a *three*-legged *race*

Our first case is one particular homoseme of the adjective-forming suffix -*ed*, which emerged when the regular, default suffix underwent a sound change A few forms were left out of the change, and now the pre-change pronunciation is an irregular morpheme that shows up with only a few roots, each of which has to be listed individually in the lexical entry for that morpheme.

In Middle English, the regular form of the adjective-forming suffix *-ed* was always pronounced with a vowel, as /əd/, no matter what the phonology of the stem it was attached to was like. Since the suffix had its own vowel, adding the suffix to a word always meant adding a new syllable to the word. (This was true not only for the derivational adjective-forming suffix *-ed*, but also for the homophonous participle-forming suffix *-ed*.) There was never any need for phonologically conditioned allomorphy of this suffix, since the phonotactic rules of English were perfectly happy with the shape of this additional syllable.

It's because the past-tense ending *used* to always be pronounced as a full syllable, as /əd/, that we spell it as "-ed," even when it's pronounced /d/ or /t/. At least, we came to consistently spell it *-ed* with some help from Samuel Johnson's dictionary-making in the 1700s. In the 1500s, the reduction of the suffix from /əd/ to /d/ was often reflected in spelling. Shakespeare often wrote -'*d* to indicate the reduced pronunciation, e.g.:

> I am constant as the northern star,
> Of whose true-<u>fix'd</u> and resting quality
> There is no fellow in the firmament,
>> (*Julius Caesar*)

> ... Herein will I imitate the sun,
> Who doth permit the base contagious clouds
> To smother up his beauty from the world,
> That, when he please again to be himself,
> Being wanted, he may be more <u>wonder'd</u> at,
>> (*Henry IV*, Part I)

After Johnson published his dictionary in 1755, no one used the apostrophe'd form any longer, except occasionally for poetic effect. Johnson's standardization of the spelling to match the older pronunciation reflects an almost universal tendency to feel that older forms are "correct" and that innovations are "corruptions."

Eventually, however, the phonological form of the suffix was shortened, from the syllabic /əd/ to the simple consonant /d/. After that shortening, adding this suffix to a stem involved forcing an additional consonant into the coda of the stem's final syllable. At that point, as we have seen, the phonotactic rules of English jumped in to create the phonologically conditioned allomorphs of /d/, in order to make the new more complex codas pronounceable.

This contraction in pronunciation happened to the suffix itself, so it should have happened everywhere the suffix was used. But in just a few cases, the older version of the affix has been preserved.

The /əd/ pronunciation was often preserved in words that were common in idioms, poems, or ritual speech, where language learners were more likely to repeat the string exactly as they heard their elders say it. In poetry, the extra syllable was often important to the meter of the poem, so reducing the suffix would hurt the poem, as in these lines of Lewis Carroll's (written long after the change occurred, but still employing the syllabic pronunciation for metric purposes):[4]

(8)   I'll tell thee everything I can; there's little to relate.
      I saw an agèd, agèd man, a-sitting on a gate.

This poem is arranged in iambic feet: I'll TELL thee EVeryTHING I CAN; there's LITtle TO reLATE. If the adjective *aged* was pronounced with the reduced suffix, as /ejdʒd/, rather than as /ejdʒəd/, the meter of the second line would be completely off.

Other examples of adjectives that retained the old pronunciation of the suffix are *learnèd* (as in *a learnèd man*), *belovèd, accursèd,* and *blessèd.* These last three are common in ritual speech – in Church liturgy – and part of the reason they were preserved is the importance people attach to the exact replication of ritual. In ritual speech, it's important to get the words exactly "right"; this usually means pronouncing them exactly the way they were learned – even if that results in archaic-sounding speech.

The independent stems that were the base of some of these adjectives in *-ed* have since dropped out of the language. The word *naked* is like that – there's no independent listeme *nake* anymore. If it still exists as a morpheme at all, it's a cran-morph, like *shevel* in *disheveled.*

The adjective-forming suffix *-ed* can also apply directly to nouns, to make an adjective meaning "having X, characterized by X" as in *toothed, moneyed, cultured, diseased, jaundiced, brown-eyed,* etc. Most of them take regular *-ed,* i.e. /d/, but there are a few adjectives formed in this way that have retained the syllabic form of the suffix: *wickèd* (related to *witch*), *raggèd, crookèd, jaggèd.* In some of these cases, like *raggèd,* or *leggèd,* (as in *a three-leggèd race* or *a one-leggèd pirate*), the root noun is still a common word of English. In other cases, as with *naked* above, the original noun from which the adjective was formed has been lost, or has become uncommon: *wick* (a variant of "witch"), *crook*, and *jag* are examples of this.

The infrequency of the root in words like *naked*, *jagged*, and *wicked* means that it might not have occurred to you before that the *-ed* in these words is a suffix at all. The combination of a cran-morph like *nake-* with the unusual homoseme of the adjectivizing suffix *-ed* may have caused your grammar to reanalyze this form as a single morpheme. (Remember back-formation? This process, *reanalysis*, is its opposite.) If you don't run into alternative forms of the root very often, and if the suffix itself is also rare and irregular, and if the whole word is a plausible English phonological word, your word-analysis machinery may decide there's just a single morpheme involved. Below, we'll see that this kind of frequency-related reanalysis might have played a role in causing Bush to produce the neologism *analyzation*.

In any case, the syllabic /əd/ pronunciation of the adjective-forming suffix has come down in the world from being the default, everywhere form, to being a very restricted homoseme of the same meaning. Here's how its listeme has changed:

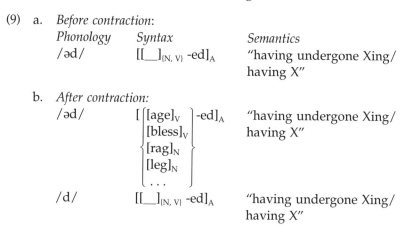

(9) a. *Before contraction*:
      Phonology   *Syntax*   *Semantics*
      /əd/ $[[\_\_]_{\{N, V\}}\ \text{-ed}]_A$ "having undergone Xing/
                                             having X"

    b. *After contraction*:
        /əd/ $\left[\left\{\begin{array}{l}[\text{age}]_V\\ [\text{bless}]_V\\ [\text{rag}]_N\\ [\text{leg}]_N\\ \dots\end{array}\right\}\ \text{-ed}\right]_A$ "having undergone Xing/
                                                  having X"

        /d/ $[[\_\_]_{\{N, V\}}\ \text{-ed}]_A$ "having undergone Xing/
                                             having X"

6.3.2 Fossils of older forms II: Incomplete application of a phonotactic change: calves, wolves, *and how they're* spelt

Above we saw a fossil of a former regular morpheme, preserved as an irregular morpheme in a tiny corner of the English vocabulary. Now we turn to a case where an irregular morpheme preserves a fossil of a former regular phonotactic rule of English. This rule is now defunct, but it has left its traces on a few common forms.

In modern English, several nouns that end in voiceless fricatives in the singular have a stem homoseme that ends in a voiced fricative in the plural, like *calf–calves*, *house–houses*, *mouth–mouths*, and *wife–wives*. Why bother? Why do we say /haws/-/hawzəz/ rather than /haws/-/hawsəz/ (as we do in the regular pair *grouse–grouses*)?

Old English, like other Germanic languages, used to have a quite general phonotactic rule which required fricatives to be voiced when they occurred between two voiced sounds. For example, *father* /fɑðəɹ/, a cognate of Latin *pater*, has a voiced interdental fricative in the middle, rather than a voiceless one, because the fricative appears between two voiced vowel sounds. Grimm's law (from Chapter 2) caused the Proto-Indo-European /t/ to become the voiceless fricative /θ/ in Germanic (as we see in the *tri-/three* cognate pair), and the P-I-E /p/ to become the voiceless fricative /f/. Now, that rule by itself would have meant that the word for *father* should have been pronounced /fɑθəɹ/, not /fɑðəɹ/. It was the phonotactic rules of Germanic that caused the /θ/ to become its voiced counterpart /ð/ in this word, because it occurred between two vowels.

Now, it so happens that the Old English ancestor of our plural suffix, like the Old English version of our past tense suffix, used to have its own vowel: it was pronounced /əz/, not /z/. That meant that when the plural suffix, complete with vowel, was added to a word like *wife*, *knife*, *house*, or *wolf*, which ended in a voiceless fricative, the resulting form would become something like /wajfəz/, /najfəz/, /hawsez/, or /wolfəz/. When the suffix was added, all of a sudden the voiceless fricative /f/ (in the case of *wife*) or /s/ (in the case of *house*) was in between two vowels. This would force the intervocalic voicing rule to kick in. When this phonotactic rule, which said "intervocalic fricatives are voiced" applied, the end result would be something like /wajvəz/ *wives*, /hawzəz/ *houses*, and /wʌlvəz/ *wolves*. (This isn't how the actual Old English words really sounded, of course, but it ought to give you the idea of how the phonotactic rule worked. See discussion in Chapter 9.)

The voicing rule no longer applies in modern English, in which intervocalic voiceless fricatives are perfectly fine. For instance, *blessing*, *facile*, *laugher*, *lifer*, and *prefer* are all English words with intervocalic voiceless fricatives. Further, the plural suffix is now just /z/, so making a plural for most words no longer involves adding an extra syllable. In /wajvz/, /wʌlvz/, /kævz/, the fricative is not intervocalic. But the intervocalic voicing rule is still with us as a fossil – in the irregular plural stem homosemes of the roots *wife*, *knife*, *wolf*, *life*, and *house*, which now have to be memorized one at a time. The lexical entry of *wife*, for instance, has changed as follows:

(10) a. *Before loss of the intervocalic voicing rule:*

Pronunciation	Syntax	Semantics
/wajf/	[wife]$_N$	WIFE

  b. *After loss of the intervocalic voicing rule:*

/wajv/	[wive]$_N$	[[WIFE]Plural]
/wajf/	[wife]$_N$	WIFE

Another example of a fossilized phonological rule is the class of past-tense irregulars like *feel–felt, dream–dreamt, mean–meant, burn–burnt.* Some other examples of this rule that are still in widespread spoken use in some dialects of American English, are *spill–spilt, learn–learnt, spoil–spoilt, smell–smelt,* and *spell–spelt.* The latter are gradually falling out of use in written English, but they still exist.

It used to be the case that the phonotactics of English required the devoiced allomorph /t/ of the past tense morpheme to appear not only after voiceless consonants, as in modern English, but also after nasals and liquids.[5] That is, the phonotactic rules for English codas didn't allow /d/ to occur after nasals and liquids. As a result, all verbs ending with a nasal or liquid got the /t/ pronunciation of the past-tense suffix, by regular phonologically conditioned allomorphy.

When the phonotactics of English changed, to allow /d/ after nasals and liquids generally, the /d/ suffix stopped changing to /t/ when it was attached to words ending in those sounds. But we retained a few of the more frequent forms with /t/ as memorized, irregular, homosemes. (Many of these verbs have stem allomorphs as well; their short vowels are a remnant of another former phonotactic rule – see Chapter 9 for discussion.) Before the change in coda phonotactics, the regular past-tense morpheme didn't have a -*t* homoseme. After codas like /nd/ and /ld/ became legal, though, and the -*t* form of the suffix was still appearing on a few diehard stems, it got one. The lexical entry for the past tense suffix changed as follows:

(11) a. *Before loss of the coda restriction:*

Phonology	Syntax	Semantics
/d/	[[__]$_V$-ed]$_{Pst}$	+Past Tense

b. *After the loss of the coda restriction:*

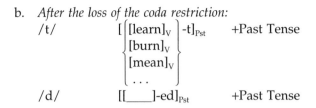

As time goes by, many of these are becoming more and more regularized, so alongside *dreamt* and *burnt* we now often see *dreamed* and *burned*. *Spill, learn, spoil,* and *smell* occur mostly with the past tense forms *spilled, learned, spoiled,* and *smelled*. However, the verbs *feel* and *mean* are still robustly hanging onto their irregular past tenses: no one talks about what they *feeled*, or what they *meaned* to say. It's possible that in the future even these fossils will erode away, and there will no longer be any record in modern English of the old phonologically conditioned allomorphy of *-ed* before nasals and liquids. In Section 6.4, we'll consider what factors are involved in the retention and loss of these irregular forms.

6.3.3 Fossils of older forms III: Borrowed suffixes from another language: -i and -s, -ity and -ness

A third source of modern English homosemes was the large influx of Latinate-origin stems and affixes that were borrowed into English between 1200 and 1700 (see the next section, and Chapter 9). Before the arrival of these elements, most of the listemes in English were provided by the native Anglo-Saxon stock.

After the influx of borrowings, though, several new homosemes had entered the language, along with the stems they applied to. We've already discussed some of the homosemes for the plural (*-i, -a,* etc.). There were also new homosemes for forming nouns of action, some of which that we've looked at: *-ation,* etc., on top of the Anglo-Saxon *-ing*. There were new homosemes for forming adjectives: *-ous* on top of the Anglo-Saxon *-ful*, and new homosemes for forming nouns of quality: *-ity* on top of Anglo-Saxon *-ness*.

Many of these were restricted to occur only with certain stems, or certain other affixes. Others were more productive. They nearly all realized meanings that the regular Anglo-Saxon vocabulary already had forms to express. They were mostly restricted to applying to stems that had also been borrowed from Latinate languages.

6.3.4 Borrowing trouble: stress-shifting and non-stress-shifting suffixes

Finally, in some cases the borrowed Latinate suffixes brought special phonological rules with them. In English, these rules became memorized morphophonological rules – rules triggered by particular morphemes – rather than general phonotactic rules. One of the clearest examples of this kind of affixal selection is particularly interesting because it's a complex result of a historical accident that changed English forever eight hundred years ago. Although most speakers of English are at best only vaguely aware of the historical events that led to the restructuring of the English vocabulary, we all have perfect subconscious command of the rules governing the word-building tools that English acquired as a result!

Different derivational suffixes have different effects on stress placement in English. To see this, pronounce the following word pairs aloud to yourself, and then transcribe a pair from each group, indicating the placement of main stress:

(12) a. | regurgitate | regurgitation |
| --- | --- |
| credible | credibility |
| artist | artistic |
| janitor | janitorial |
| compliment | complimentary |
| Canada | Canadian |

b. | guardian | guardianship |
| --- | --- |
| yellow | yellowish |
| colonial | colonialism |
| violin | violinist |
| neighbor | neighborhood |
| perish | perishable |

c. | kitchen | kitchenette |
| --- | --- |
| Reuben | Reubenesque |
| official | officialese |
| tonsil | tonsillitis |

Exercise 6.1 Transcribe three pairs of words from (12), indicating the main stress in each.

Recall that all English content words receive a main stress. For most multi-syllabic words in English, the stress falls on either the third-to-last ("antepenultimate") syllable, as in *PAradise, colLAteral, CHICkadee, REprimand,* or *MinneAPolis,* or else the second-to-last ("penultimate") syllable, as in *CANdy, ToLEdo, umBRELLa, piANo,* or *baNAna.* In one-syllable content words, of course, there's nowhere for stress to go except on the one syllable, which is both first and last.

You probably noticed that the syllable that gets main stress in the pairs in (12)a and (12)c is different for the suffixed and non-suffixed words, while the same syllable gets main stress in both kinds of words in (12)b. While the affixes in (12)a and (12)c change the placement of stress in the words they attach to, the affixes in (12)b are *stress-neutral* – they just tack onto the end of whatever word they're in, sometimes getting their own secondary stress, but never changing the placement of main stress. These affixes are very simple to treat in our mental lexicon – we don't need to indicate any special effect for them.

In the (12)c cases, the affix itself carries its own main stress, which it brings to the word it's attaching to. The stress pattern of the root is generally maintained, albeit at a reduced level. The syllable that got main stress without the suffix now gets *secondary* stress – less stress than main stress, but more than none – and the relationship between the stem word and the suffixed word seems pretty straightforward. In the IPA, just as primary stress is represented with a high-up tick before the stressed syllable, secondary stress is represented with a low-down tick before the stressed syllable. In English orthography, I'll show secondary stress with small caps. With stress and syllabification indicated, the transcriptions for the last two examples in (12)c look like this:

(13)   a.   of.FI.cial   of.FI.cia.LESE
             /ə.'fɪ.ʃəl/   /ə.ˌfɪ.ʃə.'lijz/

       b.   TON.sil   TON.si.LI.tis
             /'tɑn.səl/   /ˌtɑn.sə.'laj.təs/

These suffixes seem to be saying "Give me main stress, and reduce the stress pattern on my stem to secondary status."

In (12)a things are a little different. The main stress in the suffixed word doesn't fall on the suffix. Rather, it falls in the syllable *before* the suffix. This means that no matter where the main stress fell in the non-suffixed word, stress in the suffixed word must be on the syllable

163

right before the suffix. With stress and syllabification indicated, the transcriptions for the last two examples in (12)a look like this:

(14) a. COM.pli.ment   COM.pli.MEN.ta.ry
          /ˈkɑm.plə.mənt/   /ˌkɑm.plə.ˈmɛn.tə.rij/

      b. CA.na.da   Ca.NA.di.an
          /ˈkæ.nə.də/   /kə.ˈnej.dij.jən/

These suffixes seem to be saying, "Bring the main stress to sit over here beside me, no matter what it does to the rest of the word." Since de-stressing a syllable often involves reducing the vowel in that syllable, these stress-shifting affixes can significantly affect the pronunciation of the root. This in turn can obscure the connection between the root and the suffixed word. The pronunciation of the root in *palace* /ˈpæləs/ and *palatial* /pəˈlejʃəl/ is distinct enough that it takes a moment of thought to recognize that the latter is derived from the former.

We can clearly see the difference between the stress-shifters and the neutral suffixes when we look at a stem that can occur with both kinds. In the word *párent*, stress falls on the first syllable. *Parent* can combine with both the adjective-forming suffix *-al* and the noun-forming suffix *-hood*. Each of these suffixes is itself just one syllable, but they result in very different stress placements: *-al* shifts the stress, so that *paRENtal* has stress on the second syllable of the stem, while *-hood* leaves the stress of the stem where it found it: *PArenthood* has stress on the first syllable.

6.4 Why Some but Not Others?

Why does English have these distinct kinds of suffixes? Why don't all the suffixes affect stress placement, or none? If we look up our stress-shifting suffixes from (12)a, *-ion*, *-ic*, *-ial*, *-ary*, and *-ian* in a dictionary with etymological information, such as the OED, we immediately notice that they are all borrowed. They all entered English via French after 1100 AD. The stress-bearing suffixes from (12)c are also all borrowed, mostly quite recently, after 1800 AD: *-ette* is from French, *-esque* and *-ese* from Italian, and *-itis* was borrowed directly from Latin.

The non-stress-shifting suffixes from (12)b, on the other hand, are a mix: *-hood*, *-ship*, and *-ish*[6] have been part of English from prehistoric times, while *-ism*, *-ist*, and *-able* are early borrowings from French. None of them shift stress – but there is still a difference between the borrowed ones and the Germanic ones! The suffixes of French origin in (12)b mate happily with other suffixes from the stress-shifting list in (12)a. Nouns ending in *-ist* can usually form an adjective with *-ic*, one of the stress-shifting suffixes: *Communist-Communistic, imperialist-imperialistic*, and so on. Adjectives ending in *-able* can form a noun ending in the stress-shifter *-ity*: *perishable-perishability, readable-readability*, etc.

In contrast, our suffixes of Germanic origin, *-hood*, *-ish*, and *-ship*, cannot be followed by suffixes of Latinate origin. If we want to make an adjective out of *childhood*, for instance, we cannot add the Latinate *-ial* suffix – English speakers would be very unhappy with **childhoodial*. To make this point extra-clear, consider the difference between the suffixes *-ness* and *-ity*, both of which apply to adjectives to form nouns. The Germanic one, *-ness*, can apply to adjectives formed with the Latinate adjectival suffix *-ic*, in words like *chaoticness, rusticness*, and *causticness*. The Latinate suffix *-ity*, however, which does the same job of turning an adjective into a noun, cannot apply to adjectives formed with the Germanic adjectival suffix *-ish*: there is no *yellowishity, purplishity, freakishity*; rather, we have *yellowishness, purplishness*, and *freakishness*.

> When an affix is described as being "Latinate," that doesn't necessarily mean it was borrowed directly from Latin. It might also have been borrowed from any of the daughter languages of Latin that are the modern descendants of the Italic branch of Proto-Indo-European, such as Italian, Spanish, Portuguese, or, and most importantly, French. See Chapter 9 for discussion.

We can schematize this generalization about the ordering of these classes of suffixes as in (15):

(15)   [[[Stem]-(LatinateAffix(es))]-(GermanicAffix(es))]

The round brackets indicate optionality, as usual: most stems can occur without any derivational affixes at all, of course. They can also have Latinate affixes without any Germanic ones, and vice versa. What (15) says is that *if* a word has both Latinate and Germanic derivational affixes, the Latinate ones will occur inside the Germanic ones.

In fact, English speakers are remarkably sensitive to the fact that some of our productive suffixes "belong" with originally borrowed vocabulary. Gene Buckley, at the University of Pennsylvania, had his introductory linguistics class collect a list of words ending in the borrowed suffix *-ize* that were created in English after 1300. Of the approximately 150 newly coined *-ize* words that they found, only three are formed from stems that were originally English – *winterize, womanize*, and *weatherize*. All the others – *brutalize, compartmentalize, realize*, etc. – are formed from stems of Latinate origin. Some (like *realize*) may have been borrowed whole from the source language (in this case, French), but most of the others were formed in English by English speakers, who combined the suffix *-ize* with an independent stem. Although about 50 percent of everyday English words are Germanic in origin, only 2 percent of the new words formed with *-ize* from Buckley's list were formed using Germanic stems.

Many of the borrowed derivational suffixes of English are very productive (as we can see from Bush's ability to make up *securitize* and *analyzation* on the spot). Nonetheless, the Latinate suffixes, like *-ity*, can sometimes fail to attach even in places where we'd expect them to be fine – they're "gappy," as we saw for **deservation* at the beginning of the last chapter. When this happens, English plugs in an "everywhere" Germanic suffix to fill in the gap. So while some adjectives ending in the Latinate suffix *-ous* have nouns made from *-ity* (*curious–curiosity, pompous–pomposity, viscous–viscosity*), other *-ous* adjectives reject *-ity* and prefer the more general Germanic suffix *-ness*: from *rebellious* we can't make **rebelliosity*; rather, we must use *rebelliousness*; similarly for *vicious–*viciosity–viciousness* and *querulous–*querulosity–querulousness*. The Germanic suffix, in this case, is the catch-all which applies when the Latinate one can't.

6.5 How Do Kids Figure It Out?

Now, in fact, no one learning English as a first language knows that some derivational suffixes were originally borrowed, and some were originally native to the English spoken 800 years ago. If you know facts like that at all, it's because you learned them in school, long after you became a competent English speaker. Yet, your knowledge of English affix-placement and stress-shifting reveals that you're aware of the existence of these two very different classes of suffixes. How could you have figured this out when you were learning English?

We saw in the last chapter that infants are hyper-alert to the statistical probabilities of phoneme sequences and stress patterns. A child paying attention to the statistics will certainly notice that some roots never show up as phonological words by themselves. Some roots *always* need a suffix of some kind on them – they're bound, not free. Others can show up with or without suffixes. What a child learning English is sure to notice is that only certain suffixes show up next to bound roots – the ones we've been calling "Latinate."

So, for instance, the adjective-forming suffix /əbəl/ – one of the originally Latinate ones, spelled sometimes as *-able* and sometimes as *-ible* – appears in words like *cap-able, prob-able, dur-able, incred-ible,* and *vis-ible*, none of whose stems ever occur as words on their own. (There's no word *dur* in English!) Of course, *-able* is a very productive affix in English, and does occur on plenty of stems that are phonological words on their own (*washable, viewable, breakable . . .*) – but the crucial thing is that it occurs on some stems which aren't. The same goes for *-ity* (*authority, dignity* and *entity* are all formed on bound roots), *-ous* (*anxious, ferocious* and *frivolous*), and all the rest of the Latinate suffixes.

In contrast, Anglo-Saxon suffixes like *-ness* and *-ship* only go on stems that are actual phonological words on their own. Try and think of a word with one of these suffixes in it that isn't! *Childhood, friendship, happiness, ownership, callousness . . .* there are tremendously many, and they all have roots that are independent phonological words.[7] This distinction is a very strong clue to the existence of two classes of suffixes.

Other clues to the differences between the two kinds of suffixes are the phonological changes that some of the Latinate suffixes force on their stem, including the stress shift that we've already seen, and also others, such as requiring stem-forming morphemes like *-it-* in *competitive* and *competitor*. None of the Germanic suffixes alter the phonological shape of their stems like that.

Of course, this difference has its source in one of the major differences between languages of Latinate origin like French and languages of Germanic origin, like Dutch, or the English of 800 years ago. The former have mostly bound roots, and the latter have mostly free roots – so when Latinate vocabulary was borrowed wholesale into English, its distinct morphological properties were borrowed too. But a child learning modern English doesn't need to know that. All he or she needs to notice, and remember, is that some suffixes can go with bound roots, and trigger phonological changes, while others never do. Then he or she just has to annotate each kind of suffix as needing certain properties in its stem, and everything else follows.

6.6 Representing Complex Suffixal Restrictions

Let's say the mental lexicon entries for the Germanic suffixes need to include the information that their stem has to be an independent phonological word. This kind of restriction is rather like the unstressed, open-syllable restriction that we saw for the comparative *-er*; there, we had to include information about the syllable structure of the stem in the listeme. Here, we'll have to include information about the phonological wordhood of the stem. The usual notation for "phonological word" is the lower case Greek letter omega: ω. We'll subscript ω to the blank space that stands for the stem in the syntactic part of the entry to show that the stem has to be a phonological word for these affixes to go on. The final entry for *-ness*, then, will look like this:

(16) *Phonology*   *Syntax*   *Semantics*

/nɛs/ $[[\_\_\_\_\_ {}_\omega]_{\{A, N\}}$ -ness $]_N$ "the quality of being X"

The entries for the Latinate suffixes won't have the phonological-word restriction on them, of course, but they will impose other restrictions. In particular, to explain why Latinate affixes don't attach to words derived with Germanic affixes, there must be something that the Latinate suffixes look for in their stems that the Germanic suffixes don't have.

One such something is that many Latinate suffixes attach only to stems which are also roots. The suffix *-ify* is like that. It attaches to adjectival and sometimes nominal roots to make verbs, as in the examples in (17):

(17) | *Root* | *-ify verb* | *Meaning* |
|---|---|---|
| clear | clar-ify | to make clear |
| yuppy | yupp-ify | to make yuppy |
| magn- | magn-ify | to make big |
| simple | simpl-ify | to make simple |

The meaning of *-ify* is clear enough from the above examples; it creates verbs that mean something like "to make X." It is also clear that *-ify* is a Latinate suffix, since it attaches to a number of bound roots. But even when the part of speech is appropriate, and the meaning is clear, *-ify* can't attach to a stem that contains another suffix – not even another Latinate suffix:

(18)	*Adjective with suffix:*	**-ify verb:*	*What it would mean:*
	act-ive	*activify	"make active"
	accur-ate	*accuratify	"make accurate"
	electr-ic	*electricify	"make electric"

This last example is particularly revealing, since *-ify* CAN attach to the root *electr-*, giving *electrify*, with exactly the meaning expected for the non-word *electricify*, above. The affix *-ify* is still a productive, independent part of the language, too – it is still used to form causative verbs in modern senses, like *yuppify* and *webify*, so these made-up words in (18) don't sound bad because *-ify* isn't used to make new words anymore. We've just got to include the information about requiring a root in the lexical entry for *-ify*.

Note that *-ify* doesn't care if the root is bound or free (both *qualify*, formed on a bound root, and *personify*, formed on a free root, are perfectly good), as long as it doesn't have any affixes on it. The property of "being a root," then, isn't a phonological property, like "being a phonological word" or "ending in an unstressed open syllable."

We'll assume that being a "root" is a kind of category information, like being a noun or a verb, and include it as a label on the blank line that stands for the stem. We'll use the mathematical symbol for "root," √, to indicate the category Root:

(19)	*Phonology*	*Syntax*	*Semantics*
	/ɪfaj/	[[_____ √] -ify]	"to make X"

We're not quite done with *-ify* yet, though. It's a stress-shifting suffix – the main stress of a word formed with *-ify* falls on the syllable before *-ify*, no matter where it would fall if *-ify* wasn't there. (Consider pairs like *solid* /ˈsɑləd/ ~ *solidify* /səˈlɪdəfaj/.) We need to include this information in our lexical entry too.

We'll call the instruction to shift the stress on the stem a **readjustment rule**, and give it a special place in the listeme. Again, we'll represent syllables in the stem with the Greek letter sigma, σ. As usual, a high-up tick indicates the placement of main stress; ellipses indicate that the stem could have more syllables in it just one. The final entry for *-ify* will look like this:[8]

(20)	*Phonology*	*Syntax*	*R.Rules*	*Semantics*
	/ɪfaj/	[[_____√]-ify]	[. . . ˈσ] -ify	"to make X"

Other suffixes have other restrictions. Some attach only to stems which contain a particular suffix, or one of a few particular suffixes. For example, the adjective-forming suffix *-ic* attaches to roots (as in *electric*), to verbs formed with the suffix *-ify* (as in *terrific, specific* or *horrific*), and to nouns formed with the suffix *-ist* (as in *artistic, pessimistic* or *holistic*). It doesn't attach to nouns formed with *-er*, though they're similar in meaning to nouns formed with *-ist* (**painteric, *writeric* – they get the homoseme *-ly*: *painterly, writerly*), and it doesn't attach to verbs formed with *-ize*, though they're similar in meaning to verbs formed with *-ify* (**colorizic, *deodorizic*).

The lexical entry for *-ic*, of course, will have to encode this information:

(21) *Phonology*   *Syntax*   *R.Rules*   *Semantics*
      /ɪk/ $\left\{ \begin{matrix} [\_\_]_V \\ [\_\_\text{ ify}]_V \\ [\_\_\text{ ist}]_N \end{matrix} \right\}$-ic   [. . . 'σ] -ic   "in the manner of X"

Since *-ic* is also a stress-shifting suffix, the stress-shifting readjustment rule is also indicated in its lexical entry.

6.7 Keeping Irregulars: Semantic Clues to Morphological Classes

Irregular forms and rules just have to be memorized, listeme by listeme. For some kinds of irregular forms, though, there are clues that group the irregular listemes together. We saw above there may be semantic clues that could help with the memorization of the irregular in some cases. For instance, the null plural we see in pairs like *sheep–sheep* most often applies to domestic or game animals which travel in groups. We'll look at two other examples of semantic associations among irregulars next.

6.7.1 Pluralia Tantum

The first is the "forced plural" we see in words like *pants, scissors*, and *binoculars*. These words are made up of a root morpheme, like *pant* or *scissor*, plus the plural morpheme -*s*. They're weird because they never occur in the singular.

It's not that the singular/plural difference is there but simply marked with a null morpheme, as with *sheep*. Rather, there simply is no singular form of words like *pants*. We can see this when we compare examples (22)a and (22)b with (22)c and (22)d:

(22)　a.　That sheep is going *baaa*.
　　　b.　Those sheep are going *baaa*.
　　　c.　*That pant is lying on the floor.
　　　d.　Those pants are lying on the floor.

In (22)a, we can see that there is one sheep, both because of the singular determiner *that* and the singular agreement on the verb *to be*, which occurs in its 3rd singular present tense form *is*. And although there is no number marking on the noun in (22)b, the 3rd plural present tense form of the verb (*are*) and the plural determiner *those* gives it away: we're talking about plural sheep. In (22)c, on the other hand we can't use *pant* with a singular determiner and verb; in (22)d, we see the correct form, where determiner and verb trigger plural agreement.

What is particularly interesting about (22)d is that its *meaning* doesn't have to be plural. That is, even if there's only one pair of pants on the floor, you have to say (22)d in order to get someone to pass it to you. With *pants* there's just no way to distinguish a plural from a singular meaning, as you can in (22)a and b – you can't say **Those pants is lying on the floor*. Similarly, if you say *Hand me those scissors*, you might be asking for one pair of scissors, or many pairs of scissors – the person you're addressing has to figure it out by context. If you say *Bring me that sheep*, on the other hand, the singular nature of the noun is clear from the determiner *that*, even though there's no marking on the noun itself.

Of course, there is something that seems sort of inherently plural about the kinds of objects that occur with these mandatory plurals: *pants, scissors, binoculars, tongs*, etc. They are all made of two almost-but-not-quite-separable identical parts. This is obviously not an accident, although it's a hard criterion to define precisely. The words *panties* or *briefs*, for underwear, are inherently plural, although they don't have the Siamese-twin structure of *pants, glasses*, or *tongs*. There are a few game-names that are examples as well, where the notion of almost-separable part is really irrelevant: *billiards, skittles*, and *cards*.

Although these latter two have singular forms – *a card, a skittle* – the singular refers to one playing piece, not one game. The game-name *cards* can be used to refer to one game or more than one. Two other non-twin, inherently plural words of interest are *thanks* and *kudos*: while you can *give thanks*, you can't *give a thank*. *Thanks* and *kudos* also require plural agreement: *Thanks are in order*, not **Thanks is in order*, and *Kudos go to the director*, not *Kudos goes to the director*. The twinned-item – inherent plural rule fails in the other direction, as well: there are plenty of twinned-parts items which are *not* inherent plurals. Consider (a) *bicycle, teeter-totter, yo-yo, compass* (for drawing circles), or *barbell*. How come *bra* is singular but *panties* is plural? The word *overall* is a singular for some English speakers but a plural (*overalls*) for others. While we have a semantic clue to the irregular items, it is only a clue, not a hard-and-fast rule. We still need to memorize the inherent plural marking for each of these roots individually.

In fact, *kudos* is a borrowed Greek word that originally ended in /s/, and was pronounced /kuwdows/, not /kuwdowz/. People unfamiliar with its pronunciation read the *-s* as a plural suffix and pronounced it as /z/ accordingly; this pronunciation is now the standard one in the U.S.

Note that the roots, *pant-, scissor-* or *tong-*, can occur without the plural suffix when part of a compound: *pantleg, scissor grip, tong holder*. This shows that the *-s* suffix on these words really is the regular plural marker. Within compounds, singular or plural is simply not relevant. We say *lawn-mower*, not **lawns-mower*, even though any given lawn-mower could easily be intended to mow multiple lawns. So the existence of *pantleg* shows that the root *pant-* does exist independently of the suffix *-s*. The only strange thing in these cases is that the plural-marking is required even when the meaning is singular.

6.7.2 Mass nouns

To specify a singular number of any of the inherently-plural nouns that we just discussed, we have to use a "packaging" noun that has a proper singular, like *pair*. So we talk about *a pair of pants, a pair of scissors, a game of billiards*, etc. In this respect, these nouns have a lot in common with another class of exceptional nouns that do not make a singular/plural distinction: *mass* nouns.

This group includes nouns like *flour, wheat, rice, sand, water, money, furniture, weather*, and *cola*, as well as many abstract nouns like *advice, fun, information, knowledge*, and *peace*. To talk about particular quantities of any of these things, you also need a packaging noun: *two cups of flour, several pieces of advice, three years of peace*. The difference between these nouns and the *scissors, pants, billiards* examples, on the one hand, and the *sheep, bison, fish* examples, on the other, is that when we test them with subject–verb agreement, we find that they are inherently *singular*:

(23) a. That flour is infested with moths.
     b. *Those flour are infested with moths.
     c. That information is reliable.
     d. *Those information are reliable.
     e. That furniture is color-coordinated.
     f. *Those furniture are color-coordinated.

We also have a semantic clue to membership in this class of morphemes: the kind of amorphous, unbounded, "stuff" quality that the referents of many of these nouns (like *sand, water*, etc.) have. While this semantic property can act as a clue to mass-noun status, it again doesn't work as a definite rule. Consider the physical qualities of the referents of the words *wheat* and *oats*. Despite being almost indistinguishable to the eye, *wheat* happens to be a mass noun, while *oats* is a count noun. So you can have *one oat, many oats*, but you can't have *much oats*. In contrast, you can have *much wheat* but not *one wheat* or *many wheats*. With *wheat* you need a packaging noun again: *one grain of wheat, many grains of wheat*. Again, the morphological fact of being a mass noun must be individually learned for every root, though the amorphous quality of their referents might help as a reminder.

6.8 Really Irregular: Suppletive Forms

In all of the previous kinds of root homosemy we've seen, there was at least some phonological reason to think that the two forms of the root were related. Usually most of the consonants remained the same, even if some vowels changed: in *dream–dreamt*, for example, the consonant sequence of the root, /dɹ-m/, remains the same, even if the particular vowel in the middle changes.

For certain kinds of irregular roots, however, there is not even a hint that the two forms of the word are phonologically related. The primary examples of this in English are given in (24):

(24) a. Today, you *go*   Yesterday, you *went*
   b. Today, you *are*   Yesterday, you *were*
      Today, he *is*   Tomorrow you will *be*.
   c. good   better/best (well)
   d. bad   worse/worst

There's not even a single phoneme in common between the sequences /gow/ and /wɛnt/, yet they are present and past tense forms of the same verb. Similarly for /aɹ/, /wʌɹ/, /ɪz/, and /bij/, and for /gʊd/ -/bɛtɹ̩/-/wɛl/ and /bæd/-/wʌɹs/. How could such differentiation have come about?

It turns out that two different verbs' meanings collapsed together: where there used to be two distinct sound–meaning pairs, now there are homosemes with very different pronunciations but the same meaning. *Went* was originally a past tense form of a verb with a meaning very similar to that of *go*: the verb *to wend* (as in the expression *to wend one's way*). In the Middle English period, the past tense form *went* gradually came to displace a different past tense for *go*, *ēode*, and before long, *wend* had become quite infrequent and *went* was never used in any other context.

Similarly, the different forms of *be* in English are the result of a historical mix-and-match between *three* unrelated verbs. The present tense forms *am*, *are*, and *is* come from a verb stem *es-*, which meant "to be" all the way back to Proto-Indo-European. The past tense forms *was* and *were* come from a stem *wes-* that originally meant "remain, stay, continue to be." Those two verbs collapsed into one, using *es-* forms for the present and *wes-* forms for the past. Later, around 1200 AD, the infinitive and participle forms of a third verb, *beo-n*, "to become," were co-opted to serve as the infinitive and participle forms for the *am–was* verb. In fact, in some dialects of English, *be* made a bid at taking over the whole paradigm: there were forms like *he beeth* and *thou beest* in the south of England. However, by around 1500 the *am/are/is* group had solidified their hold on the standard dialect of English, and they've been part of the standard verb ever since.

6.9   Losing Irregulars: Producing Words on the Fly

One moral to our story so far is that "irregulars" really are irregular. While there might be a phonological or a semantic clue which reminds a speaker of English that this word *might* be a member of an irregular class, the only sure way to know if a given root is morphologically irregular is to see it used in context, and notice and remember its behavior. For every kind of irregular pattern, there are exceptions: *wolf/wolves* but *gulf/gulfs*; **a rice* but *a bean*, **billiard/billiards* but *pool/*pools*.

Now that we know something about where irregulars come from, we can ask the next question: why do they stick around? Why don't we just forget all these tricky homosemes and do everything regularly? Instead of *many children*, we'd have *many childs*; rather than *feel/felt* we'd have *feel/feeled*, and instead of *stupidity* we'd have *stupidness*.

Indeed, when children are learning a language, one of the most interesting things they do is *overgeneralize* – apply a regular morpheme to a stem that normally selects for an irregular homoseme. Children at a certain stage of language acquisition will say *falled* instead of *fell*, *feets* instead of *feet*, and *sheeps* instead of *sheep*. After they've heard the irregular often enough, they'll memorize it, and stop overgeneralizing.

An advantage to memorizing some forms is that you can often produce them faster than you could if you had to perform the extra operation of separately looking up and adding an affix. For words that you need to access often – highly frequent words – a memorized form can speed up language processing. For highly frequent words, too, there'll be more opportunities for a learner to hear the irregular form, and learn that this word is different from most. Consequently, words tend to retain their irregular forms better the more frequent they are.

Let's take our stems that call for the irregular *-t* homoseme of the past tense, *mean, feel, learn, burn, dream, spell, spoil, smell,* and *spill*. We noted above that some of them seem firmly attached to their allomorph, like *mean* and *feel*, some of them seem to be alternating with a regular form, like *learnt/learned* and *dreamt/dreamed*, and, to my ear, some are starting to sound downright archaic in the irregular, like *spoilt* and *smelt*. If the frequency hypothesis is correct, the more frequent a word is, the more likely it is to retain its irregular form, because of the greater opportunity that learners will have to memorize it.[9]

Looking at a list of the most frequent 8,000 words in the British National Corpus, a collection of modern British English texts, we see that these verbs are ordered as follows, from most frequent to least frequent.

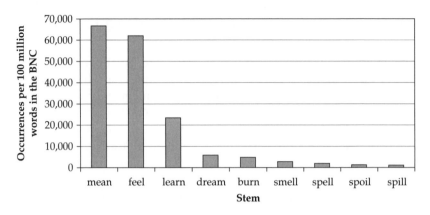

Figure 6.1 Frequency of stems that can take irregular -*t* in the past tense

(25) *Verb*   *Number of occurrences per 100m*   *Frequency rank*
     mean   66,556   134
     feel   62,185   148
     learn   23,394   432
     dream   6,050   1580
     burn   5,091   1829
     smell   3,037   2680
     spell   2,181   3300
     spoil   1,455   4373
     spill   1,296   4697

A bar chart of these numbers is given in Figure 6.1, so you can see the frequencies graphically. The ranking correlates fairly well with my own intuitions about how "natural" the -*t* past tense is with each of these stems.

Retention of an irregular form is also helped if a word has other characteristics that can help make memorization and retrieval of the irregular form faster than application of the regular affix. Any of the mnemonic clues that we considered above could help. For instance, if a certain irregular form is associated with a particular general kind of meaning, the frequency of all the similar-meaning stems with the same pattern could "add up" to quite a large number, even if the frequency of any one form is low. The meaning association could help you zero in on the memorized listed form more quickly than one might expect given the basic frequency of the word.

To explain the importance of frequency for these and other phenomena, psycholinguists propose that listemes are sorted in the mind in order of frequency. The idea is that your mental lexicon is organized so that you can get to the most frequently used listemes quickly. When you attempt to produce an inflected word, there's a sort of competition going on. You can't spend forever looking around for the right form in your mental lexicon. If you can sort through your lists and come up with an irregular form within a certain time window, then you produce an irregular. On the other hand, if the irregular listeme is farther down the frequency list, so that it takes more than your allowed time window to find it, you will give up on the hunt and just go ahead and produce the default, regular form. A diagram of this word production model is given in (26):

(26) a. Think of a meaning to convey:
       Speaker A   *Speaker B*
       HE MEAN+PastTense IT   HE SPOIL+PastTense IT

   b. Start looking for the right listemes. You're against the clock!
       A finds: *B finds:*
       . . .   .
       /mɛn/ +   /spɔjl/ +
       . . .   .
       /t/   <clock runs out>
                                nothing!

   c. *A produces*   *B produces*
       meant   spoiled
       (as soon as she finds it) (after the clock runs out)

This predicts that irregular forms should vary in how fast they are produced according to how frequent they are, but that regular forms should be produced at the same speed no matter what their frequency is. When people are tested, this prediction seems to be borne out.

6.10 Productivity, Blocking, and Bushisms

Some of the affixes we've been considering seem to hardly be "alive" in English anymore. Affixes like -*ship* (as in *friendship, guardianship, kingship, partnership*) or *-ary* (as in *visionary, missionary, secretary, adversary*) seem to occur primarily as part of a few, nonvarying words; it's not so often that someone will make up a noun ending in *-ship* or *-ary* out of thin air.

Regular affixes, though, are constantly used to form new words on the spot. Regular inflectional affixes, of course, are all used in this way, to inflect any word that comes along, whether it's made up or borrowed or whatever. Many derivational affixes are also used this way. President Bush used the suffixes *-ist* and *-ize* to make up *explorationist* and *securitize* on the spot. Perusing a few recent pages of the *New Yorker*, the *Tucson Weekly* and *The Nation*, I find the following nonce coinages, none of which are recognized by my spell-checker: *deroyalization, unfinishable, horkening, ginchy, non-city, Disneyfied*, and *regurgitant*. These words testify to the fact that that *-ation, un-, -able, -en, non-, -y, -ify*, and *-ant* are all alive and well in the hands of professional creators of English prose.

Such affixes are termed *productive*, because, of course, they are used to produce new words on a regular basis. Productive affixes are the ones which, over time, squeeze out more infrequent irregulars. Irregular affixes are not productive – they only apply to a limited set of listed stems, and if you try to apply one to a form that's not on their list, you get something quite odd-sounding. For example, if I take a verb that rhymes with *dream*, like *seem*, I can't add the irregular past-tense homoseme *-t* to it and change the stem to make **semt*, like I can with *dream/dreamt*.

Given the model of lexical production described above, when you hunt for a word form, and find an irregular in time, you won't produce the regular form, as in *mean/meant/*meaned*. In these cases, we can say the productive suffix is *blocked* by the irregular allomorph. When children overgeneralize and say *foots* instead of *feet*, or *mouses* instead of *mice*, it's because they don't know the irregular form well enough for it to block the regular one yet.

The principle of **blocking** can help us understand the funny-soundingness of a couple of the cases that we started out with two chapters ago: George W. Bush's production of *analyzation* from *analyze* and *securitize* from *security*. Here's a hypothesis about what happened during his production of these words. He wanted to convey the following meanings: a noun meaning the ACTION of ANALYZING and a verb meaning CAUSE to be SECURE. He rummaged through his listemes and found, close to the top, some frequent forms with the correct roots: *anal-yze* and *secur-ity*. However, the former is a verb, and he needed the noun of action, and the latter is a noun, and he needed the causative verb form. He began the hunt for irregular forms with the right meaning, but ran out of time before he found the noun of action *analysis*, formed with the irregular nominalizing suffix *-sis* (like *diagnosis* and *hypnosis*), and before he found the causative verb *to secure*, formed with the null causative suffix *-Ø* (like *to open* or *to clear*). Instead, he used the appropriate productive Latinate suffixes with the right meanings, *-ation* and *-ize*, as suffixes on the more-frequent stems he had originally found, *analyze* and *security*.

There's no way to test this hypothesis directly, of course, but if lexical access of irregulars is determined by frequency, then we can at least test one prediction it makes: the noun *security* and the verb *analyze* should be more frequent than the related forms *secure* and *analysis* that failed to block Bush's overregularizations. For *secure/security* this is true: *security* is quite frequent – number 644 in the BNC top-8,000 list – but the verb *to secure* is less frequent, ranked 1717. For this pair, then, our imagined sequence of events in Bush's language-generator is potentially plausible.

Unfortunately, the numbers for *analyze/analysis* go the wrong way: *analyze* is ranked 2166th of the BNC's 8,000 most-frequent words, but the noun *analysis* is considerably more frequent, ranked 732. Can we come up with another idea to explain the failure of Bush's blocking mechanism for these?

Well, one thing that is immediately noticeable about *analysis* is that it sounds very different from *analyze* – the stress is in a different place, and consequently the vowels are reduced in a different pattern. *Analyze* is pronounced /ˈænəlajz/, while *analysis* is pronounced /əˈnæləsɪs/. Further, the nominalizing suffix *-sis*, although quite common in medical terminology, is relatively uncommon in everyday speech; only 8 of the 8,000 most frequent words have it at all. Of these 8, there are only three that have causative verb forms in *-ize* besides *analysis*: *emphas-ize* from *empha-sis*, *hypothes-ize* from *hypothe-sis*, and *synthes-ize* from *synthe-sis*. For these three words, though, the change from the verbal *-ize* suffix to the nominal *-sis* suffix doesn't involve *any* change in pronunciation of the stem. In those words the *-sis* suffix is attached directly onto the same stem that *-ize* attaches to. In *analyze/analysis*, however, the stem for *analyze* is *anal-* /ænəl/, while the stem for *analysis* is *analy-* , /ənælə/. Both the infrequency of the *sis* morpheme and the homosemic stem forms could have led Bush's word-analyzing machinery to conclude that *analysis* and *analyze* are not different forms of the same stem at all, but rather are separate listemes entirely. That is, *analysis* may have undergone reanalysis by his mental lexicon. In that case, *analysis* would fail to block *analyzation* because it wouldn't even be in the competition for the noun-of-action form – and since *analyze* has the -*ize* suffix in it, -*ation* is in fact the only possible choice for the noun of action.

For English speakers whose lexical inventories do make the connection between *analyze* and *analysis*, and who are more familiar with the verb *to secure* than Bush is, Bush's failure to exhibit blocking in these cases sounds funny, like a child's failure to exhibit blocking with *foots* or *hitted*. It does, however, illustrate the fact that the order of listemes in an English speaker's mental inventory, as well as the particular set of listemes in there, will vary from person to person, depending on how much exposure to each listeme they have had, and on whether their word-analysis machinery has identified particular pieces as being related or not.

We've learned a lot about word *forms*. What about word *meanings*? We turn to this important topic in the next chapter.

Study Problems

1. Latin phonology fossilized in modern English
   Consider the following pairs of words:

magic	/ˈmæd͡ʒək/	magician	/məˈd͡ʒɪʃən/
expedite	/ˈɛkspədajt/	expeditious	/ˌɛkspəˈdɪʃəs/
rate	/rejt/	ration	/ræʃən/
artifice	/ˈaɹtəfɪs/	artificial	/ˌaɹtəˈfɪʃəl/
malice	/ˈmæləs/	malicious	/məˈlɪʃəs/

   a. What are the three consonants that occur at the end of the *unsuffixed* words on the left?

   b. Describe these consonants in terms of what they have in common, phonologically. They are all _____ .

   c. What is the final consonant in the roots of the *suffixed* words on the right?

   d. What vowel occurs in all the suffixes on the right?

   e. What *letter* occurs in all the suffixes on the right?

   f. Where does that common letter occur in all these suffixes?

   g. Describe the vowel that this letter stands for in the IPA: what is its specification for height, backness, and rounding? (See Chapter 2.)

h. What consonant is this vowel closely related to? (See Chapter 2.)

i. What is the place and manner of articulation of this consonant? (See Chapter 2.) _____.

j. What are the voicing, place and manner of articulation of the consonant you identified in (c) above?

k. These roots and suffixes are all Latinate in origin. Assume that the letter you identified in (e) was pronounced, in these Latin suffixes, as the consonant you identified in (i). In Latin, this consonant, when it occurred next to one of the consonants you identified in (b), forces a change in the (b) consonant. Fill in the blanks below to identify the phonological rule of Latin that we are seeing in action:

In Latin, when a _____ _____ was followed immediately by a _____ _____, the former became a _____ _____ _____.

When English borrowed these suffixes, it also borrowed the softening rule that went with them, treating it as a morphologically conditioned readjustment rule associated with the suffixes. The rule applies to every stem that these suffixes attach to, providing it ends in one of the "hard" consonants covered by the rule. This allomorphic readjustment rule is a fossil of a phonologically regular requirement *from an entirely different language*.

2. Here are five derivational affixes of English.
   a. -dom
   b. -an
   c. -ous
   d. -hood
   e. -ary

For each affix, do the following:
   (i) Find five words that contain the affix. (You can use a "wild card" search in the OED or other electronic dictionary, e.g. www.onelook.com, to do this if you like.)
   (ii) Give the five stems to which the affix attached. Identify each stem as bound or free.

(iii)   Does the addition of the affix affect the pronunciation of the stem? In what way?

(iv)   What part(s) of speech does this affix create? If it attaches to free stems, what part(s) of speech does this affix attach to?

(v)   In your estimation, is this affix productive in modern English? Did you find any words that seem to have been coined using this affix in the past 50 years?

(vi)   Give a definition for the affix (use "X" to stand in for the meaning contributed by the root). How well does your definition work for your examples? Have any of your example words undergone idiomatization?

3.   Consider the following list of bound roots and words which contain them. With the help of a dictionary containing etymological information, look up the original source language and meanings of these roots. Are any of these words compositional?

-ceive	-vert
-cur	-port
-duce	-gress
-fer	-ject
-fine	-mand
-form	-mit

perceive, deceive, receive, conceive
incur, occur, recur, concur
deduce, produce, reduce, induce
infer, defer, prefer, offer, confer
define, refine, confine,
reform, deform, conform, inform, perform
avert, invert, revert, extrovert, pervert
report, deport, import, comport
ingress, egress, progress, regress, digress
object, inject, deject(ed), reject
demand, command, remand
commit, remit, permit, emit, omit

4.   Here are some verbs, normally regular, that have been inflected according to the pattern of an *irregular* verb. Each one is given in the future tense, the past tense and in the past participle form. (They sound weird, don't they?) For each strangely inflected verb, identify an actual English verb that follows this pattern.

a. *rig*: He will rig it so it works. He rug it so it works. He has rug it so it works.
b. *pet*: I will pet the dog. I pot the dog. I have potten the dog.
c. *try*: I will try to do it. I trew to do it. I have trown to do it.
d. *care*: He will care for you. He core for you yesterday. He has corn for you in the past.
e. *peep*: The chick will peep when it sees its mother. The chick pept yesterday. It has pept.
f. *trim*: The stylist will trim my hair. She tram my hair yesterday. She has trum it often.
g. *mind*: I won't mind! I mound it very much that you didn't come. I have mound your antics in the past, but not today.
h. *pee*: I'll pee before we leave. I paw already, we can go now. I have peen in the bushes before now.
i. *call*: I will call you tomorrow. I cell you yesterday. I have callen you 10 times today!
j. *link*: The photograph will link the candidates together. It lank them together. It has lunk them together inexorably in the minds of the voters!

Further Reading

On irregulars:
Pinker, Steven (1999) *Words and Rules: The Ingredients of Language*. New York: Basic Books.

On learning morphology:
Pinker, Steven (1995) "Why the child holded the baby rabbits: a case study in language acquisition," in Lila Gleitman (ed.), *An Invitation to Cognitive Science*, vol. 1: *Language*. Cambridge, MA: MIT Press.

On productive morphology:
Bauer, Laurie (2001) *Morphological Productivity*. Cambridge: Cambridge University Press.
Plag, Ingo (1999) *Morphological Productivity: Structural Constraints on English Derivation*. Amsterdam: Mouton de Gruyter.

On the the irregular morphophonology of English.
Chomsky, Noam and Halle, Morris ([1968] 1991) *The Sound Pattern of English*. Cambridge, MA: MIT Press (technical!).

Notes

1   These Greek and Latin plurals illustrate a phenomenon we touched on briefly, earlier – the existence of *bound stems*. In the word *symposium*, or the word *cactus*, the plural is not formed by simply adding *-a* or *-i* to the singular form. If we did that, we'd get *symposiuma* and *cactusi*. Rather, the plural is formed by subtracting *-um* from *symposium*, or *-us* from *cactus*, and substituting *-a* or *-i*. That is, the root of *symposium* is *symposi-*, and the root of *cactus* is *cact-*, neither of which can occur on their own as words – they're bound roots.

2   Actually, *child* will have to have a stem homoseme, *childr-*, to make this rule produce the form *children*, rather than *childen*. See discussion of stem homosemes in the next section.

3   The form "brother" here, and "ax" in the *-es* plurals above, should make you notice that the information that picks out the relevant stems here is not just phonological. Rather, it's the stem's whole listeme, complete with semantics, that determines the application of these particular plural affixes. The word *brother* that gets the *-en* suffix isn't the word that means "*male sibling*," but rather the (historically related) word that means "monk" or "a male member of a religious or ritualistic organization." Similarly, the "ax" that takes the /ijz/ plural is a bound Latin root that means something like "line of reference," as in *axis*, not the homophonous free root *ax* that means "instrument for chopping."

4   Syllabic pronunciation of the *-ed* suffix is sometimes indicated with a grave accent; I'll follow this convention here.

5   This rule is also the source of the adjectival participles *gilt*, *pent*, and *girt*.

6   Actually, *-ish* and *-esque* are cognate, according to the OED – Latin originally borrowed *-esque* from Old High German *-isc*, which is the source of Modern English *-ish*.

7   There are a few exceptions. One is *worship*, which was originally formed from *worth+ship*, but for obvious pronunciation reasons the /θ/ was lost. Others are *gormless*, *wistful*, *grateful*, *reckless* and *gruesome*.

8   Since there's a whole group of suffixes that have this stress-shifting effect, a more economical way to represent this rule would be to write it separately, as "[(σ") 'σ] -Affix," give it a number (e.g. "Readjustment Rule 1"), and just include a note with *-ify* and the other affixes to the effect that they are subject to Rule 1 (and any other rules of this type – there are several).

9   For some speakers, the irregular past tense variant with *-t* has acquired a slightly different meaning than the regular variant with *-ed*. These speakers use the *-ed* form when they are describing an event that took a certain amount of time, e.g. *The house burned all night*. They use the irregular form in *-t* when they are describing an event that is instantaneous, or punctual, as in *My finger burnt when I touched the hot stove*. See the *Cambridge Encyclopedia of the English Language* for further discussion.

7

Lexical Semantics: The Structure of Meaning, the Meaning of Structure

/'lɛksəkl̩ sə'mæntɪks: ðə 'stɹʌktʃəɹ əv 'mijnɪŋ, ðə 'mijnɪŋ əv stɹʌktʃəɹ/

In this chapter we take a first look at the kinds of meanings that listemes have. We look first at function listemes – those whose meaning is an intrinsic part of the grammar of English – and then at content listemes, whose meanings flow and change over time. We look at how content listemes' meanings are related to each other and we learn that there are certain generalizations and classifications of content listemes that we can make based on argument structure. Finally, we look at the ways the different classes of content listemes interact with function listemes.

In the previous two chapters, we've seen a lot about certain kinds of restrictions that morphemes impose on their immediate neighbors – phonological restrictions (like comparative *-er* has), and morphological restrictions (like causative *-ify* has). But there are other kinds of restrictions that listemes are subject to, even when all their phonological and morphological requirements are happily met. Consider the following groups of examples:

(1) a. Defenseless fuzzy bunnies run quickly.
 a'. #Colorless green ideas sleep furiously.

 b. I asked whether she likes him. / *I asked that she likes him.
 b'. I know whether she likes him. / I know that she likes him.

b″. *I hope whether she likes him. / I hope that she likes him.

c.   He emptied the tub.
c′. The tub emptied.
c″. He cleaned the tub.
c‴. *The tub cleaned.

d.   The crash killed the driver.
d′. #The crash murdered the driver.

> Recall that the * marker in front of an example indicates morphological or syntactic ungrammaticality. Here we also use the # marker, which indicates syntactic well-formedness but *semantic* oddity – syntactically it's OK, but its meaning is confused.

Some of these sentences are fine examples of English, and some of them aren't. Whatever the problem is with the not-fine ones, though, it's clear that it isn't phonological or morphological. In this chapter, we begin to look at the lexical knowledge you have that tells you which of the above sentences are good and which are bad.

We'll consider questions like the following: In compositional words, how do the meanings of the parts combine to make the meaning of the whole? Are there any restrictions on what the parts themselves can mean? And how are the meanings of listemes organized in the mind?

7.1   Function Meaning vs. Content Meaning

We've observed before that there are two main categories of listemes: function and content. Content listemes carry the meanings that are summarized in dictionary entries; they carry the "meat" of the message we want to send. Function listemes restrict and organize those meanings, providing the structure that lets us communicate better than Tarzan. Although one can be explicitly instructed about the proper meanings and uses of content listemes (that's what dictionaries are for, after all), almost no one is ever explicitly instructed in the meaning and use of a function listeme in their first language.

Exercise 7.1 Think about how you would explain the meanings of the following function listemes. Which ones seem difficult to define and which easy? Provide a definition for the easy ones.

a, but, every, had, his, I, if, me, what, and, -s (as in *(two) dogs*), that (as in *He said **that** I lied*), them

---

Notice that the "that" in *He said that I lied* is different from the determiner article "that," as in *that girl*, though they are written the same way. For one thing, they are usually pronounced differently. Unless it is emphasized, the *that* in *He said that I knew him* is pronounced /ðət/, while the *that* in *I know that girl* is invariably pronounced /ðæt/, with a full vowel.

For many function listemes, the only definition that can possibly be helpful is a description of how it is used in a sentence. Below, I give the first definition in the long list of "definitions" that the OED provides for the word *that*, which occurs in phrases like *He said that I lied*:

that: Introducing a dependent substantive-clause, as subject, object, or other element of the principal clause, or as complement of a n. or adj., or in apposition with a n. therein.

Now, very few people in the English-speaking world know enough grammatical terminology to be able to understand this definition, (which, despite being very complicated, is in fact quite inadequate to accurately capture the distribution of *that*, as can be seen from the 10 or so other definitions the OED provides and the separate entry for *that* in contexts like *The girl that I saw* – that is, in relative clauses). Yet, every English-speaking 5-year-old has mastered this word. At the other extreme, the function listeme -s, as in *two dogs*, doesn't even rate a definition in the OED (although *-ed* and *-ing* do). The *Cambridge Advanced Learner's Dictionary* gives the following definition:

-s: used to form the plural of nouns: *books, sandwiches*

Even quite a young English speaker, who didn't know what "plural" meant, or what a noun is, could do a good approximation of this definition – they'd probably say that it means "more than one of something," which is pretty much a paraphrase of the official definition above.

With content listemes, there's much more of a continuum of difficulty in writing definitions. Some seem hard to define, others easy, others in-between. Compare, for instance, the subtleties involved in appropriately deploying a word like *matron* or *dame* with the general-purpose word *woman*, or the somewhat more restricted *lady*. How about *pooch* or *hound* compared to *dog*?

Despite the gradience of content meanings, there are strong connections between the concept named by a content listeme and the kinds of structures (and function listemes) that the content listeme can occur with. For instance, verbs like *say* and nouns like *belief* can be followed by a clause introduced by *that*, but verbs like *fall* or nouns like *touch* really cannot:

(2) a. Ancient scholars didn't say [that the world was flat].
    b. Ancient scholars didn't really hold the belief [that the world was flat].
    c. *Ancient scholars didn't fall [that the world was flat].
    d. *Ancient scholars didn't really hold the touch [that the world was flat].

More subtly, as we saw above, while a word like *hope* can be followed by a clause introduced by *that*, it can't be followed by one introduced by *whether* – and words like *ask* work in exactly the opposite way:

(3) a. I hoped that she liked it. / *I hoped whether she liked it.
    b. I asked *that she liked it. / I asked whether she liked it.

Exercise 7.2 What do you think is the difference between *that* and *whether* in example (3)?

It must be that the meanings of these content words put restrictions on the kinds of function words that can go with them. In this chapter, we'll first look briefly at the meanings (aka functions) of function listemes, so that we have a more sophisticated understanding of structure to go on with. Then we'll look at the meanings of content words and the kinds of relationships that they have to each other. Finally, we'll consider the interactions between function and content words, and how their meanings can affect one another.

7.2   Entailment

Some of the best-understood meanings are those of function listemes. A few of these listemes have had their meanings investigated since the dawn of philosophy and before, as part of the study of logic.

> **logic**, *n*. From Greek, *log-* "word, reason." The branch of philosophy that treats of the forms of thinking in general, and more especially of inference and of scientific method.

Before we proceed to our first meanings, however, we need some tools for investigating meaning. One of the most powerful ones that we have is the logical idea of **entailment**, which is closely connected to the notion of truth. If we assume that a given statement is true, its entailments are the other statements that "logically" follow – things that *must* be true,[1] given the meaning of the first statement. Since statement meaning is made up of listeme meanings, we can often get a handle on listeme meanings by looking at the entailments of statements that contain the listeme we're wondering about.

To illustrate the idea of an entailment, think about what else would necessarily have to be true if the statement *Flossie is a brown cow* is true. One of the entailments of that statement is *Flossie is a cow*. What other ones can you think of? (Remember that entailments are *necessary* truths, not simply quite probable ones. *Flossie has horns* may be probable if *Flossie is a brown cow* is true, but it's not necessarily true, so it's not an entailment of *Flossie is a brown cow*.)

Exercise 7.3   List as many entailments of the sentence *Flossie is a brown cow* as you can.

7.3   Function Words and their Meanings

7.3.1   Conjunctions

Conjunctions are words that stick two elements of the same type together (they *conjoin* them). For instance, *and* and *or* conjoin two sentences in the examples in (4):

(4)   a.   [She studied] and [she failed].
     b.   [She studied] or [she failed].

In the first case, with *and*, the meaning of the whole conjoined sentence is true if both of the conjuncts are true. In the second, with *or*, the whole sentence is true if at least one of the conjunct sentences are true. (If the person *she* refers to in the above sentences didn't study, and failed, then sentence (4)a is false but (4)b is true; similarly if she did study, and didn't fail.)

The meanings of *and* and *or* specify what the conditions are that make a sentence with them in it a true sentence. That's one central way of thinking about word meaning: a word's "meaning" consists of a specification of the conditions in which it can be used truthfully – its **truth conditions**. If you know that the word *and* can be used to make a true sentence out of two other sentences as long as both of the other sentences are true, then you know just about everything there is to know about the meaning of *and*.

To see how word meanings can specify more than just truth conditions, though, consider the two conjunctions *but* and *although* in (5):

(5)   a.   She studied, but she failed.
     b.   She studied, although she failed.

In order for these sentences to be true, both conjuncts have to be true (you couldn't say (5)a or (5)b truthfully if she hadn't studied, or if she hadn't failed) – but these conjunctions carry a certain amount of extra information as well. This extra information tells something about the attitude of the speaker towards the conjuncts. *But* implies that the speaker thinks the truth of the second statement is unexpected, given the truth of the first. *Although* implies that the speaker thinks the truth of the first statement is unexpected, given the truth of the second. In a sentence of the form *A but B*, B is unexpected; in a sentence of the form *A, although B*, A is unexpected.

All conjunctions are able to conjoin two sentences, but only some of them can conjoin nouns, verbs, or adjectives (or the phrases built on them):

(6)   *Noun Phrases*
    a. I saw [the girl] and [the boy].
    b. *I saw [the girl] but [the boy].

    Verbs
    c. I [saw] and [liked] the new model.
    d. ?I [saw] but [hated] the new model.

    Adjectives
    e. I saw the [athletic] and [short] boy.
    f. ?I saw the [athletic] but [short] boy.

In (6), we see that *and* can conjoin elements of several different syntactic categories. *But* is more restricted; it can't conjoin nouns, although it may be able to conjoin verbs and adjectives. (What is your own judgment about (6)d and (6)f? I find them somewhat literary, but not ungrammatical.) The lexical entries for *and* and *but*, then, will look something like this. (In the syntax for *and*, the subscripted "X" stands for any syntactic category – noun, noun phrase, verb, adjective, sentence, etc. In the syntax for *but*, "S" stands for "Sentence," "V" for "Verb" and "A" for "Adjective"; the curly braces stand for "choose one of," as usual.)

(7)   *Phonology*   *Syntax*   *Semantics*

/ænd/	$[[\_\_]_X$ and $[\_\_]_X]_X$	Both conjuncts are true.
/bʌt/	$[[\_\_]_{\{S, V, A\}}$ but	Both conjuncts are true,
	$[\_\_]_{\{S, V, A\}}]_{\{S, V, A\}}$	and the second is
		unexpected, given the first.

7.3.2   Determiners and their meanings

Another set of function words whose meanings are fairly well understood are the **determiners**, sometimes called *articles* or *quantifiers*. (Before this chapter, you may have noticed that we've used the term *determiner* *article* to refer to these items.) These are the words that occur in front of nouns, or nouns that are modified by adjectives or other words.

> A noun together with its determiner, plus any adjectives or other modifiers, is called a **noun phrase** and is sometimes abbreviated "NP." The string of words *A big black cat* is a noun phrase, for example.

Determiners can be fussy about the sorts of nouns they go with. As we saw in the last chapter, there are two main classes of nouns in English: mass nouns and count nouns. Mass nouns usually describe things that are amorphous – substances, like *water* or *metal*, although there are abstract ones too, like *happiness* and *spontaneity*. Count nouns usually describe things that can be individuated – counted – words like *cup* or *dog*, although again there are abstract ones, like *idea* or *compliment*. We'll come back to mass and count nouns below.

Some examples of determiners with their nouns are given in (8):

(8) a. *Some determiners that require count nouns:*

a fish	each cat	every dog
several fries	three apples	many shirts
few doctors	which student	

   b. *Determiners that require a mass noun:*

   much rain   little snow   (*much dog)

   c. *Determiners that require a mass noun or a **plural** count noun:*

   Mass noun   *Count noun*
   enough food   enough nails   (*enough nail)

   d. *Determiners that don't care whether the noun is count or mass:*

Count nouns	*Mass nouns*
the coat	the coffee
this computer	this rice
that mountain	that beef
my house	my sugar

The determiners in (8)a–c tell you how much or how many of the noun are being referred to; they're usually called *quantifiers* (since they specify quantity). One of the most interesting properties of quantifiers is the way they interact with each other. Think about the truth conditions of the following sentence. What kind of situations can this sentence truthfully describe?

(9) The president has a reason for everything he does.

This is true if the president has one reason that motivates all his actions, of course, but it's also true if, for each action, he has a different, unique reason. (There's a joke that illustrates the same point: "Did you know that someone is hit by a car every three minutes in the United States?" "Oh, that poor person!")

The last set of determiners, in (8)d – the determiners that don't care about quantity – carry another kind of meaning. They tell you the status of the noun with respect to the conversation. If the speaker expects the hearer to know exactly which instance of a particular noun she's talking about, she uses the definite determiner, *the*. If a noun under discussion is relatively close to the conversation, the speaker uses the demonstrative determiner, *this*. Possessive determiners, like *my*, specify who owns the noun, and their meanings depend on who's in the conversation and what's been said so far: *my* refers to me if I'm talking, but to you if you're talking. Meanings that vary depending on the conversational context this way are called **deictic** meanings.

A lexicon entry for the determiners *every* and *the* might look something like this:

(10) | *Phonology* | *Syntax* | *Semantics* |
|---|---|---|
| /ˈɛvɹi/ | [every [___]$_{NP}$]$_{NP}$ | All instances of "NP" |
| /ˈðə/ | [the [___]$_{NP}$]$_{NP}$ | The unique instance of "NP" that is most relevant to the discourse |

An enormous amount of research has been done on the semantics of determiners; for us, though, the main thing is to recognize the existence of the two main types: quantifying and deictic, and to recognize that the quantifying ones care about whether the noun they attach to is a mass noun or a count noun, while the deictic ones don't.

7.3.3   Pronouns

Pronouns stand in for a noun or a noun phrase. As we saw for the possessive determiners above, their meanings are *entirely* deictic. What a pronoun refers to varies depending on the identity of the person speaking, and the conversation that they're used in.

The first and second person pronouns *I* and *you*, and their plural counterparts, *we* and *you*, have meanings that depend on who in the conversation is talking. The speaker, no matter who it is, uses *I* and *we* to refer to himself and his associates, and *you* to refer to the person or people he's talking to.

The third person pronouns are a bit trickier. They specify more than singular or plural; they also include information about the gender of the noun that they're standing in for (*he*, masculine, *she*, feminine, and *it*, inanimate). They usually refer back to the topic of the conversation – the thing under discussion – although if the speaker and hearer disagree about what the topic of the conversation is, there's lots of room for misconstrual, as shown by the joke in the panel below.

> An old blacksmith realized he was getting on in years and would quit work soon, so he took on an apprentice. The old fellow was crabby and exacting. "Don't ask me a lot of questions," he told the boy. "Just do whatever I tell you to do." One day the old blacksmith took an iron out of the forge and laid it on the anvil. "Get the hammer over there," he said. "When I nod my head, hit it good and hard." The boy did as he was told . . . and now the town is looking for a new blacksmith.

Pronouns also specify one other thing – their form is sensitive to the structure of the sentence that they occur in. If the speaker wants to refer to herself in the following two sentences, he or she has to use a different pronoun in sentence (11)a and sentence (11)b. Fill in the blanks as if you were saying the sentences. What pronoun do you use?

(11)   a.   "Jake saw ____."
      b.   "____ saw Jake."

If you are a native speaker of English, you put *me* in (11)a, and *I* in (11)b. English pronouns specify whether or not the noun phrase that they're standing in for is the subject of the sentence. Pronouns like *he, I, she, they* . . . etc., are subject pronouns. Pronouns like *me, him, them, us,* etc., show up everywhere else. "Being the subject" is a grammatical property, so it must be included as part of the syntactic information attached to the listeme.

Since they stand in for a noun phrase, like *the cat* or *my head,* pronouns are themselves noun phrases, as far as their grammatical category goes. Lexical entries for *we, them* and *it* might look like this:

(12) | *Phonology* | *Syntax* | *Semantics* |
|---|---|---|
| /wij/ | [we]_{NPSubj} | The speaker and others. |
| /ðɛm/ | [them]_{NPNonSubj} | The plural topic of conversation. |
| /ɪt/ | [it]_{NP} | The non-human topic of conversation. |

7.3.4   Complementizers

Words that introduce a whole complement clause – a whole extra sentence – are called **complementizers**. Some examples are below:

(13) a.   I believe <u>that</u> [she studied]_S.
   b.   He wondered <u>whether</u> [she studied]_S.

---

complement, *n.* From Latin *com-,* 'intensive' + *plēre* 'full' → *complere,* "to fill up, fulfill," + *-ment,* "result or instrument of V." That which completes or makes perfect. Grammatically, one or more words joined to another to complete the sense. Note the distinct spelling of the homophonous word *compliment,* which is derived from the same source as this word but has come to have quite a distinct meaning. (The English word *full* and the Latin word *plēre* are Indo-European cognates, where the fricative in the former is related to the stop in the latter by Grimm's law – remember Chapter 2?)

Another famous pair of complementizers are the conditional *if,* as in *I'll go if you go,* and *because,* as in *I went because you went.*

Traditional grammars often use the term *subordinating conjunction* for complementizers. Sometimes the question–pronouns *who, which, why, when,* and *where* can function like complementizers when they're used to form **relative clauses** – whole sentences that modify a noun: *the man [who left], the reason [why he left], the place [where he lived].* All these alternate with the real complementizer *that* in these contexts. Interestingly, *what* varies – some dialects of English allow it as a relative pronoun, as in *the chair what broke* – but no dialect of English, to my knowledge, allows *how* as a relative pronoun: *the way that/*how he did it.*

Complementizers have the interesting semantic property of indicating the truth-conditional status of the complement clause that they introduce. Recall, above, that we asserted that statements have a truth value: they're either true, if they correctly describe the real world, or false, if they don't. But what is the truth value of a question, as in *Did she study*? It's neither true nor false, of course; rather, it's a request by the speaker for someone else to inform him of the truth value of the statement. Some verbs that take a complement clause require that clause to be a question – verbs like *ask* or *wonder* are like this. The special complementizers *whether* and *if* explicitly indicate that the clause they introduce is a question – that is, they indicate that the truth value of the clause that they introduce is unknown, as in *I wonder if/whether she studied.* The complementizer *that*, on the other hand, indicates that the clause it introduces has a definite truth value.

The bigger clause created by adding a complementizer to a sentence isn't a sentence by itself, of course; the complementizer forces that sentence to be a *complement* to something else (hence the name). We'll label this bigger clause, formed of a complementizer plus a sentence, CP, for "Complementizer Phrase." With that in mind, here are lexical entries for *that* and *whether*:

(14) | Phonology | Syntax | Semantics |
|---|---|---|
| /ðət/ | [that [___]$_S$]$_{CP}$ | S is true. |
| /ˈwɛðəɹ/ | [whether [___]$_S$]$_{CP}$ | The truth-value of S is unknown. |

There is much more to say about the meaning and behavior of all of the functional items we've discussed above, and there are several that we haven't touched on at all (for instance, the meanings of tense and aspect listemes, like *is going* or *has gone*, or the meanings of modal auxiliary verbs, like *may, can, should* and *might*), but this is enough to go on with. Let's now turn to the kinds of meanings expressed by content words – the meanings, in short, of *roots*.

7.4 Content Words and their Meanings

Content words, as we've seen before, are the words which carry the meat of our messages. They are the nouns, verbs and adjectives that form the bulk of our vocabulary. What kinds of meanings do they have?

Traditional grammars of English claim that contentful syntactic categories convey certain kinds of basic meanings. Nouns are supposed to refer to a "person, place or thing"; verbs are "activities" and adjectives are "properties." In fact, as we saw in the Appendix to Chapter 1, this characterization is very problematic. For one thing, the words *activity* and *property* are themselves nouns! And what about nouns like *work, nap, fear, idea, touch, whistle, pleasure, completion, bend, threat, conversation* . . . ? Are these, and thousands of nouns like them, people, places, or things? And what about the mass nouns we've seen, like *rice, water,* and *emptiness*?

In fact, noun meanings can name people (*girl*), places (*home*), concrete things (*screwdriver*), abstract things (*idea*), properties (*intelligence*), activities (*work*) – if we can think of it, we can give it a name that's a noun.[2]

Adjectives and verbs, on the other hand, are not so free. Adjectives always name properties, even when they're formed out of nouns, as in *wimpy* (from the noun *wimp*), or *penniless* (from the noun *penny*). Verbs always name either *events* (as in *to fall, to sleep, to build*) or *states* (as in *to know, to want, to seem*), even if they're formed out of nouns (*to hammer, to corral*).

Meaning-wise, then, nouns are the freest category. We could, roughly speaking, think of possible noun meanings as simply the possible *concepts* – the concepts that humans can invent words for, anyway.

7.4.1 Concepts: definitions or atoms?

The meaning of a content word is often explained in terms of its entailment relationships with other content words. To take one common example: it's supposed to be self-evident that if you know the meaning of *bachelor*, you will recognize that the entailment relations in example (15) hold:

(15) a. Statement: Chris is a bachelor.
      b. Entailment 1: Chris is a man.
      c. Entailment 2: Chris is not married.

If you were trying to teach someone else what the word *bachelor* meant, you might very well say, "A bachelor is an unmarried man." Lexical entailments like this – entailments that come from within the meaning of a word[3] – are clearly a very important part of our knowledge of meaning.

There are basically two approaches to these kinds of lexical entailment relations. The first holds that the entailments of a lexical item *are* the meaning of that item. That is, instead of having a concept BACHELOR, we have the complex combination of the more "basic" concepts UNMARRIED and MAN making up the semantic content of the listeme $[/\text{'bætʃlər}/]_N$. On this approach, although there is a listeme $[/\text{'bætʃlər}/]_N$, there is no "basic" concept BACHELOR; there's only UNMARRIED MAN. If this idea is right, most listeme meanings are made up of a combination of other concepts from a basic inventory of "fundamental" concepts. We could call this the "definitional" theory of meaning – meanings really are definitions, as you might find in a dictionary, and the entailment relations of *bachelor* reveal its mental definition. Everybody who knows the word *bachelor* must also know, at a minimum, the concepts UNMARRIED and MAN.

The second approach holds that lexical entailment relations are facts you learn *about* a listeme, but these relations aren't the meaning itself. On this view, listemes mean what they mean, e.g. $[/\text{'bætʃlər}/]_N$ means BACHELOR. All concepts are primitives; one could call them "atoms of thought." The list of entailment relations associated with a given concept, often called "meaning postulates," are just facts you learn (or discover) about that concept. This is the "atomistic" theory of meaning.

One point in favor of the atomistic view is the fact that it seems clear that in most cases, not knowing all the entailments of a word doesn't disqualify you from knowing the word. For instance, you can know and use the word *dog* accurately even if you don't know the word *canine* or *mammal* – but both of those concepts are entailments of *dog*. If the meaning of *dog* is made up of its entailments, it's hard to see how you could know *dog* but not *mammal*. We might conclude that concepts don't consist of their entailments, but are independent atoms.

On the other hand, in favor of the definitional theory of meaning is the fact that it would explain exactly how lexical entailment works. If definitional theories are right, lexical entailment works exactly the same way as regular entailment. Recall that *Flossie is a brown cow* entails *Flossie is brown*. This syntactic entailment follows, obviously, because the concept BROWN is directly included in the meaning of both sentences – they both have the listeme [/brawn/]$_A$ in them. If the meaning of *bachelor* is made up exactly from the concepts UNMARRIED and MAN, which define it, then the fact that *Chris is a bachelor* entails *Chris is unmarried* can be explained in the same way as *brown cow* entailing *brown*, above – the first sentence about Chris directly invokes the concept UNMARRIED, and so entails the second sentence.

Both theories of meaning hold that lexical entailments are an important part of our knowledge of or about concepts. Many researchers think that lexical entailment relations reveal important facts about the basic structure of the mental lexicon – the way that words are organized in the brain.

7.4.2 The semantic web

One way of thinking of the relationship between the word *bachelor* and its entailments is illustrated in the Venn diagram in Figure 7.1. Thinking of *bachelor* as picking out a certain subset of all the things in the world, and other words as picking out other subsets of things, allows us to mathematically define the special relationship between the word *bachelor* and the words it entails: it's the subset relation. The set of things picked out by *bachelor* is a subset of the sets of things picked out by *man, unmarried*, and *human* – that's why these concepts are entailments of *bachelor*:

There is no entailment relationship between the concept "bachelor" and the concept "lawyer" – if Jim is a bachelor, it doesn't follow that he's a lawyer. This is reflected in Figure 7.1, which shows that bachelors are not a subset of lawyers. On the other hand, there is an entailment relationship between being a lawyer and being human (lawyer jokes aside), and this is reflected in the fact that the set picked out by the concept "lawyer" is a subset of the set picked out by the concept "human."

There's a problem with this way of thinking about meaning, though. Imagine that it so happened that, at some particular point in time, all the bachelors in the world also happened to be lawyers. Our intuitions tell us that that situation wouldn't suddenly change the lexical entailments of *bachelor* – we wouldn't suddenly think that *lawyer* is now part of the meaning of *bachelor*. It would just be a coincidence – in another second, some new bachelor could turn up who isn't a lawyer. But no new bachelor could ever turn up who wasn't male – if someone's not male, they just *can't be* a bachelor! We need a way to capture

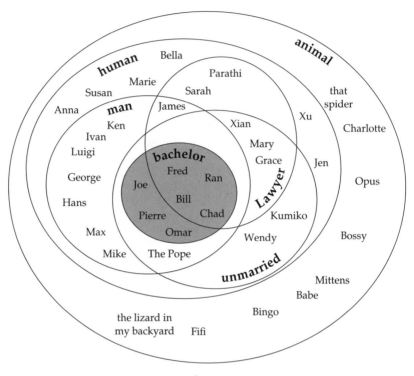

Figure 7.1 Entailment as the subset relationship

lexical entailments that talks about the relationships between word meanings, not just the relationships between different groups of things in the world.

A more psychologically revealing approach adopts the metaphor of a semantic web. Concepts are points in our mental space. Two points, like *jockey* and *horse*, are connected to each other in the web if some other concept defines a characteristic relationship between them. For instance, the concept *riding* defines a characteristic relationship between jockeys and horses. The concept *eating* defines a characteristic relationship between horses and hay, and horses and carrots, and horses and sugar cubes. The concept *pulling* defines a characteristic relationship between horses and carts. The concept *having* defines a characteristic relationship between horses and manes. We could just think of the *is* (or *being*) concept as another potential connecting point between two other concepts. In that case, then, *is* will define a characteristic relationship between horses and animals, and between bachelors and

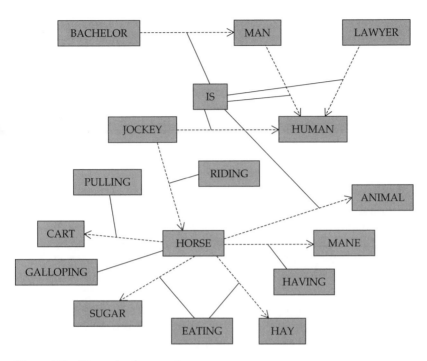

Figure 7.2 The web of concepts

men and between lawyers and humans. We could represent this kind of web of relationships graphically as in Figure 7.2.

In Figure 7.2, connections between concepts are represented as lines. Connections between two concepts that depend on a third concept are drawn with a dotted line, and the relational concept that tells you what relation the dotted line represents is connected to it with a solid line. So, for instance, *jockey* and *horse* are connected by the relational concept *riding*, so a dotted line connects *jockey* to *horse* and a solid line connects *riding* to the dotted line. In the same way, *man* and *bachelor* are connected by the relational concept *is*, so there's a dotted line that joins *man* to *bachelor*, and a solid line connecting *is* to the dotted line. (The connection between horses and galloping, on the other hand, is direct – no other entities are involved in galloping – so that line is solid.) As you learn new facts of this type – e.g. if you learn that "horses are mammals" – your web acquires more connections.

The lexical entailments we've been discussing are the ones defined by the *is* relation. We could extract all the connections defined by the *is*

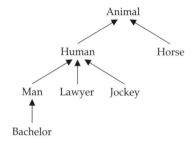

Figure 7.3 The *is* relations from Figure 7.2

relation out of the semantic web and have a representation of just the lexical entailments between concepts – a **taxonomic** representation. Taking just the *is* relations out the web in Figure 7.2, we get a taxonomic relation similar to that in Figure 7.3. Here, the *is* relation is just represented by the line connecting the lower concept to the upper concept.

> **taxonomy**, *n*. From the Greek roots *taxis* "arrangement" and *nomia* "name." A classification of anything.

We could just as well extract another kind of relation from the web, and diagram that. For instance, if we were to extract the relation *eating* from our semantic web, we would end up with a diagram that is a representation of the food chain (or "food web" as it is also, more accurately, called). A sub-part of such a diagram is shown in Figure 7.4.

Here, each line represents an *eating* relationship, rather than an *is* relationship. Since definitions are concerned with what things *are*, the *is* relationship has a privileged kind of status in the semantic web for people interested in meaning – but it's far from the only kind of relationship that's worth considering![4]

Exercise 7.4 Consider a semantic web made up of the following concepts: leg, hoof, knee, paw, dog, horse, mane, tail, claw. Draw a diagram of the *have* relationships in this web (e.g. *dogs have legs*). In your diagram, the lines connecting the concepts should represent the relation *have*. (The technical term for this kind of *having* – where the thing possessed is a part of the possessor – is **meronymy**.)

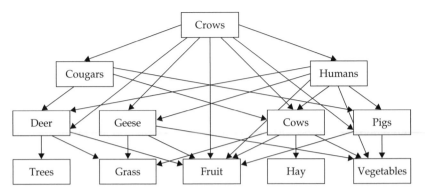

Figure 7.4 Some *eating* relationships

One important difference between the *is* relationship and the *eating* relationship is that *is*-ness is inherited from one pair of relations to another. If Dalmatians are dogs, and dogs are canines, then we can conclude (because we know the meaning of *is*) that Dalmatians are canines, right? But that's not true for eating relationships. If crows eat cows, and cows eat hay, that doesn't mean that crows eat hay, right? The meaning of *eat* doesn't allow such transfer of properties.

Relations that behave like *is* have the mathematical property of **transitivity**. (This is different from syntactic transitivity, which only applies to verbs and which just means they take a direct object – see section 7.5.) Mathematical transitivity is a property that any relation can have – not just verbs. So, for instance, the relation denoted by the preposition *above* is transitive: if the book is above the desk, and the desk is above the carpet, then we can conclude that the book is above the carpet, right? Other relations that have this property are *sibling of, equals, greater than, less than, taller than, hotter than,* etc.

Exercise 7.5 Another mathematical property that relations can have because of their meaning is *symmetry*. If a relation is symmetric, the statement "X RELATION Y" entails the reverse, "Y RELATION X." So, for example, the relation *beside* is symmetric: If we use the noun phrase *the book* for X and *the cup* for Y, we see that "The book is beside the cup" entails "The cup is beside the book." The relation *marry* is also symmetric: the statement "Mary married John" entails the statement "John married Mary." Consider the relations below, and decide if they are symmetric, transitive, both, or neither:

meet, sibling of, brother of, ancestor of, play (with), in contact (with), converse with

---

There are other properties besides symmetry and transitivity that relations can have by virtue of their meaning, but these are enough for you to get the idea. Most relational listemes in natural languages have neither of these properties, but the ones that do are fairly special. For one thing, they are the relations that enable us to reason about numbers – they reflect our inherent mathematical understanding.

In this section, we have examined the notion of word meanings, trying to decide if word meanings are made up of other, more basic word meanings, or if they are atoms. We tentatively concluded that they are atoms, but that they are intricately interconnected in a web-like fashion, in which some concepts define relationships between other concepts. The *is* concept defines the important set of relationships that we call *lexical entailments.*

> The relationships represented by the semantic web are the ones that encode a lot of what we think of as "common sense." In trying to get computers to process and produce human language, one important sub-goal is to provide them with an adequate semantic web of concepts to work with. The WordNet project at Princeton University (wordnet.princeton.edu) is one example of an attempt to build a knowledge base like this.

7.5   Relationships and Argument Structure: Meaning and Grammar

Let's think about our categories of concepts again for a minute (still without worrying about syntactic category). In our diagram, we had two fundamentally different kinds of concepts: the ones (like *eat* or *is*) that necessarily involve a relationship with other concepts, and the ones that just seem to be independent units (like *horse* or *bachelor*). The independent ones can be connected to each other via a relationship concept, but they themselves don't connect other concepts.

Relationship concepts can themselves be connected to each other by another relationship concept, as in the sentence *Seeing is believing* – in this sentence, the relationship concept *seeing* is connected to the relationship concept *believing* via the relationship concept *is*. So relationships can connect other relationships. But independent concepts can't connect other concepts – there's no way, for instance, for the concept *wallet* to indicate a relationship between two other concepts. We have two fundamentally different kinds of concepts: ones that are necessarily relations, and ones that aren't.

The meanings of relational concepts specify how many other concepts they relate to. It can be just a single one, like *gallop* – *gallop* only needs one other concept (like *horse*) to relate to. Verbs like this are called **intransitive** verbs. We've seen many concepts that need two other concepts – *eating* and *riding* are two examples; neither eating nor riding would make sense if there wasn't both an eater and a thing eaten, or a rider and a thing ridden. Verbs like this are called **transitive** verbs. (Again, be careful not to get this notion of transitive mixed up with mathematical transitivity, discussed above!) Some concepts specify a relationship between *three* other concepts – *put* and *give* are like that. In order to make sense, *put* needs to express a relationship between a putter, a thing put, and a location; *give* expresses a relationship between a giver, a thing given, and a recipient. Verbs like this are called **ditransitive** verbs. A very few concepts seem to relate four other concepts: *trade*, for instance, needs a trader, a thing traded, someone to trade with, and a thing to trade for.

If you look back at the the semantic web in Figure 7.2, you'll see that it has one feature that we haven't discussed yet. Some of the dotted lines connecting concepts are not just lines – they're *arrows*. What do you think this is trying to indicate?

If we just used a non-directional dotted line to indicate the *riding* connection between *horse* and *jockey*, how would we know who's the rider and who's the ridee? The relation might be *horses ride jockeys*, not *jockeys ride horses*. Relational concepts not only tell you how many other concepts they connect to, they tell you who does what to whom. That's why *John loves Mary* doesn't mean the same thing as *Mary loves John*. Borrowing a term from logic, linguists call the concepts that are connected by a particular relation the **arguments** of that relation. A relation like *gallop* takes one argument, a relation like *eat* takes two arguments, and a relation like *give* takes three arguments. In each case, the arguments must be of particular types. The structure the relation imposes on the other concepts is called its **argument structure**.

205

This use of the word *argument* is very different from its most common meaning, where it refers to a disagreement or debate ("They had a terrible argument!"), or a statement intended to prove a point ("The debater's argument for his position didn't make sense"). The meaning here is derived from the term *argument* as it is used in predicate logic and math, where a given function's value may depend on one or more independent variables. The variables are called the *arguments* of the function because their value determines the output of the function, by analogy with the way a particular point in a chain of reasoning may determine the outcome of that chain of reasoning.

7.6   Argument Structure

There are only a few kinds of argument structures that relational concepts can have. Once we define a few general kinds of argument structure, we can categorize practically any new relational concept that comes along. Relations tend to impose particular kinds of *roles* on their arguments. That is, relations require arguments with certain semantic properties.

7.6.1   Mary kissed John: *Agent–Theme verbs*

Perhaps the most typical kind of argument structure a relation can have is one where one argument is doing something to another argument. Examples of relations that involve this kind of argument structure are *eating, riding, twisting, kissing, poking, crushing, lifting*, etc. The argument that's doing the action is usually called the *Agent* (or sometimes *Causer*, especially if it's inanimate), and the argument that's having the action done to it is usually called the *Theme* (or sometimes *Patient*). The subject bears the Agent role, and the object bears the Theme role.

7.6.2 Bill ran *and* Bill fell*: Agent-only verbs and Theme-only verbs*

As we noted above, sometimes a relation involves just one other argument. Relations that involve just one other argument fall into two broad classes: one where the single argument is in control of what's happening, and one where the single argument is not in control. So, for instance, *running, singing, galloping, fidgeting, partying,* and *smiling* are cases where the single argument is in control; the single argument of these relations is called an Agent. On the other hand, *collapsing, growing, happening, shining,* and *blushing* are cases where the single argument isn't in control; the single argument of these relations is usually called a Theme. Sometimes it's difficult to tell the difference between the two. (Where do you think *laughing* belongs? What about *appearing* or *sleeping*?) We'll see below that there are some morphemes that are sensitive to the difference.

7.6.3 Mary knows French*: Experiencer–Theme verbs*

There are also two-argument relations where neither argument is an Agent. In the sentence *John likes dogs, John* isn't actually doing anything, and the dogs aren't having anything done to them. Similarly for the relations expressed by the verbs in these sentences: *Mary knows French, Bill wanted the apple, Sue doubted the evidence, Bob believed the story, Jill hates custard.* In all these cases, the relation expresses a feeling or attitude on the part of one argument with respect to the other argument. Here, the argument doing the feeling is called an Experiencer, and the argument that is the target of the feeling is again called a Theme.

7.6.4 Mary knows that Bill is coming*: Experiencer–Proposition verbs*

One thing that's interesting about these two-argument relations with Experiencers is that they all allow their other argument to be something besides a simple Theme – they can express a relationship between an Experiencer and a Proposition, as well. A proposition is a complete statement about some state of affairs. As well as *Mary knows*

French, we can say *Mary knows <u>that Bill is coming to the party</u>*, where instead of a Theme, we have the Proposition "Bill is coming to the party." Similarly, we can say *Sue hated (it) <u>that Bill was coming to the party</u>*, or *John wanted <u>Bill to come to the party</u>*, or *Jane doubted <u>that Bill was coming to the party</u>*, or *Bob believed <u>that Bill was coming to the party</u>*. This isn't true of the Agent–Theme verbs we described above: there's no way to make sense of a statement like **John kissed that Bill came to the party* or **Mary lifted (it) that Bill was coming to the party*. It seems to be systematic that relational concepts with Experiencers and Themes can also relate their Experiencers to Propositions.

7.6.5   Mary said that Bill left: *Agent–Proposition verbs*

There are also relational concepts that connect Agents to Propositions, for example, *John said that Mary left, Mary claimed that Joe had done his homework, Bill demanded that Jack apologize, Sue inquired whether Bill had left*. Some of these also accept the Agent–Theme structure, where instead of a proposition, they take an appropriate direct object: *John said the words, Bill demanded an apology* – but some don't: **Sue inquired the question, *Mary claimed Joe's completion of his homework*.

7.6.6   Mary donated a present to the library:
Agent–Theme–Location, Agent–Theme–Proposition

Finally, some verbs express relations between *three* arguments: an Agent (doing the action), a Theme (undergoing the action) and a Location (receiving the Theme). *Give* is like this, as in *John gave Bill a book*, and so is *donate*, and *send, pass, throw, convey, put, transfer*.

Some of these verbs, if their meanings are appropriate, also allow a Proposition, as well as a Theme (just like *say* does, above): *John told Mary <u>that Bill left</u>* (vs. *John told Bill the story*), *Mary asked John <u>whether Bill left</u>* (vs. *Mary asked John the question*).

Exercise 7.6   Categorize the following verbs into the eight categories of argument structure listed above, also given below. (Warning: some verbs belong in more than one category!) Write a sentence illustrating each of the argument structures associated with a given verb.

Argument Structures to use:
(1) Agent-only (2) Theme-only (3) Agent–Theme (4) Agent–Proposition
(5) Experiencer–Theme (6) Experiencer–Proposition (7) Agent–Theme–
Location (8) Agent–Theme–Proposition

Verbs to categorize:
break, eat, insist, invite, wink, divide, ask, repeat, think, bake, inform,
explode, scream

7.7 Derivational Morphology and Argument Structure

Now we can understand the semantic effects of some of the derivational morphemes we considered in the last chapter. Many of these
morphemes' meanings refer directly to argument roles like Agent,
Theme, etc. Consider the derived nouns in (16):

(16) a. employer, climber, fighter, rider, writer, sleeper, singer
     b. actor, bettor, operator, instigator, abductor, agressor
     c. alarmist, contortionist, cartoonist, journalist, activist

As we've seen before, the *-er* nominalizing suffix refers to "someone
who does X." Now we know the name for it: *-er* makes nouns referring
to the Agent or Causer of the verb it attaches to. The homophonous
suffix *-or* does the same thing. The suffix *-ist* does the same thing –
with one interesting difference: it attaches only to nouns or adjectives:
active-ist, not *act-ist*, *contortion-ist* not *contort-ist*. Nonetheless, it still
refers to the Agent of the action named by the stem it attaches to.

Other suffixes refer to the argument structure of verbs as well. We've
seen that *-ed* and *-en* can make adjectives from verbs: *The assigned
homework is due on Friday, The beaten team left the field slowly, The well-
written book won the Pulitzer Prize*. But it can't do this for just any
verb – we can't talk about **the laughed baby* or **the blushed man*. And
the adjective that is formed from *-en* or *-ed* can't describe just any
argument of the verb. A verb like *write* involves an Agent (the author)
and a Theme (the book), but the adjective *written* describes only the
Theme argument of *write*, not the Agent – we can talk about *the
unwritten book* but not *the unwritten author*.

7.8 Subtleties of Argument Structure

The above types of argument roles are not an exhaustive character-ization of verbal semantics, of course. There are a number of further refinements that are worth mentioning, but we'll only discuss two: verbs that require *intentional* subjects, and verbs which express the *creation* or *destruction* of their object.

7.8.1 *In control of the situation: intentional subjects*

There's a subtle difference in meaning between *killer* and *murderer*, which you can also see at work in the following set of examples:

(17) a. John killed Bill.
   b. The crash killed Bill.
   c. John murdered Bill.
   d. #The crash murdered Bill

Obviously, only a certain kind of Agent can *murder* someone, while just about anything can *kill* them. The crucial difference is that *murder* requires an intentional Agent for a subject, while *kill* does not. This distinction is even partially encoded in the legal system, in the differ-ence between the two crimes *murder* and *manslaughter*. It seems, per-haps, as if we need to distinguish between true Agents (like *John*, who can do things on purpose) and mere Causes (like *the crash*, which can't do anything on purpose).

We can also see this difference showing up in more subtle ways in the use of the English verb *have*:

(18) a. John has a plastic bag.
   b. John has a big nose.
   c. #The tree has a plastic bag.
   d. The tree has a thick trunk.

It sounds odd to talk about the tree *having* a plastic bag, doesn't it? If we add a location preposition phrase *in it* to the sentence, it's fine (*The tree has a plastic bag in it*), but just by itself, the sentence is odd. When we're talking of a person, like John, however, it's quite natural to say that he has a plastic bag.

The difference between John and a tree is that John can possess things *on purpose* (just like he could murder someone on purpose), while a tree can't. It's OK for a tree to possess something just because that's the way it's built – inanimate items can possess things *meronymically* – the "part-of" relation you diagrammed in Exercise 4 – as in (18)d, but it can't possess something that's not a part of itself. Intentional subjects of *have*, though, can do either kind of possession.

7.8.2 Being created or being affected? Two kinds of Themes

There's a *Buckets* cartoon, depicting a kindergarten classroom with students all standing beside easels, on which they've painted various kindergarteny things. Little Eddie, though, is standing next to a classmate, who's all covered in paint. The teacher is looking at this in disbelief. By way of explanation, Eddie says, "Well, you said we could paint anything we wanted! I wanted to paint *him*!"

In the cartoon, there's been a difference of opinion between the teacher and Eddie about which meaning of *paint* was intended. The teacher meant something like *create a picture (of anything you want!) by painting*, while Eddie chose to interpret her as meaning *cover (anything you want!) with paint*.

Paint is ambiguous in this regard. *You can paint anything* might be discussing either an act of creating whatever is the object of *paint* (as the teacher intended) or an act of putting paint on whatever is the object of *paint* (as Eddie interpreted). But there are lots of verbs where only one or the other meaning is available.

(19) a. Verbs of creation
          build, write, create, invent, devise, imagine, produce, construct.
      b. Verbs of location change
          water, oil, saddle, string, butter, varnish, blindfold, shoe, salt.

You can't use *write* to mean *put writing on* (#*John wrote the sheet of paper*); and you can't use *butter* to mean *create something from butter* (#*John buttered a model airplane*, meaning "made it of butter").

In the set of roles we currently have available, this distinction, between creating something or affecting something, isn't captured. For reasons like this, some linguists distinguish between Patients (preexisting things that are the recipients of some action) and Themes (items which are created or destroyed as a result of the verbal action).

ANTHONY DODGES THE LAW WHILE KEN DUCKS THE COPS

Figure 7.5 Verbing nouns in *Bizarro*. © Dan Piraro. King Features Syndicate.

It's worth noting that all the location verbs mentioned above are formed from already existing nouns. This process of verb formation ("conversion") is very productive in English today, and is exploited to good purpose on a daily basis. Sometime when you're reading, notice how many of the verbs you run into can also be used as nouns! The cartoon in figure 7.5 shows this principle taken to extremes.

7.9   Function vs. Content Meanings: The Showdown

We've looked in some detail at the semantics of verbs and other relational content words. Let's look in a little more detail at the semantics of non-relational content words – the meanings of nouns – and see how they interact with some of the function words that go with them. It turns out that the meanings of the function words are pretty inflexible, while the meanings of content words can be molded more easily: when a function word and a content word don't go together naturally, the one whose meaning changes to accommodate the meaning of the other is the content word, not the function word.

We saw above that there are two kinds of nouns in English: mass nouns, like "dough" and count nouns, like "cookie." And we saw that certain determiners can go with one kind of noun but not the other – *many* goes with count nouns, but *much* goes with mass nouns. Similarly, if we want to use a noun without a determiner, we have to add plural *-s* to count nouns but we can use mass nouns without determiners just as they are.

Given enough imagination, though, we can also use mass nouns with count determiners and count nouns in mass environments. Sometimes it takes a lot of imagination, sometimes not so much. For instance, *coffee* is a mass noun, because it goes with the determiner "much" (*I don't drink much coffee*), and because you can use it without a determiner and without a plural *-s* (*Coffee makes me jumpy*). But it's not too hard to understand what someone means when they say *I bought two coffees this morning*, or *The coffees you ordered will be ready in a minute* – you automatically imagine that the person is talking about either packaged coffee, in cups or (if not prepared) in bags. On the other hand, when you try this with mass nouns which are not so easily imagined in units, it gets a little weirder; it's strange to say *I bought two paints this morning*, to mean "I bought two cans of paint." Here, you're more likely to imagine that the speaker is talking about two *kinds* of paint.

The point is that when you force a mass noun to go with a count determiner, you have to massage the meaning of the noun in your mind so that it is packaged up into some kind of countable unit. The meaning of the noun bends to accommodate the meaning of the determiner. Of course, the particular units you imagine will be affected by general knowledge you have about the noun in question, like the fact that *coffee* is usually served in cups and *paint* comes in different colors and textures. You are employing what some psycholinguists call the Universal Packager.

The same thing goes for count nouns used in mass contexts. If I say something like *That baby has cookie all over his face*, you know I don't mean individual cookies, but rather cookie crumbs – the amorphous substance that cookies are made of. Similarly, looking at your windshield after a long road trip, you might say, *There's bug all over the windshield*, to express the idea that there's bug-substance on there, rather than individual bugs. But again, one has to use one's imagination – this time, exploiting the Universal Grinder.

The notions of "unit" vs. "substance" ("packaged" concepts vs. "amorphous" concepts) reveal something very important about the core meanings of nouns. Substances, like "dough," have properties which don't depend on the *shape* of the thing being referred to. Substances are unstructured – the quality of "doughiness" of any given thing has to do with its texture and function, but it doesn't matter what size or shape it is. The quality of "tableness," though, depends on shape, as well as function: non-table-shaped things aren't tables.

One way of thinking about meaning difference between count nouns and mass nouns is to sort them out by whether they have inherent *boundaries* or not. The boundaries that define an instance of "telephone" are important – half a telephone is not a telephone – but the boundaries that define an instance of "water" are *not* important – half of a puddle of water is still water.

7.10 How Do We *Learn* All That?

We've covered some pretty complex information in this chapter – and we've only scratched the tip of the iceberg. We've seen that function words' meanings are relatively formal and inflexible. We've seen that argument structure is a fundamental characteristic of the meaning of relational concepts, and substance vs. shape naming is a fundamental characteristic of the meaning of independent concepts. But there's plenty of other things to worry about. *Jogging* and *walking* involve using legs, but *swimming* and *flying* don't specify any particular instrument of locomotion. *Dogs* and *cats* have four legs, *robins* have two, and *snakes* none. *Conjecturing* and *cogitating* involve some kind of mental activity, while *believing* or *liking* are just states of mind, no effort required. *Peeing* and *pooping* are informal and childish kinds of words, while *urinating* and *defecating* are technical, scientific kinds of words. When we learn words, we figure out *all* these aspects of meaning, usually automatically, without having to be explicitly told. Certainly no one is ever explicitly taught the meaning of a function word. Only very rarely does anyone need to have the argument structure of a verb explained to them, or the substance vs. shape-naming properties of a noun. Relatively infrequently, guidance is given with respect to finer distinguishing characteristics of some content words – a child might need to be told that *robins* have red breasts, for instance – but the vast bulk of all this subtle information is picked up without any instruction. How does it happen? We turn to this question in the next chapter.

Study Problems

1. In the text, we described the conjunction *or* as entailing truth if either or both of its conjuncts are true. The following questions ask you to think a bit more about the meaning of *or*:

   a. In a sentence like *We'll stay inside if it's cold or if Susan's sick; otherwise we'll go out*, the conclusion is that if it's cold, we'll stay inside. We'll also stay inside if Susan's sick. What will happen if Susan's sick *and* it's cold? Will we stay inside or go out?

   b. Imagine a restaurant menu says *Entrées come with soup or salad*. You can be sure that if you order soup with your entrée, it'll be free. Similarly, if you order salad with your entrée, it'll be free. What will happen if you order both soup *and* salad? Will they both be free?

   We're seeing a difference here between "exclusive *or*" and "inclusive *or*." Inclusive *or* is being used in the sentence in (a), while exclusive *or* is being used in the sentence in (b).

   c. Describe the difference in meaning between inclusive and exclusive *or*.

   d. Look at each of the sentences below and categorize each use of *or* as more likely to be inclusive or exclusive:

      (i)   Boss to employee: *You can have Tuesday or Thursday off.*

      (ii) Child A to child B: *I can't swim or ride a bike.*

      (iii) Doctor to patient: *When was the last time you drank beer or wine?*

      (iv) Student to teacher: *Should I do problem 6 or problem 7?*

2. Draw a taxonomic hierarchy showing the *being* relation ("X is a Y") between the following words:

   animal, bird, canine, cat, chihuahua, dog, dolphin, feline, fish, fox, hamster, invertebrate, jaguar, mammal, oyster, penguin, rabbit, rat, rodent, shark, snail, sparrow, St Bernard, swallow, vertebrate, wolf, worm

3. Consider the pairs of transitive and intransitive sentences, each using the same verb, below:

	Transitive	*Intransitive*
a.	John opened the door.	The door opened.
b.	The sun melted the ice.	The ice melted.
c.	Susan dropped the ball.	The ball dropped.
d.	Jane tore the paper.	The paper tore.
e.	John grew the tomatoes.	The tomatoes grew.
f.	Bill sang a song.	Bill sang.
g.	Mary ran the race.	Mary ran.
h.	The student wrote a paper.	The student wrote.
i.	Jill ate a cookie.	Jill ate.
j.	The housekeeper vacuumed the room.	The housekeeper vacuumed.

(i)   In sentences a–e, which argument of the transitive sentence disappears in the intransitive version?

(ii) In sentences f–j, which argument of the transitive sentence disappears in the intransitive version?

(iii) In sentences a–e, does it seem likely that the event described by the transitive sentence would take the same amount of time as the event described by the intransitive sentence?

(iv) In sentences f–j, does it seem likely that the event described by the transitive sentence would take the same amount of time as the event described by the intransitive sentence?

(v)   On the basis of your answers in (iii) and (iv), what do you conclude about what kinds of arguments matter more in determining the temporal duration of an event?

Further Reading

On lexical semantics:

Jackendoff, Ray S. (1990) *Semantic Structures*. Cambridge, MA: The MIT Press.

Partee, Barbara (1995) "Lexical semantics and compositionality," in Lila Gleitman (ed.), *An Invitation to Cognitive Science*, vol. 1: *Language*. Cambridge, MA: MIT Press.

On argument structure:

Dowty, David (1991) "Thematic proto-roles and argument selection," *Language* 67.3: 547–619 (technical!).

On the formal semantic treatment of conjunctions, determiners, etc.:
DeSwart, Henriette (1998) *Introduction to Natural Language Semantics*.
Palo Alto, CA: CSLI Press, Stanford.

Notes

1 What does "true" mean, you may ask? Let's (at least initially) assume
"describes the actual state of the world" (so far as it can be accurately
determined, barring existential doubts, etc.).

2 Some languages, like modern Persian (also called Farsi), get by with just
a few verbs – between 50 and 200 – and express most of the ideas that
English expresses with verbs by using a noun–verb combination. To get a
feel for this, it would be as if we always said "give an invitation to" rather
than "invite," or "take a fall" rather than "fall," or "have a belief that . . ."
rather than "believe that. . . ."

3 Lexical entailments like this contrast with *syntactic* entailments, like the
entailment between *Flossie is a brown cow* and *Flossie is brown*, where you
don't even have to know the exact meaning of "brown" to know that it's
entailed by *Flossie is a brown cow*. Syntactic entailments are due to the
structure of the sentence; lexical entailments are due to the meaning of the
word itself.

4 Would one say that *eats cows* is an entailment of "human"? Of course not,
right? This suggests that eating relationships are not as central to the meaning of words as *is* relationships are – every *is* relationship that "human"
enters into is true of all humans; all humans are mammals, for instance.
However, every human does enter into *some* eating relationship with *something*. The key is that we drew our *is* diagram assuming that the lines
meant "ALL Xs are Ys," while we've drawn our *eats* diagram assuming
the lines mean "**SOME** Xs eat Ys." If we drew an *eats* diagram with the
"all" meaning, we might well end up with a diagram that looks more
definitional – "humans" connected to "food," say. Is a human human if he
or she never eats?

8

Children Learning Words

/'t͡ʃɪldrən 'lɜːnɪŋ 'wɜːdz/

In this chapter, we look at what kind of process word-learning is – what children must be doing when they figure out word meaning from observed word use. Among other things, children have to be able to recognize objects, make guesses about what the people around them are talking about, and assume that concepts have only one name. It turns out that some of the most valuable clues about content words' meanings come from the function words they combine with.

8.1 How Do Children Learn the Meanings of Words?

As we've seen, when you're listening to someone speak a language that you don't know, you can't even tell where the individual phonological words begin and end. Babies are faced with this problem initially, but over time, as they hear more and more speech, they come to recognize the phonotactic patterns of English and begin to parse the speech stream into phonological words. They begin to track and remember recurring patterns. Before long, they have an inventory of highly frequent phonological sequences in their memory – morphemes. They probably even have information about what kinds of morphemes often go with what other kinds of morphemes. That's a pretty amazing accomplishment in itself. But now they have an even harder problem to solve.

As we learned in Chapter 1, the sound–meaning relationship is arbitrary. That is, the particular phonemes a morpheme is made out of don't provide any hint about what the morpheme might mean. The

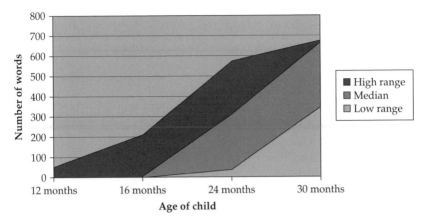

Figure 8.1   Range of variation in normal toddler vocabulary acquisition, by age

child has to figure out the meaning of individual morphemes and groups of morphemes on his own – he has to turn his statistically discovered morphemes into real listemes. How can he do this? How do children learn the meanings of words?

Children, and people generally, are phenomenally good at it. The average young adult has command of between 50,000 and 100,000 listemes, counting affixes, roots, and word-sized and phrase-sized idioms. Babies whose language development is proceeding normally can start producing words as early as one year of age or as late as two years (see Figure 8.1). They start off fairly slowly, learning about one new word every three days. On average, by about 18 months, they're producing a new word almost every day. Then comes the real spurt: between the ages of 2 and 6, they're up to four new words a day, and by the time they're 10 years old, they're learning about 12 new words a day. Most people top out between 50,000 and 100,000 listemes because they stop running into new ones on a regular basis, not because they lose their ability to learn new words. The more words you encounter, the more you will learn.

So the average 6-month-old baby has command of no listemes, and the average 18-year-old can deploy about 50,000. In between, she learned it all, mostly without noticing. Only very occasionally is a learner explicitly instructed about listeme meaning (usually when she uses the listeme in a way that reveals that she has come to an incorrect conclusion about what the meaning is). For the most part, the learner comes up with a meaning for a novel word by simple induction: given a linguistic sound sequence and a context, the learner assigns a meaning to the sound sequence based on what it must mean, given the context.

Let's be sure we understand why this is a hard problem. For a long time, people didn't really think it *was* a hard problem at all. As soon as anyone wondered about how children came to attach certain sound combinations to certain meanings, the association hypothesis was born.

The philosopher John Locke (1690) assumed that all babies had to do to learn a word was notice co-occurrences of sound sequences and their referents. If a baby saw a rabbit go by, and Mother said /ˈɹæbət/ at that moment, and that happened more than once, eventually the baby would come to associate the sound /ˈɹæbət/ with real-world rabbits, and would hence know the meaning of the listeme.

This general picture of learning by association fit in well with behaviorist models of learning, the earliest modern theory of how learning occurs. After all, if you ring a bell before feeding them enough times, dogs will involuntarily begin to salivate at the sound of bells, as the psychologist Pavlov found out. Why shouldn't word learning work the same way? Pronounce /ˈɹæbət/ in the presence of an actual rabbit enough times, the theory goes, and a child will involuntarily begin thinking of a rabbit when he hears the sound /ˈɹæbət/. Better yet, if some reward is given for demonstrating the correct sound–meaning association, like a smile from Mom, or getting a bottle when baby says /ˈbɑbɑ/, the positive reinforcement will help the association mechanism operate even faster.

Behaviorism is an approach to the study of psychology that originated in the early twentieth century. It focuses on the relationships between things and events in the environment, on the one hand, and behaviors in organisms, on the other – the relationship between a stimulus and a response. The most famous early behaviorist was B. F. Skinner, who studied how positive and negative reinforcement changed the behavior of animals. One of his most famous experiments involved providing food pellets at regular intervals to pigeons, quite independently of what the pigeons were doing. What happened was that the pigeons did more of whatever they happened to be doing at the time the food arrived – the food was a positive reinforcement of whatever behavior they happened to be exhibiting at that moment. For instance, if a pigeon happened to be lifting its head at the moment the food arrived, it would lift its head more often – which would make it more likely that the next piece of food would arrive when it was lifting its head, which would reinforce the head-lifting behavior more, and so on – until he had a whole group of pigeons, each one repeatedly performing its own little "superstitious" behavior, which it had come to associate with getting food.

It seems clear that sound–object association must play a role in children's word learning to a certain extent. It's equally clear, however, that it can't possibly be the whole story.

To consider the most basic kind of objection first, let's look at the following quote from the philosopher W. V. O. Quine, discussing the problem of matching up sound sequences and real-world items:

> The recovery of a man's current language from his currently observed responses is the task of the linguist who, unaided by an interpreter, is out to penetrate and translate a language hitherto unknown. All the objective data he has to go on are the forces that he sees impinging on the native's surfaces and the observable behavior, vocal and otherwise, of the native. . . . A rabbit scurries by, the native says "Gavagai", and the linguist notes down the sentence "Rabbit" (or "Lo, a rabbit") . . . Who knows but what the objects to which this term applies are not rabbits at all, but mere stages, or brief temporal segments, of rabbits? In either event the stimulus situations that prompt assent to "Gavagai" would be the same as for "Rabbit". Or perhaps the objects to which "gavagai" applies are all and sundry undetached parts of rabbits; again the stimulus meaning would register no difference. When from the sameness of stimulus meaning, the linguist leaps to the conclusion that a gavagai is a whole enduring rabbit, he is just taking for granted that the native is enough like us to have a brief general term for rabbits and no brief general term for rabbit stages or parts. A further alternative . . . is to take "gavagai" as a singular term naming the fusion, in Goodman's sense, of all rabbits; that single though discontinuous portion of the spatiotemporal world that consists of rabbits. . . . And a still further alternative in the case of "gavagai" is to take it as a singular term naming a recurring universal: rabbithood. The distinction between concrete and abstract object, as well as that between general and singular term, is independent of stimulus meaning. (1960: 29, 52)

Substitute "child" for "linguist" and "mother" for "native" in the discussion above, and the discussion is exactly applicable to first-language acquisition. Why does the learner assume that /ɹæbət/ (or /gævəgaj/) refers to a rabbit, and not to a rabbit leg and/or rabbit fur, or a rabbit for a 30-second period, or a rabbit plus the inch-thick envelope of air surrounding the rabbit? Quine's point is that there is an infinite number of things in any given environment that a sound sequence could be associated with. Even tracking the occurrence of a sound sequence across several different occurrences in several different environments will never eliminate all the available referents. How does the learner know which thing he should associate the new sound with? The string "gavagai" could refer to anything. It could even, for instance, be saying something about the learner himself in conjunction with a rabbit. In principle its impossible for a hearer to proceed by remembering all the details of all the circumstances in which a word was heard, cross-classify the circumstances, and come up with the one element common to them all that the word must refer to; there will always be an infinite number of logical possibilities. Word learners – babies – must be making some additional assumptions that let them narrow their hypothesis space a bit.

8.2 Learning Words for Middle-Sized Observables

Obviously, in any given encounter with a new sound sequence, a baby's word-learning machinery *doesn't* consider *every* possible association with that sound sequence. Rather, it makes educated guesses about what's the most likely association, given what else the baby knows about the situation. Then the question is, what else does a baby know? What assumptions are they basing their educated guesses on?

Experimenters have become very good at inferring what assumptions babies are making about the way the world works. Many of the experiments that have been conducted to investigate this problem are based on the length of time a baby looks at a scene or listens to a sound, in experiments like the ones described in Chapter 3. Sometimes experimenters will also measure the rate at which the baby sucks on her pacifier – faster sucking indicates more excitement, slower sucking shows less. The basic idea is that longer looking at a scene, or faster pacifier-sucking, indicate feelings of surprise at or interest in something in the scene. Surprise or interest result when things don't turn out the way the baby expects them to – so they reveal what the baby is expecting to see: they reveal what its basic assumptions are. So what are some of the basic assumptions that babies approach word-learning with?

8.2.1 Whole-object bias

It turns out that Quine's imaginary linguist was doing what babies normally do, when faced with an unknown content word. All else being equal, babies tend to assume that novel sound sequences refer to entire objects (like rabbits), not to some subpart of the object (like ears), or to some property of the object (like softness), but to the whole object itself.

Experiments have determined that babies automatically assume several things about objects. They assume that an object is not attached to its surroundings (babies are surprised by scenes that show a solid object-looking thing is stuck to the wall or the floor). They assume that objects move as a solid unit rather than piece by piece (babies are surprised if something that looks solid comes apart into several separate bits). They assume that objects must be supported from below (babies are surprised if an object doesn't move when something is taken away from under it – but they're not surprised if it doesn't move when something touching it from above is removed). If you construct a situation where an apparently object-like item violates any of these basic assumptions, even very young babies will exhibit surprise. They know how objects work.

Furthermore, babies prefer to assume that novel sound sequences name objects. They'll reject that assumption if other clues in the scene contradict it (see below), but for her initial guess, Locke's hypothetical baby would be likely to prefer the rabbit itself as the referent of /ˈræbət/. She would certainly prefer the rabbit as a referent than its parts, its properties, or some element of the background. The whole-object bias is what Quine is referring to when he says, "[the linguist] is just taking for granted that the native is enough like us to have a brief general term for rabbits and no brief general term for rabbit stages or parts." That's what babies take for granted too.

8.2.2 Mind-reading bias

The best clues about what a particular utterance is intended to refer to come not from the environment, but from the utterer herself. If the person speaking is referring to an object in the immediate domain, her gaze will tend to go to that object during the utterance. If a baby can learn to follow eye gaze, and infer that the person he's listening to is thinking about the thing that her eyes are gazing at, he's got a great clue about what the utterance is intended to refer to. If the mother of Locke's hypothetical baby were looking right at the rabbit when she said /'ræbət/, and if the baby noticed where her eyes were looking at the time, he'd have one more reason to prefer the actual rabbit as the referent of /'ræbət/, rather than any other object in the environment.

Their ability to follow someone else's eye gaze is one argument for the hypothesis that young children have developed a *theory of mind* – that is, that they understand that other humans have feelings, thoughts and desires in the same way that they themselves do. The idea is that when a child follows an adult's eye gaze, he does so because he knows that the adult is looking at something that interests her. Since the child knows that the adult has feelings and thoughts like his, he follows her gaze because if she's interested in it, there's a good chance that it will interest him as well.

Learning to follow eye gaze, and using that ability to make inferences about a speaker's intended reference, is a sophisticated cognitive skill. Not many animals can do it, if any. Babies learn to do it between about 12 and 14 months of age, right around the time that they begin producing words for the first time.

8.2.3   Mutual exclusivity bias

Imagine that there's a mouse very close by the rabbit. The child can't tell which of the two the speaker is looking at, and they're both perfectly good and equally interesting objects. How can he choose between these two possible referents for /'ræbət/?

Well, imagine that he already knows the word for the mouse. That is, on the basis of former experience with mice when no rabbits were around, he has associated /'maws/ with mice. But he's never seen a rabbit before. It turns out that in situations like this, children assume the new sound corresponds to the novel object. Unless there is good evidence to the contrary, they won't imagine that a single object can correspond to two different sound sequences. Because they know the mouse goes with /ˈmaws/, they'll assume that /ˈræbət/ can't go with the mouse. Consequently, they conclude, it must go with the rabbit. This is called the *mutual exclusivity* bias – children assume that different sound sequences have to go with different referents.

8.2.4 The taxonomic and meronymic biases

The mutual exclusivity bias gives kids a leg up in trying to figure out the cases where a different sound sequence is applied to an object they already know a word for. Let's say that Locke's hypothetical baby, who knows the word *mouse* already, is hanging around with his mother when a mouse comes by, and she looks at it and says /ˈɹowdənt/, or /ˈgrej/, or /ˈijɹ/. Her eyes are on the mouse, and there's nothing else around she might be talking about. In this situation, he *knows* she has to be talking about the mouse, but she's not using the word he's familiar with. Mutual exclusivity rules out the possibility that the new sound sequence might mean the same thing that /ˈmaws/ means. What else might it mean?

It might be a word that names a type of object that mice are an instance of, but not the only instance of – it might name a bigger class of objects than *mouse* names. This would be the right guess in the case of /ˈɹowdənt/ – a mouse is a kind of rodent, although there are others. If mutual exclusivity tells the baby to abandon the whole-object hypothesis, they could adopt this *taxonomic* hypothesis – using the *is* relation – and get the right answer sometimes.

Alternatively, it might be a word that names a subpart of the mouse – something that comes along with mice, but which doesn't make up the whole mouse by itself. This would be the right guess in the case of /ˈijɹ/. If mutual exclusivity tells the baby to abandon the whole-object hypothesis, they could adopt this *meronymic* hypothesis.

Some interesting experiments have shown that the taxonomic bias is specific to the word-learning situation. Experimenters show children a picture of a cow, a pig, and a glass of milk. (These are kids who already know the words for all three things.) In one condition, the experimenters just ask the children to sort the pictures into groups. The children tend to put the cow and the milk together. After all, the cow and the milk are naturally associated with each other, so the kids use the association as the basis for their sorting. In the other condition, the experimenter first points to the cow and names it with a nonsense word, by saying something like *That's a dax!* Then the experimenter asks the kids to sort the pictures into groups of daxes and non-daxes. In this situation, the kids tend to put the cow and the pig together, rather than the cow and the milk. That is, they have assumed that *dax* must mean something like "animal," rather than something like "cow-related item" – even though their previous sorting showed that they are predisposed to sort according to cow-related items and non-cow-related items. Kids apparently assume that word meanings are related in taxonomic ways, rather than in purely associative ways.

8.3 When the Basics Fail

What if the mother of Locke's hypothetical baby, who was faced with a rabbit for the first time ever, *hadn't* said "rabbit"? What if she had been thinking about animals in general, and had said /ˈænəməl/? What if she'd been thinking about ears, or fur, and said /ˈijr/ or /ˈfʌɹ/? What if she knew the rabbit was named Peter, and had said /ˈpijtəɹ/? Her eye-gaze clue would have been the same, and the whole-object bias would operate in the same way. The exclusivity bias wouldn't apply, because the baby had never seen the rabbit before, or learned the meaning of the sound sequence. Given everything we've said, the baby would have to assume that the new sound sequence referred to rabbits – and he'd be wrong.

In fact, kids do occasionally make this kind of mistake. There are many stories of children who assumed that *rover* was the word for all dogs, not just the name of the family pet – or vice versa: kids who've assumed that the family pet's name is Dog. But they don't make it as often as you might think. The kids are also exploiting other clues to inform their guesses.

8.4 Morphological and Syntactic Clues

There's a crucial ingredient missing from this puzzle. Locke's hypothetical baby's mother is very unlikely to just say "rabbit" or "ear" or "fur" or even "Peter" as an isolated utterance. Nearly every content word a baby hears will be embedded in a sentence, like *There goes the rabbit!* or *Do you see Peter?* or *Look how long his ears are!* It's almost never the case that an utterance will consist of just a single content word.

Remember that kids are not just trying to figure out the meanings of content words this whole time. Their pattern-matching statistics will have zeroed in on the *function* morphemes as well – determiners, plural markers, pronouns, complementizers, conjunctions – the lot. In fact, because the function morphemes recur so much more frequently than content words, kids are very likely to have isolated them as units very early on. In the Brown corpus of English – a million words of written English text – the first 62 most frequent words are function words. The most frequent content word that appears in the corpus is ranked 63rd. (It's *new*.) The top ten most frequent words in the corpus, in order, are *the, of, and, to, a, in, that, is, was, he*. (Of course, the frequency count on a corpus like this doesn't take into account sub-word-sized listemes, but we can be sure that affixes like *-s, -ed*, and *-ing* would appear in the top ranks if they were included.) Children's statistical analyzers will certainly detect and remember not only stand-alone function listemes like *to* and *the*, but also affixal function listemes. Having isolated the function words early, language-learning children are bound to start noticing when they show up and when they don't.

Even if they haven't attached any meaning to the function words yet, for instance, they may have noticed that different content words co-occur with different function words. Here are two very similar utterances that our hypothetical mother might have made in the presence of the rabbit:

(1) a. It's a rabbit!
     b. It's Peter!

Our hypothetical baby will notice whether the function morpheme *a* is present or absent. His statistical tallies will have told him that *a* can co-occur with some content words but not others – *girl, bottle, apple*, but not *Jimmy, Susan*, or *juice*. He can immediately put /ˈɹæbət/ in the same class as the other words he's heard with *a*. If he's learned the meanings of some of those words already, he might guess that /ˈɹæbət/ names the same kind of concept that those other words do. Since *a* goes with count nouns, and object names are the quintessential examples of count nouns, he might find that his object-name guess about the meaning of /ˈɹæbət/ was reinforced.

In contrast, since there's no *a* (or any other determiner) with the word "Peter," if he heard the utterance in (1)b he might be able to conclude that /ˈpijtəɹ/ is *not* a count noun. It would take a little more evidence to decide what kind of thing it was – it might be a mass noun

(*It's fur!*) or an adjective (*It's gray!*) as well as a proper name – but at least the absence of a determiner would be a good clue to steer the word-learner away from a count-noun type of meaning for /'pijtəɹ/.

8.5 Learning Words for Non-Observables

It should be clear by now that word learning isn't a trivial problem, even word-learning of words for easily observable, everyday middle-sized objects. We have seen that in order to winnow down the myriad possibilities for the meaning of any new sound sequence, a child must be making several quite strong tacit assumptions. Even when learning words for middle-sized observables, children have to be applying some fairly structured cognitive principles to the problem – it can't just be straight sound–stimulus association.

What's even worse is that Mom may even say /'ræbət/ when no rabbits are around! Quine discusses the problems that this situation poses for his imaginary linguist:

> The difficulty is that an informant's assent to or dissent from "Gavagai" can depend excessively on prior collateral information . . . He may assent on the occasion of nothing better than an ill-glimpsed movement in the grass, because of his earlier observation, unknown to the linguist, of rabbits near the spot . . . More persistent discrepancies of the same type can be imagined, affecting not one native but all, and not once but regularly. There may be a local rabbit-fly, unknown to the linguist, and recognizable some way off by its long wings and erratic movements; and seeing such a fly in the neighborhood of an ill-glimpsed animal could help a native to recognize the latter as a rabbit. (1960)

Here, Quine is imagining that the linguist is asking his informant, "Gavagai?", and trying to deduce from the informant's yes or no response what the precise meaning of *gavagai* is. What if the informant says "yes" to *gavagai* even when there's no rabbit around right at the moment, because he saw a rabbit there recently? What if he says "yes" because he can see, in the distance, a rabbit-fly, and knows that where there is a rabbit-fly, there also is always a rabbit? The same problem applies to children learning language. How can a child know in advance when the referent of /'ɹæbət/ is present in his field of view and when it's not? The association between utterances of a word and the physical presence of its referent is far from perfect.

In fact, there are many words – perhaps most – for which it is simply impossible to detect the physical presence of their referent. Huge numbers of words, of all parts of speech, refer to non-observable entities. That is, a large piece of anyone's vocabulary actually consists of words for *abstract* concepts, which have no concrete physical manifestation in the actual world. How could anyone learn the meaning of a word like *tomorrow* by simple association? There are never any *tomorrows* physically present for the speaker to gaze at, or for the hearer to automatically associate with the sound sequence /tə'maɹow/.

The sound–referent association problem arises for even very simple and concrete verb meanings, like *sleep* or *eat* or *wash*. Observation of adult–child interaction shows that in fact most verbs in child-directed speech are used when the event referred to is *not* happening. Utterances like *Go to sleep!* or *What would you like to eat?* or *Let's wash your face* are almost never made while the relevant activity is going on. If the child were to use straightforward association to deduce the meanings of these words, they might think that *sleep* referred to the action of lying down in bed, or that *eat* referred to the action of opening the refrigerator. In fact, they almost never make mistakes like this. How are they learning verb meanings?

8.6 Syntactic Frames, Semantic Roles, and Event Structure

As noted above, words are almost never uttered in isolation. They nearly always appear surrounded by the functional apparatus that makes up a complete proposition – a declaration, a question, or a command. Even when a word appears as an answer to a question, it nearly always has some functional material attached to it. If older brother says, "What's that?" as the rabbit hops by, Mom isn't likely to say "Rabbit" as her entire answer. Rather, she'll say, "It's a rabbit," or just "A rabbit." At least one of the functional listemes associated with count nouns *has* to appear with any utterance of the content word *rabbit* – it really can't be said on its own. Similarly when answering a question like "What's it doing?", the answer will be "It's hopping" or "Hopping" – not just "hop." The suffix *-ing* will invariably appear along with the root verb. As noted above, the only content words that can grammatically appear in an utterance completely free of overt functional listemes are adjectives (Q: "What color is it?" A: "Red."), proper nouns (Q: "Who is it?" A: "Peter.") and mass nouns (Q: "What's that?" A: "Grass").

The mere appearance of surrounding structure with a content word can be a powerful clue to the child about what general class of content words the utterance belongs to – mass noun, verb, adjective, etc. – and after learning just a few examples, the child can begin to make generalizations about the likely kinds of meanings that go with items of each class. For instance, *-ing* only attaches to stems that are verbs. If a child hears a new word with *-ing* attached to it, he will confidently sort it into "the class of words that can have *-ing* attached to them." Once the child learns even just one or two verb meanings, he can begin to make guesses about what kinds of meanings words in the *-ing* class can have. If the child has already concluded that words of this particular class don't refer to concrete objects, then he can narrow down the possible meanings for any new word with *-ing* on it, completely independently of whatever is going on around him at the time. He can be pretty sure that whatever the new word's meaning is, it'll have to be a "property" or an "event" or some other abstract notion.

If the child has just a little bit of knowledge about the kind of meaning we discussed in the last chapter – argument structure – he can restrict the search space of possible meanings for novel verbs even more, again based just on the grammatical context, essentially independent of any actual observations about the real world at the time of the utterance with the novel verb in it.

Remember that verbs tend to fall into general classes according to how many arguments they have, and what kinds of semantic roles those arguments bear. If a child can sort out noun-words from verb-words based on their co-occurrence with certain function morphemes, he could begin to assign verbs to different classes depending on how many nouns the verbs tended to co-occur with.

For instance, consider the sentences with mystery words in them listed in (2):

(2) a. The blah will fimble the floop.
     b. The gau lammaned the pon the rall.
     c. He pangled that she fawed.
     d. The windle is pating copan.

Assuming that a child can sort the content words into classes according to the function listemes they co-occur with, these sentences fall into the following kinds of patterns:

(3) a. The X_A will X_B the X_A.
    b. The X_A $X_B$ed the X_A the X_A.
    c. He $X_B$ed that she $X_B$ed.
    d. A X_A is $X_B$ing X_C.

Now, suppose the child has learned a few basic nouns already, and has noticed that they are members of class A, according to the function elements that they can co-occur with – anything that can go with *the* is a class A element. Based on the nouns he knows already, he knows that words of class A can refer to concrete things in the world – objects, animals, people, etc. So even though he doesn't have the foggiest idea of what *blah, floop, gau, pon, rall,* or *windle* actually mean, he could guess that they might have concrete-item meanings.

Then he's got to figure out what *fingle, lamman, pangle,* and *pate* could mean. Assuming that the sentences are conveying complete propositions, he can figure out that *fingle* must have a meaning that can relate two concrete items to each other. Similarly, *lamman* must have a meaning that could relate three concrete items together. The child has figured out that *fingle, lamman, pangle,* and *pate* must have relational meanings, and he's figured out how many arguments each of these relations takes. That is, he knows that *fingle* can have a meaning like *hit, touch,* or *cook* but not like *sleep* or *laugh*; he knows that *lamman* can have a meaning like *give, send,* or *bring,* but not like *fall, pat,* or *sit*; and he knows that *pate* can have a meaning like *run, eat,* or *drink,* but not *put* or *think.*

These discoveries may not seem like much, but they do reduce the search space for possible relational meanings enormously. In combination with a few additional bits of knowledge, children could narrow the search space even further. Psycholinguists are in the process of discovering that it seems very likely that children do have and use the additional bits of knowledge required.

8.7 Agent–Patient Protoroles

For instance, if kids generally assume that S–V–O sentences fall into a semantic pattern of Agent–Verb–Patient (rather than Patient–Verb–Agent), they'll have a leg up in figuring out the meaning of the verb. To take a concrete example, if the child hears *Mary fingled the dog,* in a situation where Mary's patting the dog and the dog's licking Mary, the assumption that the subject Mary is the Agent of *fingle*, rather than the Patient, will allow the child to zero in on a meaning for *fingle* like PAT, rather than LICK. In the same scenario, if the child had heard *The dog fingled Mary*, assuming that the dog is the Agent would cause the child to zero in on a meaning for *fingle* like LICK.

Indeed, there aren't many transitive verbs in English (or any language) where the Subject = Agent, Object = Patient assumption will lead the child to a wrong meaning. The main class of exceptions to this are the Experiencer–Theme predicates – usually, predicates that describe psychological states. Consider the following sentences:

(4) a. Mary feared the dog.
　　 b. Mary knew French.
　　 c. Mary liked green beans.

These are verbs whose subject is not an Agent, but an Experiencer. Here, the Agent–Patient assumption will induce the child to make a wrong guess about the meaning of /'fijr/ – they'll think that it describes a situation where Mary was doing something to the dog, rather than a situation where she had a certain emotional reaction to them.

In fact, though, there is a way for children to sort out these verbs into a separate class from event-denoting verbs, and again, it has to do with the functional listemes that they can co-occur with.

8.8　Functional Listemes Interacting with Content Listemes

Verbs that refer to states of being interact with tense and aspect marking differently from verbs that denote dynamic, happening events. The sentences in (5) illustrate this:

(5) a. Mary is kissing John.　　(The event is happening right now)
　　 b. #Mary is liking John.
　　 c. Mary kisses John.　　　(Mary has a habit of kissing John)
　　 d. Mary likes John.　　　 (The state holds right now)

In (5)a and (5)b, the verb is in the progressive present tense: the verb *be* plus the progressive participle *-ing* indicate an event is going on right now. Interestingly, only dynamic, happening events can be marked with the progressive *be* + *-ing* combination. Verbs that refer to states, such as *like* in (5)b, don't combine with the progressive at all in most dialects.[1]

The regular present tense, in (5)c and (5)d, interacts differently with dynamic verbs and stative verbs too. When a dynamic verb is in the regular present tense, as in (5)c, it doesn't get a true "present tense" reading – it doesn't get interpreted as happening right now. Rather, it gets a "habitual" reading – (5c) means something like "Mary kisses John on a regular basis – she has a habit of doing it." On the other hand, a stative verb in the true present tense *does* get a real "present tense" reading – (5d) means that Mary likes John right now, right at the moment of speech.

Consequently, a child is very likely to hear verbs that denote activities in the present tense with progressive aspect (*be* + *-ing*). Verbs that denote states like *like, know, want, have,* etc. almost never occur in the progressive aspect. Instead, they occur in the "true" present tense, with no aspectual marking at all. Assuming that children are keeping track of which functional morphemes verb stems can co-occur with, they'll sort event-denoting verbs and state-denoting verbs into separate classes.

Now, it so happens that Experiencer–Theme verbs are all state-denoting verbs – they describe a state the Experiencer is in, not any kind of a dynamic event. Since the functional morphemes that go with each class of verbs is different, a child has the necessary clues to understand that the Agent–Subject/Patient–Object semantic pattern only goes with verbs in the Event class, and that a different semantic pattern – Experiencer–Subject/Theme–Object goes with verbs in the State class.

Similarly, children can sort nouns into two classes, corresponding to mass and count nouns, based on whether they co-occur with the indefinite determiner *a* or *some*, or the plural suffix *-s*. Once that sorting has happened, and the meanings of a couple of examples of each class has been figured out, the child has a good clue that can help narrow down their guesses about new items in the future.

8.9 Simple Co-Occurrence? Or Actual Composition?

Above, we saw that even without knowing what each function listeme means, children could use them as markers when they're parsing the speech stream. Flanking function listemes mark the boundaries of the content listemes between them. Furthermore, children can remember, for each content listeme, which function listemes it co-occurs with.

We supposed that when a child learns the meanings of one or two content listemes from each class, he could generalize certain properties of those meanings, and use those general properties to guide future guesses about meanings for other content words from the same class.

That's the most associationistic way of looking at these kinds of effects – for that idea to work, the function words don't have to have any meanings at all; they could just be class markers. But there's another possible way to think about it. What if children know more than just "this function word occurs with this set of content words"? What if it's something about the *meanings* of the function words that allows them to combine with certain kinds of content words, but not others? For instance, it's *because* count nouns name discrete, bounded entities that they can form a plural with -*s* – they can form a plural because there can be more than one discrete, bounded entity. And it's similarly *because* mass nouns name amorphous, stuff-like entities that they *can't* form a plural: there can't be more than one amorphous stuff. It's the interaction of the *meaning* of the function word with the *meaning* of the content word that causes the restrictions on co-occurrence to appear, and allows children to detect the classes of nouns in the first place.

To see the difference between meaning-based co-occurrence restrictions and purely arbitrary, class marking co-occurrence restrictions, we have to turn to other languages. Romance languages, like French, Spanish or Italian, use different determiners with different classes of nouns.[2] In French, for instance, *le* goes with "masculine" nouns, like *crayon* "pencil" and *chien*, "dog," while *la* goes with "feminine" nouns, like *chaussure*, "shoe" and *souris* "mouse." Unlike the mass and count classes in English, however, the feminine and masculine classes of nouns have essentially nothing to do with meaning. Whether a noun is feminine or masculine is entirely arbitrary. A child learning French must learn and remember which determiner goes with which nouns, but in this case the co-occurrence restrictions will not help the child make more accurate guesses about the meaning of a new noun. Indeed, if the child tries to base his meaning guesses on the gender categories indicated by the determiner, he'll be sadly misled. It seems clear that the only co-occurrence relationships that a child can use to guide his guesses about meanings are the ones that are the result of semantically significant interactions between function words and content words. In order for *that* to work, the child must also know what the function word means.

The first person to investigate whether children actually *do* use clues from the syntactic context to figure out word meaning was Roger Brown, in 1957. He showed three sets of 3- to 5-year-olds a picture of some unrecognizable spaghetti-like stuff being poured into a bowl. He told the children from the first group, "Point to some blick." The second group of kids were told "Point to a blick." The third group were told "Point to blicking." Sure enough, the children from each group, presented with the same picture, formed different ideas about the meaning of *blick*. The first group thought that *blick* meant the spaghetti-like stuff, the second group thought that *blick* meant the bowl, and the third group thought that *blick* meant the pouring action. The only thing that could have caused them to develop these different ideas about what *blick* meant is the meanings of the different function listemes in the sentences they heard the word in; everything else about the context was the same. It seems pretty clear that the children were basing their guesses about *blick* on the meanings of the function words it was combined with.

The tricky thing about this idea is that function listemes' meanings are the *most* abstract kind of meanings there are. It's reasonably clear that a child can learn the meaning of a noun referring to a concrete thing, like a rabbit, just by associating the sound and the object, especially if the child makes a few general assumptions about objects and eye gaze and so on. Many animals can learn this kind of association without difficulty. (An awful lot of dogs know what /wɑk/ means, for instance!) But how could a child learn the meaning of *the*, or *-ing*, or *some* from a word-to-world mapping? There *is* no real-world observable entity, action, relation, or property that corresponds to the meaning of function listemes. No animal has ever learned the different meanings of *the* and *a*, or the progressive aspect *be -ing* and the perfective aspect *have -en*, no matter how frequent they are. Yet kids can achieve subconscious mastery of these listemes as early as two or three years of age.

The only guess that linguists have so far about how children learn the meanings of function listemes is that they're predisposed to look for items expressing those particular kinds of meanings. In other words, certain kinds of grammatical meanings are *innate*. Children come pre-wired to know that whatever language they are exposed to will probably have ways to indicate tense, aspect, number, definiteness, mood, person, case, and other functional meanings. If that's true, then their job is just to figure out which of this limited set of functional meanings their language actually marks with function listemes, and to match up the most frequent morphemes they hear in their input with these predetermined functional meanings. This idea is called the *innateness hypothesis*.

8.10 Yes, but Where Do the Words Come from in the First Place?

We now have the beginnings of a grasp on how children can go from an unparsed speech stream to a complete inventory of function and content listemes, each with their own meaning attached. The child's job is to extract morphemes from the speech stream and induce what their meanings are. If they did it perfectly – if they always arrived at the exact same idea of the meaning of a word that the adults around them had – words' meanings would stay exactly the same from generation to generation.

But a quick perusal of Shakespeare or Milton, or even watching a movie from the 1930s or the 1940s, will reveal that some listemes that look the same as listemes of modern English actually have quite a different meaning than they do now. Further, some listemes that used to be common have dropped out of the language, and others that are currently very common are absent from the older forms of English. A trip to another English-speaking country, or another part of your own English-speaking country, or even hanging out with a different group of people in your own English-speaking town, will introduce you to new words and new uses of old words, and cause you to wonder where other words went. Changing circumstances, changing fashions, and historical accidents will mean that no two children will get exactly the same input from generation to generation, and consequently the meanings they arrive at for many content words will change from generation to generation. A little semantic "slip" can go a long way over time. Consequently, the contingencies of history can have a big impact on the development of a language's lexicon and grammar, and English is one of the best examples of just how big an impact it can be. We turn to this topic next.

Study Problems

1. One important guide to word-learning that was discussed above was the *mutual exclusivity* bias: the idea that, if a child already

knew that one sound sequence referred to a particular something, he would assume that different sound sequence could not refer to that exact same thing.

The morphological phenomenon of *suppletion*, from Chapter 6, poses a particularly difficult problem for language acquisition, given the mutual exclusivity hypothesis.

  a. Why? Discuss, explaining what suppletion is, giving examples of it, and explaining how it would pose a problem for a child who was operating under the mutual exclusivity hypothesis.

  b. What kind of factors might help a child overcome this problem and learn the suppletive form accurately?

2. Imagine that child who doesn't know the word *cat* sees a scene containing both a cat and an elephant, as in the following:

His mother says, "Look at the cat! What a big cat!"

  a. What are five possible meanings that the word *cat* might conceivably have in this context?

  b. What are three meanings that the word *cat* could NOT have in this context? Why couldn't it mean those things?

3. (For discussion.) Have you ever noticed that you thought a word meant one thing while someone else thought it meant something else? What was the word? What did you each think it meant? Did you try to correct the person? How did you try to decide who was right? What would have happened if you had never happened to discuss the topic with each other?

Further Reading

Bloom, Paul (2000) *How Children Learn the Meanings of Words.* Cambridge, MA: MIT Press.

Gleitman, Lila and Newport, Elissa L. (1995) "The invention of language by children: environmental and biological influences on the acquisition of language," in Lila Gleitman (ed.), *An Invitation to Cognitive Science*, vol. 1: *Language*. Cambridge, MA: MIT Press.

Golinkoff, Roberta M. and Hirsh-Pasek, Kathy (1999) *How Babies Talk*. New York: Penguin.

Quine, W. V. O. (1960) *Word and Object*. Cambridge, MA: MIT Press.

Notes

1   Some varieties of English do use the progressive form to indicate the present tense of stative verbs such as *like*; Indian English (spoken in India) is like this, accepting progressives such as *I am understanding that* as the present tense form of 'understand'.

2   As we'll see in the next chapter, Old English was like this as well, but it is likely that more of you are familiar with one of the Romance languages than with Old English, so I'll use them to illustrate here.

9

Accidents of History: English in Flux

/'æksədn̩ts əv 'hɪstəɹij: 'ɪŋgləʃ ən 'flʌks/

In this chapter, we look at a broad outline of the history of English, or rather, the history of those people who have spoken English since it *was* English. Understanding their history helps us understand why the English vocabulary and spelling system are the way they are today. We learn about the sources of much of the English vocabulary, the reasons for some of the vagaries of English spelling, and about some of the reasons why languages change and continue to change in general.

9.1 Linguistic Change, and Lots of It

English is really not the same language it was a thousand years ago. All languages change over time, but few languages have changed as much in as short a time as English has. Speakers of modern French or Icelandic can read prose written in Old French or Old Icelandic without too much special training. Speakers of modern English, however, usually need to take one or more university-level courses before they can even begin to read Old English texts.

To get a feel for how much the language has changed over the years, have a look at the Old English text I've provided and glossed below, and then read the free translation of the text following it.[1]

The excerpt is from one of the documents that the English king Alfred the Great had written for him around 900 AD. It's a description of what a Viking trader told Alfred about a northward voyage he had made. The Viking's name was Ohthere, and he came to see Alfred sometime after 890, when he made the voyage. Ohthere had sailed north to a latitude of 71° 15′, which was farther than anyone had sailed before and farther than anyone would again for more than 500 years. The excerpt describes what he told Alfred about the people of the very northernmost lands, where he met both Finns and a people called the Beormas, and collected a tax from them. The text is revealing about the contemporary culture both of the Finns and the Norwegian Vikings, and also about that of the English who were writing it down.

Now, to make some sense of the Old English text below, you need to know just a few things about the Old English writing system. It was generally fairly phonetically accurate. Almost all the recognizable symbols represent the same sounds that they represent in the IPA. In particular, the vowels generally have their IPA values: "o" = /o/ as in *boat*, "e" = /e/ as in *gate*, etc. The consonant symbol "ð" represents the same thing it does in IPA, the voiced interdental fricative /ð/, as in *father*.

There are a few symbol–sound relationships in this text that will be new to you, which are summarized in Table 9.1. Try to get a little

Table 9.1 Symbol–sound relationship in OE

Symbol	Sound (features)	Sound (IPA)	Example OE word(s)	Modern English sound-alike word
þ ("thorn")	Interdental fricative	/θ/ or /ð/	*þæt*, "that"	*that*
c next to a front vowel	voiceless palatal affricate	/tʃ/	*micle*, "much"	*Mitchell*
sc before a front vowel	voiceless palatal fricative	/ʃ/	*sceall*, "shall" *scip*, "ship"	*shall* *ship*
g next to a front vowel	palatal glide	/j/	*twentig*, "twenty" (also *gyt*, below)	*twenty*
y	high, front, rounded vowel	/y/	*gyt* "yet"	Not in modern English – an /i/ with lip-rounding
h in middle of word	voiceless velar fricative	/x/	*eahta*, "eight"	Not in modern English – Like German "ch" in *Ich, Bach, Buch*.

familiar with them before looking at the text, as it'll help sort out things that are *really* different from modern English from things that just *look* different.

The following represents approximately the second quarter of the complete text of *The Voyage of Ohthere*:

1 Fela   spella him sædon þa Beormas ægþer ge of hiera agnum
   Many stories him said   the Beormas both   of their own
   lande ge   of
   land [and] of

2 þæm landum þe   ymb hie utan   wæron, ac he nyste
   the   lands   which about them outside were   but he not knew
   hwæt þæs
   what the

3 soþes wæs, for þæm he hit self ne geseah. Þa Finnas, him
   sooth was, for that he it self not seen.   The Finns, him
   þuhte, ond
   thought, and

4 þa Beormas spræcon neah an geþeode.
   the Beormas spoke   nigh one language.

5 Swiþost he for   ðider, to ecan þæs landes sceawunge, for þæm
   Especially he fared thither, besides these lands surveying   for the

6 horshwælum, for þæm hie habbaþ swiþe æþele ban on hiora
   horsewhales, for that they have   very noble bone in their

7 toþum – þa teð hie brohton sume þæm cyninge – ond hiora
   teeth – the teeth they brought some to the king –   and their
   hyd bið swiðe
   hide is very

8 god to sciprapum. Se   hwæl bið micle læssa þonne oðre
   good for shipropes. This whale is much less than   other
   hwalas: ne
   whales: not

9 bið he lengra ðonne syfan elna lang. Ac on his agnum lande is
   is he longer than   seven ells long. But in his own   land   is

10 se betsta hwælhuntað: þa beoð eahta and feowertiges elna lange,
   the best   whalehunting: they are eight and forty   ells long,

241

11 and þa mæstan fiftiges elna lange; þara   he sæde þæt he, syxa
   and the biggest fifty   ells long; of them he said that he, six
   sum ofsloge
   some, slew

12 syxtig on twam dagum.
   sixty in two   days.

13 He wæs swyðe spedig man on þæm æhtum   þe   heora speda
   He was very rich   man in those possessions which their riches
   on beoð,
   in are,

14 þæt is on wildrum.   He hæfde þa   gyt, ða   he þone cyningc
   that is in wild [animals]. He had   then yet when he the   king
   sohte,
   sought,

15 tamra deora unbebohtra syx hund. Þa   deor hi   hatað
   tame beasts un-be-bought six hundred. Those beasts they called
   "hranas"; þara
   "hranas"; there

16 wæron syx stælhranas, ða beoð swyðe dyre mid   Finnum, for
   were six decoyhranas, that are very   dear among Finns, for
   ðæm hy
   that they

17 foð   þa wildan hranas mid. He wæs mid   þæm fyrstum
   capture (the) wild   hranas with. He was among the   first
   mannum on
   men   in

18 þæm lande; næfde he þeah ma   ðonne twentig hryðera and
   that land; not had he yet   more than twenty cattle   and
   twentig sceapa
   twenty sheep

19 and twentig swyna, and þæt lytle þæt he erede he erede mid
   and twenty swine, and that little that he plowed he plowed with
   horsan. Ac
   horses. But

20 hyra ar   is mæst on þæm gafole þe   ða Finnas him gyldað.
   their property is mostly in that   tax   which the Finns them yielded.

21 Þæt gafol bið on deora fellum and on fugela feðerum and
    That tax   is   in beasts' skins   and in   fowls' feathers and
    hwales bane
    whales' bone

22 and on þæm sciprapum þe   beoð of hwæles hyde geworht and of
    and in those shipropes   which are   of whales' hide wrought and of

23 seoles. Æghwilc gylt be hys gebyrdum. Se byrdesta sceall
    seals. Each   pays by his birth.   The top-birthed shall

24 gyldan fiftyne mearðes fell and fif hranes and an beran fel
    yield   fifty   martens' skins and five hranas' and one bear's skin
    and tyn
    and ten

25 ambra feðra   and berenne kyrtel oððe yterenne and twegen
    ambers' feathers and bearskin kirtle   or   otterskin and two
    sciprapas;
    shipropes

26 ægþer sy   syxtig elna lang: oþer sy   of hwæles hyde
    both   being sixty ells long: either being of whales' hide
    geworht, oþer
    wrought, either

27 of sioles.
    of seals.

Free translation

The Beormas told him [Ohthere] many stories, both of their own land
and of the lands around them, but he didn't know what the truth was,
because he did not see it for himself. The Finns and the Beormas seemed
to him to speak nearly the same language.

Besides surveying the land, he mainly went there for the walruses,
because their teeth contain very fine bone – they brought some of the
teeth to the king – and their hide is very good for ship-rope. This whale
[the walrus] is much smaller than other whales, it doesn't reach more
than 26 feet in length. However, the best whale-hunting is in his own
land [Norway]. [There], they are a hundred and eighty feet long, and
the biggest a hundred and eighty-eight feet; he said that he and five
others killed sixty of them in two days.

He was a very rich man in those things that their riches are in, that is
in wild beasts. He still had, when he sought the king, six hundred

unsold tame beasts. They called those beasts "reindeer"; there were six decoy reindeer that were very costly among the Finns, because they use them to capture the wild reindeer. He was among the leaders of the land, even though he didn't have more than twenty cattle and twenty sheep and twenty swine, and what little land he ploughed, he ploughed with horses. But his riches are mostly derived from the tax that the Finns paid them. That tax is paid in beast skins and in feathers and whale bone and in ship-rope made of whale and seal skin. Each pays according to his rank. The highest ranked shall pay fifty marten skins and five reindeer skins and one bear skin, and 320 gallons of feathers and a bearskin or otterskin coat and two ship-ropes, each being 225 feet long, made either of whale hide or of seal hide.

What are some of the differences you notice between Old English and modern English, besides the orthographic and phonological differences mentioned above? There are significant differences at every level: differences in syntax, morphology and vocabulary. For instance, have a look at all the noun phrases below. They are the NPs in the text that are modified by a relative clause. I've provided glosses and identified the syntactic categories of each listeme:

(1)   Syntactic differences between OE and Mod E
   a.   þæm landum   þe   ymb hie   utan   wæron,   (Line 2)
        those lands   which about them outside were
        Det   N   [$_S$ Comp P   Pron Adv   V   ]

   b.   þæm æhtum   þe   heora speda on beoð,   (Line 13)
        those possessions   which their   riches in are
        Det   N   [$_S$ Comp Pron N   P V   ]

   c.   þæm gafole   þe   ða Finnas him   gyldað. (Line 20)
        that tax   which the Finns them yielded.
        Det   N   [$_S$ Comp Det N   Pron V   ]

   d.   þæm sciprapum þe   beoð of hwæles hyde geworht (Line 22)
        that ship-rope   which be   of whales' hide wrought
        Det   N N   [$_S$ Comp Aux P N   N   V]

In all these cases, the determiner and noun are followed by a modifying relative clause, introduced by the complementizer *þe*, "which". But the words in the relative clause are not in the same order they would be in their modern English equivalent! In all the OE examples above, the main verb in the relative clause comes at the end – but that's not where we put it now. To say (1)c in modern English, for instance, we would say *that tax which the Finns yielded*[2] *to them*, not *that tax which the Finns to them yielded*. In modern English, the verb directly follows its subject, in this case *the Finns*, and precedes the object, rather than coming at the end of the sentence, as it did in Old English. Similarly for the others: the modern English equivalent of (1)d is *that ship-rope which is wrought*[3] *of whales' hide*, with the main verb preceding the object, not *that ship-rope which is of whales' hide wrought*, with the main verb following the object. For (1)b, we'd say *those possessions which their riches are in*, not *which their riches in are*. And (1)a would be something like *those lands which are about them*, not *those lands which about them are*. If you know any German or Dutch, you may notice that this Old English word order, with the verb at the end, is like the word order of those languages in the same kind of clause. So it's clear that the syntax of English has changed in the past thousand years.

There are many, many morphological differences between Old English and modern English. To take one example, let's see if we can figure out how nouns were pluralized in Old English. There are several plural nouns in the text above, and a couple that occur both in singular and plural form. If we look at all these nouns together, we see that many different suffixes seem to do the job of representing plural number. I've extracted all the plural nouns in the text, and any corresponding singulars, and listed them below. They are subscripted with the line number(s) in which they appear in the text, so you can find them in context:

(2)   *Morphological differences: plural nouns*

Sg. noun	Plural noun	English gloss	Suffix(es)?
?	horsan$_{19}$	horses	*-an*
?	spella$_1$	stories	-a
?	sceapa$_{18}$	sheep	*-a*
?	hryðera$_{18}$	cows	*-a*
?	swyna$_{19}$	swine	*-a*
?	speda$_{13}$	riches	*-a*
man$_{13}$	mannum$_{17}$	men	*-um*
?	æhtum$_{13}$	possessions	*-um*
?	wildrum$_{14}$	wild (beasts)	*-um*

Sg. noun	Plural noun	English gloss	Suffix(es)?
?	$dagum_{12}$	days	*-um*
?	$elna_{9,\ 10,\ 11,\ 26}$	ells	*-na*
$hwæl_8$	$hwalas_8$, $horshwælum_6$	whales, horsewhales	*-as, -um*
?	$sciprapas_{25}$, $sciprapum_{8,\ 22}$	ship-ropes	*-as, -um*
$lande_{1,\ 9,\ 18}$	$landes_5$, $landum_2$	lands	*-es, -um*
?	$Finnas_3$, $Finnum_{16}$	Finns	*-as, -um*
?	$teð_7$, $toþum_7$	teeth	*-Ø, -um*
fel_{24}	$fell_{24}$, $fellum_{21}$	skins	*-Ø, -um*
?	$feðra_{25}$, $feðerum_{21}$	feathers	*-a, -um*
?	$deora_{15}$, $deor_{15}$	beasts	*-a, -Ø*

For some nouns, we have both singular and plural forms. For others, we have only plurals, but many of these words have made it through to modern English, so we can identify which part is the suffix and which the root without too much trouble. In *horsan*, for instance, it seems clear that *-an* is a suffix on a root *hors-* (especially if we compare it to the first part of *hors-hwalum₆*, literally "horse-whales", referring to walruses.) Assuming that much, it is probably safe to conclude that even in the unrecognizable words *hryðera* and *æhtum*, the *-a* and the *-um* are suffixes, since we see them in other words too.

If that was all there were to it, we might be able to decide that *-an*, *-a*, *-um*, and *-as* were all just different plural suffixes that went with different sets of stems, like *-s* (*horse-s*), *-i* (*almun-i*), and *-Ø* (*sheep-Ø*) in modern English. But things start to get very confusing when we look at the last seven plural nouns. There, it seems like we've got *two* possible suffixes that mark plurality! Six nouns show up once with *-um* and once with some other suffix from the list above. The last shows up with the null suffix (*-Ø*) and the *-as* suffix from the list above What's going on?

It turns out that the noun suffixes on Old English nouns included other information as well as plurality. Remember, from Chapter 7, that English pronouns have different forms depending on where in the sentence they appear? The third person pronoun is pronounced *he* as a subject, but when it's a possessor, it's *his*, and anywhere else in the sentence, it's *him*. Old English marked these and other distinctions on *all* nouns, not just pronouns, rather like German or Latin does. The suffix attached to the various nouns above is indicating both plurality and *case* – the role the noun is playing in the sentence.[4]

Exercise 9.1   Locate in the text all the nouns in the list above that end in *-um*. (The line numbers where they occur are given in the subscripts.) Can you figure out what common syntactic environment all the *-um* words share?

Finally, there are obviously plenty of vocabulary differences. Old English clearly had a lot of suffixal listemes that modern English lacks. Besides the noun suffixes discussed above, there were similar adjective suffixes that agreed with the nouns they modified, like the *-um* in *fyrst-um mann-um*$_{17}$, "first man." Verbs also seem to have a number of affixes that no longer exist in modern English either: for example the *-e* in *soht-e*$_{14}$, "sought" and *þuht-e*$_3$, "thought"; the *-on* in *wær-on*$_2$, "were" and *sæd-on*$_1$ "said"; and the *ge-* in *ge-worht*$_{26}$, "wrought" and *ge-seah*$_3$, "seen." Just looking at the single verb *gyld-*, "yield," we see the following forms in the text: *gyld-að*$_{20}$, *gyl-t*$_{23}$, and *gyld-an*$_{24}$. Looking at the verb *be*, "be," we see the following: *wær-on*$_2$, "were," *wæs*$_3$, "was," *bið*$_7$, "is," *is*$_9$, "is," *beoð*$_{10}$, "are," *sy*$_{26}$, "be." Some of these suffixes might be a bit familiar to you, because they lingered on into the Early Modern English period. The King James Bible (1611) often uses the 3rd person present *-th* suffix, which we see here in the *-að* in *gyld-að* and the *-oð* in *beoð*. Here are the first few lines of the 23rd Psalm from the Bible:

(3)   The Lord is my shepherd, I shall not want.
      He mak<u>eth</u> me to lie down in green pastures,
      He lead<u>eth</u> me beside the still waters,
      He restor<u>eth</u> my soul.

Other function listemes are also different. The pronouns are different – *hie*$_6$ for "they" and *heora*$_{13}$ for "their." The complementizers are different – *for þæm*$_6$, literally "for that," instead of modern English "because." The conjunctions are different – *ac*$_9$ instead of "but." The quantifiers are different or changed in function – *fela*$_1$ instead of "many," for example. *Ægþer* (which became modern English "either") meant "both" in Old English.[5] The prepositions are different or changed in function, so we see *mid*$_{16}$ for "among" and also *mid*$_{19}$ for "with," *on*$_9$ for "in," and *to*$_8$ for "for." We also see many function listemes we recognize in the text (*him*, *þæt*, *of*, and *and*), but many – probably most – are not familiar to speakers of modern English.

There are, of course, many obvious differences in content listemes as well. There are content listemes that are simply completely different from their modern English equivalents, like *hataþ₁₅,* "called," *hryðera₁₈,* "cattle," *erede₁₉,* "plowed," and *fel₂₄,* "skin, hide." There are others that may be recognizable to some of you but are archaic, obsolete or dialectal in modern English: *kyrtel₂₅,* "kirtle (coat, tunic)," *ðider₅,* "thither (there)," *soþes₃,* "sooth[6] (truth)." And there are others that you may recognize but whose meanings have changed significantly. The word *deor₁₅,* which became our modern English word *deer,* used to mean just "(wild) beasts, animals," not "deer." Similarly, *þuhte₃* has became our modern verb "think," but in Old English its meaning was "seem." (The Shakespearean word *methinks* meant something more like "it seems to me that . . ." than "I think that. . . .") Finally, the words *spedig₁₃,* "rich," and *speda₁₃* "riches," have become the modern English word *speedy* and *speed,* but they've lost their former meaning of "wealth," "success" or "good fortune" and retained only the meaning "fast." The archaic farewell expression, *Godspeed,* originally conveyed a meaning like "God give you success," not "God give you speed."

Despite these differences, there are clearly many very recognizable words in the Old English texts, whose forms and meanings have changed very little, setting aside the different spelling conventions, and all those suffixes. Some listemes like this are *hors-, hwæl-, man-, feðr-, scip-, swyn-,* and many others. The main difference in content words between Old and modern English is an *absence*: in Old English texts, there are very few words from Latin, Greek, French or other Romance languages. Indeed, there are few borrowings of any sort: the vocabulary is basically Germanic in origin. In modern English, on the other hand, it is estimated that about 50 percent of the words in common use are of non-Germanic origin.

Exercise 9.2   In the preceding sentence (the last one of the previous paragraph), 6 of the 14 nouns, verbs and adjectives are of Latinate origin. Which ones? One of the words is of indeterminate origin. Which one? Find out by using the OED.

Where did all those new words come from? And where did all those affixes go?

9.2 Layers of Vocabulary and Accidents of History

In Chapters 5 and 6, we saw that the English vocabulary is partitioned into two main groups – Latinate and Germanic – which behave differently with respect to certain morphological patterns. English is historically a Germanic language, related to Swedish, Dutch, German, and other languages of that group. How did English come to have so many words of Latinate origin in it? And how did it even get to England in the first place? All the other Germanic languages are spoken in the northern part of mainland Europe, where the Germanic tribes had settled, sometime before 1000 BC.

The accidents of history have forced English into very intimate contact with several other European languages. In those situations, the other languages often had the upper hand, so to speak – they were spoken by the socially and culturally prestigious, and by those in political and military power. The early political history of England is one of repeated conquest and subordination, and the profound changes in the language between 1000 AD and 1500 AD, which created Modern English out of Old English in the relatively short time span of 500 years, are a direct consequence of those political events, which we'll review next.

9.3 A Brief History of England, as Relevant to the English Vocabulary

There are essentially four main periods in the history of English, once it had arrived in England:

1. 600–1000 AD: Old English
   1000–1100   *transition*
2. 1100–1400 AD: Middle English
   1400–1500   *transition*
3. 1500–1750 AD: Early Modern English
4. 1750–present: Modern English

We'll look at each period in turn, looking mainly at the events that had an effect on the English vocabulary. First we answer the question: How did the English get to England?

9.4   55 BC to 600 AD: **How the English Came to England**

Before 449 AD, the primary inhabitants of the British isles were *Celts*,[7] who had invaded from the east hundreds of years earlier and driven out earlier, non-Indo-European tribes. They spoke Celtic languages: Welsh, Manx, Gaelic, and Briton. In fact, before the Roman Empire began to seriously expand around 125 BC, most of Europe was inhabited by Celts.

In 55 BC the Romans finally got around to invading Britain. Caesar's first invasion wasn't successful, but a century later Romans came again. They ruled southern Britain from 43 AD to 410 AD. The Celtic Britons under Roman rule were converted to Christianity by Roman missionaries, but they otherwise retained their own essentially separate identities and language during this period. The Romans left Britain in the late fourth and early fifth centuries, partly because their empire was under attack in mainland Europe from rebelling Germanic tribes: Goths, Franks and Vandals, all former Roman allies, were now attacking the Romans. In 410, Visigoths, led by their king, Alaric, burned Rome.

The departure of the Romans left the Britons without the military shield they'd become used to. In that same year, 410, they were being attacked by Picts and Scots, other Celtic tribes who lived in Scotland. The Britons begged Rome for military aid, but Rome had no resources to spare.

The beleaguered Britons, looking around for allies, noticed that just across the Channel, three German tribes – the Jutes, Saxons, and Angles – had military strength to spare. In 449 the Britons invited them to come over and help protect Britain against the northerners, in exchange for a piece of land in the east.

Here's a translation of a description of this period, the *Ecclesiastical History of England*, written by St. Bede around 730 AD, explaining how the Germanic tribes were given an inch and took a mile:

> Then the nation of the Angles, or Saxons ... arrived in Britain with three ships of war and had a place in which to settle assigned to them ... in the eastern part of the island. Accordingly they engaged with the enemy, who were come from the north to give battle, and the Saxons obtained the victory. When the news of their success and of the fertility of the country, and the cowardice of the Britons, reached their own home, a more considerable fleet was quickly sent over, bringing a greater

number of men, and these, being added to the former army, made up an invincible force.

Those who came over were of the three most powerful nations of Germany – Saxons, Angles, and Jutes. . . . In a short time, swarms of the aforesaid nations came over into the island, and the foreigners began to increase so much, that they became a source of terror to the natives themselves who had invited them. . . . Public as well as private buildings were overturned; the priests were everywhere slain before the altars; no respect was shown for office, the prelates with the people were destroyed with fire and sword; nor were there any left to bury those who had been thus cruelly slaughtered. Some of the miserable remnant, being taken in the mountains, were butchered in heaps. Others, spent with hunger, came forth and submitted themselves to the enemy, to undergo for the sake of food perpetual servitude, if they were not killed upon the spot. Some, with sorrowful hearts, fled beyond the seas. Others, remaining in their own country, led a miserable life of terror and anxiety of mind among the mountains, woods and crags.

By 600 AD, Germanic tribes controlled Britain. The Celts were driven south, west, and north, into Wales, Cornwall, Devon, and Scotland. Irish Celtic raiders attacked the hapless Britons from the west, and carried off prisoners. (One of the Briton prisoners was St. Patrick, who converted Ireland to Christianity.) The southern part of Britain, ruled by the Germanic invaders, came to be called by the name of one of the tribes: Angle-land, or *England*.

9.4.1   *Loanwords from before English was English*

The Angles, Saxons, and Jutes, *before* they came to Britain, had had lots of interaction with Roman military personnel, merchants, and colonists. Even before they came to England, they had borrowed some Latin words from them: *wine* (Latin *vīnum*), *street* (Latin *strata*), *mile* (Latin *mille (passum)*, "thousand (paces)"), *pan* (Latin *panna*), *wall* (Latin *vallum*).

Once they had arrived, the Anglo-Saxons were not talking much to the resident Celts – more often, killing them – and, as rulers, were certainly not speaking Briton. Hence only a few loanwords from Celtic languages entered English at this time: *bin* and *druid* are a couple of examples that have made it to Modern English; others were borrowed and later lost. Lots of British place names are Celtic, though: *Avon*, *Thames*, *Wight*, etc.

9.4.2 The Anglo-Saxons and Christianity

Although the Anglo-Saxons, like all the residents of Europe, had been in contact with Latin-speaking Romans over the previous several hundred years, they didn't get very intimate with Latin until they adopted Christianity. Then they heard considerably more Latin, as it was the language of the Church.

The original Anglo-Saxons were pagans, holding religious beliefs similar to those you may be familiar with from the Norse legends. The Norse theology, whose pantheon includes Odin, Freya, Thor, Loki, etc., is the source of some of our names for weekdays: *Woden's day* (Wednesday), *Thor's day* (Thursday), *Freya's day* (Friday). The subjugated Celts were Christian, but they weren't interested in ministering to their oppressors, and the Roman Church had other things to worry about at first.

However, in the late 500s, Pope Gregory saw a couple of beautiful Anglo-Saxon slaves in the marketplace in Rome (when he supposedly made a famous Latin play on words: *Non Angli, sed Angeli* – "not Angles, but angels") and sent a mission to Britain to convert them. The Angles were hard to convert, partly because the church structure imposed priests from abroad, rather than promoting locals, but after a hundred or so years the Celtic Christians got into the act too, and the resulting conversion was close to total.

Loanwords from Latin during this period, then, mostly have to do with the church: *apostle, deacon, demon, pope, school, hymn* were all borrowed around this time. Keep in mind that up to this point written records in OE were very sketchy: literacy and books were for the rich only, and Latin was the lingua franca, so everything was written in it. It wasn't until after 800 AD that a number of substantial texts became available in OE. By then, most Anglo-Saxons had become Christian. Many were interested in learning to read so they could read the Bible. King Alfred, who attached great importance to literacy, observed that it was easier to just learn to read than to have to learn to read *and* learn Latin at the same time, so he had a number of texts translated into Old English. Before then, although England was a relatively cultured place – in fact, with the Roman missions, great centers of learning had arisen, and many people came from all over Europe to study in England – there was nothing written in the English language. Prior to Alfred, it was all in Latin.

9.5   600–900 AD: **The English and the Vikings**

The Anglo-Saxons established a stable government and defended England against incursions for the next three hundred years. The biggest threat came from the north. From around 790 to 880, England was repeatedly raided by Scandinavian Vikings (also called Norsemen, or Danes), who essentially ruled the northern and eastern parts of Britain under a system now called the *Danelaw*. Old Norse was spoken widely throughout this area, because the Vikings not only landed and extracted tax, but moved in and married Englishwomen. Old Norse was a household language in the northern half of the island.

When the Viking raiders came south, they had a very bad effect on the archival material of the day. Most of the loot worth taking in southern England was in the churches and monasteries, so these buildings attracted visits from the Vikings. Once they were done looting, they usually burned the buildings, along with all the books in them.

King Alfred, who ruled England from 871 to 899, defeated the Vikings decisively. More importantly for us, Alfred was a scholarly man who attached great importance to literacy and learning. Because Alfred had many important texts translated into Old English, he provided some of the most extensive written evidence that we have now about what Old English was like (including the excerpt about the Viking trader Ohthere that we looked at above).

After Alfred's death, England remained united and independent for a century. Then the Norsemen returned. This time, the English were beaten into submission, and Canute, king of Denmark and Norway, became ruler of England.

9.5.1   *Old Norse and Old English*

During this period, a lot of Scandinavian loanwords entered English, although it's hard to tell sometimes exactly which words those were, because Old Norse and Old English were closely related Germanic languages and much of their vocabulary sounded very similar. There were a couple of sound changes that distinguished the two languages, however, so it is possible to distinguish some of them. If a word exhibits a sound pattern that belongs to Old Norse but not Old English, we know it must have been borrowed. Some examples: OE *æg*, "egg," became early Middle English *ei*. (Remember that the OE spelling "g" represented a velar fricative in this kind of environment, and such fricatives are easily lost in coda position.) By late Middle English, though, the Old Norse word *egg*, with a genuine voiced velar stop in it, had replaced *ei* as the usual word for EGG in English. OE *sweostor*, "sister," became Middle English *suster*. This word was replaced by Old Norse *systir*, which is the source of our modern *sister*.

Old English also borrowed some function words from Old Norse, which is itself extremely remarkable. Content words are borrowed back and forth between languages all the time, but it is rare for a new function word to enter a language via borrowing. (Remember the failure of the introduction of a non-gendered 3rd person pronoun into English discussed in Chapter 6?) Nonetheless, one thing Old English got from Old Norse was a set of pronouns.

If you look at the third person plural pronouns in our *Ohthere* text, you'll see that in Old English, they all began with an /h/, not with /ð/. OE had a masculine subject pronoun, *he*, and its object variant, *hine*, its indirect object variant *him* and its possessive variant, *his*. Similarly, it had a feminine subject pronoun *heo*, a feminine object pronoun *hiere* (the source of ModE *her*), and a feminine possessive *hie*. All the Old English third person plural pronouns also began with /h/. The reason we now have *they*, *them*, *their*, instead, is because the original Old English third person plural pronouns were replaced wholesale by their Old Norse counterparts, which began with the interdental fricative /ð/. Similarly, on the way to ME, the feminine singular subject form *heo* was replaced by the Old Norse *she*, although English kept the object form *her*.

Sometimes a borrowing from Old Norse didn't displace the equivalent Old English word. Rather, one or the other would take on a more specific meaning, and the two words would continue to coexist. Some pairs like that are *shirt/skirt*, and *shy/scare*. In Old English, the original Proto-Germanic /k/ sound had disappeared entirely from consonant clusters beginning with /s/; rather, the whole cluster became the palatalized fricative /ʃ/. (That's why the spelling "sc" in Old English was pronounced /ʃ/.) But when the Old Norse speakers interacted with the English, the English picked the /sk/ clusters right back up in a number of borrowed words. Old Norse *skirt* came to mean a garment for the lower half of the body, even though it had originally been entirely equivalent to Old English *shirt*, referring to a tunic worn over the torso. Similarly, Old English *shy*, "to take fright," and Old Norse *scare*, with a similar meaning, came to coexist with meanings "to take fright" and "frighten."

Exercise 9.3 Using the OED or another dictionary containing etymological information, see if you can find any other *sh/sk* pairs of this type, where one is etymologically English and the other etymologically Norse.

Some other borrowings from Old Norse during this period include *aloft, anger, bag, bang, club, die, flat, gift, husband, ill, knife, leg, outlaw, sky, skin, skill, until, cut*.

What is particularly worth noting is that the kind of borrowings we see from Old Norse differ markedly from borrowings from the Latinate languages that we've seen so far and will see more of in a minute. These Old Norse words are everyday words that name concepts that Old English certainly already had words for – things like *sister, sky, leg, knife*, and *club*. Old Norse even contributed some function words to Old English, as we've seen – the pronouns. This pattern of borrowings speaks of a very different kind of contact between Norse speakers and English speakers than between English speakers and Latin, French or Celtic speakers. Latin and Celtic borrowings, before the Norse came, were limited pretty much to things the English didn't have words for: place names and religious concepts. Those borrowings are entirely typical: languages are generally very happy to borrow content words for novel concepts. English just took what it needed in those cases. The Old Norse borrowings, on the other hand, seem to reflect a history of two similar languages intermingling, trading everyday terms and function words because both languages were in use by similar people in everyday contexts. Because many of the Danish settlers intermarried with the English, Old Norse and Old English were both household languages, used in an often bilingual environment.

The Danes ruled England from 1016 to 1042, but then their empire disintegrated, and the English line returned to the throne once more – but not for long. For just 24 years, in fact.

9.6   1066–1200: Norman Rule

In 1066, England's King Edward died without an heir. Duke William of Normandy, in France, was a distant relative – the Norman French were French-speaking descendants of Danes who had invaded France centuries before.[8] William took advantage of the opportunity to challenge the English nobility's choice of a successor, King Harold: he declared himself the rightful king of England, with the Pope's support, and invaded. He conquered the English that same year, had himself crowned, and by 1070 controlled all of England (though not Wales or Scotland). He's known as William the Conqueror, or sometimes William the Bastard, depending on perspective. The most important foreign language in England was now emphatically French.

For the next 150 years, the Norman French ruled England, as well as their holdings in France. William took land from the English nobility and redistributed it to his French followers or appropriated it to the crown. The language of the courts and the nobility was exclusively French.

French became the official language of government: it was used in the courts, the schools, the parliament. French was also important in the Church, because many of the highest ecclesiastical posts were given to William's followers, as well as the estates of rebellious (and hence dead) English nobility. Also, French artisans, monks, priests, soldiers, traders and workmen tagged along to England. Everyone who was anyone, socially and politically, spoke French: it was the language of an entire socioeconomic class. Trade with Normandy was booming, because William was still also Duke of Normandy. His realm crossed the Channel: the French speakers were citizens of a sort of international state, while the English speakers remained tied to the English soil.

Literacy was the province of the French speakers. Not much lexical change happened to English during this time – the situation was somewhat similar to that of the Romans ruling the Celts 900 years earlier: a conquering people ruling a conquered people, with only as much linguistic or cultural exchange as absolutely necessary. The wholesale intermingling of the two vocabularies had not yet really begun.

9.7   1200–1450: Anglicization of the Normans

In 1200, though, John, King of England and Duke of Normandy, married the wrong woman. She had been engaged to a French nobleman, who appealed to the king of France. John was rude when called to account by the king, and was punished for his social shortcomings by having the French crown confiscate his Norman holdings. The kings of England were no longer Dukes of Normandy: the French connection had been severed. The holdings of other English nobles in France were also confiscated by the king of France. Relations worsened between the the two countries, and it became politically expedient to take an "England for the English" stance. By 1295, Edward I was complaining that the king of France nefariously meant to wipe out the English language. In 1327, the historian Higden complained that the teaching of French in England had led to the "corruption" of the English language. And then England and France went to war – the Hundred Years' War – and French was really out. In 1362, the Statute of Pleadings made English, rather than French, the official language of the courts and Parliament.

9.7.1   The Norman French borrowings

Suddenly, the ruling class of England, who had been native speakers of French, were now true residents of England. They began to speak English more and more. The stage was set for French vocabulary to begin pouring into English at a tremendous rate. The upper classes, speaking English, used French vocabulary when they needed to refer to a concept that that they didn't know the English word for, or that English didn't have a word for. Since social climbers tend to emulate the speech of the upper classes to which they aspire, native English speakers began to use these French terms too. Some 10,000 French words entered English during this period. 75 percent of these words are still in use.

These borrowings include words from government – *parliament, minister, territory, counsellor, council, people, power;* from finance – *treasure;* from titles – *duke, sovereign, royal, monarch, prince, count, princess, principality, baron, baroness, noble;* from the military – *sergeant, peace, battle, admiral, captain, lieutenant;* from the law – *judge, jurisdiction, advocate, jury, court, law, prison, crime, accuse;* from the arts – *tragedy, comedy, ballad, artist, critic, dance;* from medicine – *surgeon;* from cuisine – *dinner, supper, sauce;* from the Church – *religion.* In fact, the very words *government, finance, military, law, art, medicine,* and *cuisine* are themselves all borrowings from French during this period. Some other examples of general borrowings from Norman French include *gentle, blame, catch, mercy, puny, mountain, lunatic, vinegar, mustard, salad.*

The class distinction encoded between French vocabulary and English vocabulary at this time is often illustrated with the following list of French-origin/English origin word pairs:

(4) *Meat*   *Animal*
    beef   cow
    veal   calf
    mutton   sheep
    pork   pig
    venison deer

The words for the meats come to us from the French-speaking people who got to eat it; the words for the animals come to us from the English-speaking people who had to raise them. English is unusual in having etymologically unrelated words for these two kinds of concepts; most languages use the same name for both the meat and the animal, as English does with *chicken* and *lamb*.

> **French**, *n.*, *adj.* The people or language of France; pertaining to the people or language of France. From Old English *frencisc*, "Frankish," with palatalization of /k/ and umlaut of /æ/ in the root /frænk/ triggered by the high front vowel of the suffix /ɪʃ/.

9.7.2   The loss of Old English inflection

This period also saw the completion of another, perhaps more important change in English: the almost total loss of the rich inflectional system that is so characteristic of most other Germanic languages. The distinct class, gender, and case suffixes on nouns, adjectives, and determiners disappeared almost entirely, leaving only the modern possessive inflection *'s* and the plural *-s*; the verbal suffixes showing agreement with the number and person of the subject, as well as tense and mood, were also completely lost, leaving only the past tense marking *-ed*, the 3rd singular present tense *-s*, and the progressive *-ing*. The 3rd singular *-eth* ending and the 2nd singular *-est* ending hung around in religious texts for a while, because of the conservativeness of ceremonial language that we've remarked on before, but by 1400, the entire complicated system had essentially disappeared. In the space of 200 years, English went from being a highly inflected language with relatively flexible word order to being an almost completely isolating language with quite fixed subject–verb–object word order.

It's hard to say why this change was so fast, radical, and complete. One major contributor was a new phonological trend of reducing vowels to /ə/ in unstressed syllables. Since the inflectional endings were all unstressed, the vowel reduction blurred acoustic clues to the different inflectional classes and made them much more difficult to distinguish. It may have also been helped along by the number of second language speakers of English during this time: both the native speakers of French in the south and the native speakers of Old Norse in the north had different systems of gender and inflection in their own languages. Given that the English inflectional markings were hard to hear because of reduction, and given that a complex inflectional system is one of the most difficult aspects of a new grammar for a second language learner to master, it may be that the second language speakers of English helped spread the use of uninflected bare root forms. Whatever the reason, by 1400, no one learning English as a first or second language had to worry about noun class, case, or gender, and the complexity of the verbal inflection was also severely reduced.

9.7.3 Middle English borrowings from other languages

Latin was still the language of religion and scholarship, and borrowing from Latin continued in ME just as it had in OE: *scribe* and *baptist* were borrowed from Latin during this period. Besides Latin, there was considerable trade with the people of the "Lowlands" (the Netherlands, Holland) during this period – the Dutch. Some common words to do with commodities, seafaring and commerce were borrowed from Dutch at about this time: *mart, market; pickle, spool, sled, buoy,* and *dote.*

9.8 1450–1600: The English Renaissance

> **renaissance**, *n.* From French *re-*, "again," and *naissance*, "birth." The great revival of arts and letters, under the influence of ancient Greek and Roman models, which began in Italy in the fourteenth century and continued during the fifteenth and sixteenth.

Although the Norman French borrowings were very significant, expanding the total recorded vocabulary of English from about 35,000 to

45,000 words, that number seems small when compared to the influx of words that was to come.

Under the reign of the Tudors, culminating with Elizabeth I, English really came into its own as a language of culture and literature. With the advent of the printing press, invented by Gutenberg in 1452 and brought to England by Caxton in 1476, literacy on a wide scale became possible, and a much larger population began to write books, as well as read them.

The Renaissance was a period of renewed interest in classical Greek and Roman culture, and the huge collection of learning they had amassed. In the Renaissance, any university-educated man was conversant with both Greek and Latin, and would often choose to write in the latter. Newton, for example, composed his *Principia Mathematica* entirely in Latin (although his later work *Opticks* was in English). Writers who are now considered masters of English prose or poetry, like John Milton and John Donne, also wrote in Latin. Scholars associated literary and rhetorical excellence with Latin, which was the standard educated language of Europe. English came under intense criticism for being too rude, base, and inadequate to express refined thoughts and ideas with eloquence. Certainly it lacked terms referring to technical details of grammar, logic, rhetoric, arithmetic, astronomy, and geography, which were primary topics of study among the scholarly Renaissance men. And English didn't yet have an established literature, no "great books" to demonstrate how well suited it was as a medium of expression. Greek and Latin, then, were in a prime position to influence the development of prestige English.

9.8.1   Greek and Latin borrowings: Inkhorn terms

Whenever a scholar needed a technical term to refer to a concept that English didn't have name for, they would import one from Greek or Latin. If Greek or Latin didn't have name for the concept either – a situation that became increasingly frequent as scientific knowledge rapidly expanded beyond the dreams of the ancients – they would make up a name for the concept out of Latin and/or Greek roots, rather than from English roots. This practice continues to this day. As a result, many borrowed Latin terms, and newly formed words from Latin roots as well as affixes that had never been uttered in Cicero's time, entered English in this period. Many such words fell out of use almost immediately, but many others were picked up by contemporaries and are still with us today. These words were often derisively called "inkhorn" terms; "inkhorn" referred to the vessel made of horn that a scribe would keep his ink in, and came to connote pedantry and obscurantism.

Here's a sampling of successful inkhorn terms that were borrowed or coined during this period: *expend, celebrate, extol, clemency, relinquish, contemplate, dexterity, refine, savage, education, dedicate, obscurity, intimate, insinuate, explicate, inclination, politician, idiom, function, asterisk, asteroid, disaster*[9] ... and many, many, *many* others. Some made it, some didn't. Some that didn't make it were *splendidious, adnichilate, continguate, collaude, obtestate, fatiguate*, and lots of others. It's often mysterious why one version of a word made it and another didn't. Why did people like *magnificent* but not *magnificate?* We have *filter, filtrate*, and *filtration* – why not *register, *registrate*, and *registration?*

9.8.2   English borrowing from itself

The influx of non-English terms and the often expressed disdain for English's expressive capacity caused something of a backlash among English writers who were beginning to have a sense of pride in the English literature already extant. Influential poets, such as Spenser, looked to older authors like Chaucer, and to non-standard English dialects, to expand their expressive vocabulary without going foreign, and a few of these revived words remain in the language: *astound, doom, filch, flout, freak, askew, squall, don, belt, glance, endear, disrobe, wakeful*, and *wary*. Sometimes the revived word was misinterpreted, since people were unfamiliar with it. When Shakespeare wrote about *wyrd sisters* he was using an Old English noun, *wyrd*, which meant "happening" and also "force that decrees or forsees what happens." That is, they were "fate sisters" or "fortune sisters." But the term was obsolete when he used it, and playgoers understood it as an adjective, not a noun, taking it to mean something like "far-out" – because the witches were so freaky – hence the meaning of *weird* today.

9.8.3   Borrowings from other languages

French was still a prestige language in this period, especially after the end of the Hundred Years' War. It remained the language of polite correspondence between nobility – and between lovers. The prestigious French, though, was different from the Norman French that had come over with William: it was Parisian French. The children of English nobility began to take French lessons in "polite" French, as a foreign language, not a native tongue. French lingered in the courts (because the lawyers were reluctant to speak understandably lest they lose their monopoly on the job), and in correspondence. For a long time, for educated English speakers, French was the *langue d'amour*.

Besides Latin, Greek, Old English, and French, this period saw an increase in significant contact with the languages of other seafaring nations of Europe. There had already been some borrowing from far-away languages during the Middle English period, due to importation of new commodities: *cinnamon* (Hebrew), *musk* (Persian), *lemon* (Arabic), *silk* (Chinese), *pepper, sugar, indigo, ginger, sandal* (Hindi), and *damask* (from Damascus) are a few examples. Increased trading resulted in the importation of words from other European languages, in particular Spanish and Portuguese. From Spanish came *armada, embargo, sherry, mosquito,* among others, and from Portuguese, *molasses, Madeira.* Also, because ships from Spain and Portugal were world travelers, bringing back commodities from all around the world, English acquired some words from other, non-European languages *via* Spanish and Portuguese, which had borrowed them first: *yam, cocoa, canoe, hammock, hurricane, potato, maize, tobacco, chocolate, tomato, banana, avocado.*

Trade with the Netherlands continued apace, and so there were more borrowings from Dutch around this time: *skipper,*[10] *huckster, booze, dock, smuggle, gin, dollar.* The Dutch school of painting gave *landscape* and *sketch.* And, since the Dutch were also out there trading in the Far East, English also got a couple of words from other languages via Dutch: *paddy, rattan, amok, tea, coffee.*

9.9 1600–1750: Restoration, Expansion

In this period, the English monarchy was temporarily abolished and then restored. Early on, Elizabeth I's navy, commanded by Sir Francis Drake, defeated the Spanish Armada, establishing England's naval preeminence among the nations of Europe. English monarchs then began a program of exploration, trade, and expansion that ultimately created the British Empire. In 1583, Elizabeth claimed the island of Newfoundland, on the north-east coast of North America, creating the first official British colony. In 1600, she chartered the East India Company, granting it a monopoly on trade with the Far East. In 1607, the Jamestown colony was founded in Virginia, and 13 years later, the Pilgrims landed at Plymouth. This was the beginning of the extraordinary chain of events by which English has become the most widely spoken language in the modern world.

During this period, the different Englishes of the different English colonies began to diverge somewhat. The English in India brought home several Hindi words: *curry, bungalow, chintz, dungaree, punch, mongoose, cash, pajamas, cot, pagoda, tattoo, polo, loot, juggernaut,* also *sahib, rupee, coolie.* English speakers in America were interacting with the indigenous population, and borrowing words for the new places, animals and plants they encountered: *oppossum, raccoon, skunk, squash, hickory, tamarack, pecan, moccassin, succotash, toboggan, coyote, totem, woodchuck, quahog, Mohawk, Ohio, Massachusetts, Mississippi, Connecticut.* But in neither India nor America did the cultures interact in such a way that the English speakers borrowed large quantities of words. The invaders had the upper hand, so like the Romans and Anglo-Saxons in Celtic Britain, the Vikings in England and the first generation of Norman French in England, the conquerors spoke their own language and disdained to learn more than a necessary handful of words from the languages of the subjugated natives.

9.10   1750–Modern Day

With the continued development and prosperity of the colonies in America, India, Australia, Canada, New Zealand, and Africa, English became a true world language. Besides the several dialects that were flourishing in the British Isles, the varieties of English spoken in each of the colonies began to acquire their own unique characteristics of pronunciation and vocabulary.

No matter the variety, speakers of English are able to communicate with more people now than has ever before been possible, for speakers of any language. The recent astonishing prosperity of the English-speaking world, particularly the United States, has forced English to function rather like Latin did in Europe at the height of the Roman empire, as a kind of lingua franca, spoken as a second language by millions of people. The scientific publications upon which techno-logical success depends are generally published in English. Literature written in English is accessible to a wider audience than literature in any other language. Among modern languages, English is now one of the superpowers.

Table 9.2 summarizes the main points of the history provided above.

Table 9.2 History of England, 443–1755

Period	Dates	Historical events	Linguistic characteristics	Spelling
Old English 450–1000	443	Romans leave Britain	**Phonology:** velar fricatives, short/long vowel contrast, /sk/ onset clusters borrowed from Old Norse	Use of þ, ð, æ. No k, v, j. Velar fricative represented with h, palatal fricative with sc, front rounded vowel with y.
	449	Angles, Saxons, Jutes arrive, drive out Celtic Britons	**Morphology:** robust inflectional system with case marking, noun gender, verbal agreement	
	790–880	Viking raiding, *Danelaw* in northern Britian	**Syntax:** Germanic; SOV in embedded clauses	
	871–899	King Alfred defeats Danes, orders Old English to be written	**Vocabulary:** Mostly Germanic; a few Latinate borrowings for religious words, Celtic place names, some common Old Norse words	
	1016–1042	Danish rule of England		
1066–1200	1066	Norman conquest, French becomes official language of government	**Vocabulary:** Old Norse pronouns *she*, *they*, *their*, *them* established in English	

Period	Date	Historical event	Phonology / Morphology / Syntax / Vocabulary	Spelling
Middle English 1200–1400	1200	King John loses lands, titles in Normandy	**Phonology:** reduction of unstressed vowels **Morphology:** loss of gender, noun class, most of case system **Syntax:** SVO order begins to emerge as dominant **Vocabulary:** approx 10,000 borrowings from Norman French,	loss of þ, ð, æ. Appearance of th, sh, gh for interdental, palatal, velar fricatives, ch for palatal affricate. Respelling of *love, come, woman* with o for readability.
	1362	English becomes the official language of government		
	1387–1400	Chaucer writes *Canterbury Tales*		
1400–1500	1476	Caxton brings moveable-type press to England	Great vowel shift occurring	Spelling begins to be standardized
Early Modern English 1500–1750	1564	Shakespeare born	**Phonology, Morphology, Syntax:** Relatively stable. GVS completed in various dialects at different times during this period. Final remnants of complex inflectional system disappear. SVO word order firmly established. **Vocabulary:** Rampant borrowing from Greek and Latin for scientific, scholarly, and technological terms; coining of new Greek and Latin words using never-before combined roots. Continued cultural borrowing from French and Italian, names for imported goods and ideas from Spanish, Portuguese, Dutch, American Indian Languages, Hindi, and other colonial languages.	Some new spelling conventions borrowed with Greek and Latin roots (ps for /s/, ph for /f/, etc.) Alteration of some spellings to mirror their Latin roots (*debt, island*, etc.) Spelling standardization largely established.
	1583	First British overseas colony		
	1600	East India Company founded		
	1607	Jamestown colony founded		
	1600–1700	General flowering of English scholarship, both literary and scientific.		
	1755	Johnson's *Dictionary* published		

> **lingua franca**, *n.* /ˈlɪŋgwəˈfræŋkə/ From Italian *lingua franca*, "tongue of the Franks," referring to a mixed language or jargon used in the Middle East in the 1700, consisting largely of Italian words deprived of their inflections. Any of various languages used as common or commercial tongues among peoples of diverse speech.

9.11 The Rise of Prescriptivism: How to Really Speak Good

With the Restoration of the monarchy around 1600 came an increased sense of pride in the accomplishments and potential of the great authors of English literature. With that new pride, however, came a sense of dismay at the inevitable process of language change, and the beginnings of grammatical prescriptivism began to appear – the notion that there is a "proper" usage, and the idea that the language is debased by "improper" use. Samuel Johnson, when initially pitching the first English dictionary to potential investors, stated that his goal was to "fix" the language in place – he wanted to establish correct usage for all time, based on the usage of the most respected writers of the day. By the time he finished it, however, he had come to recognize that any dictionary can only be a record of a language, not a rulebook for it. Nonetheless, the idea of "correct" usage, once it had taken hold, became one of the most tenacious myths of academia. Looking at the model of the Académie Française, the legally sanctioned authority on correct usage of French, many English scholars felt it was important to establish usage rules for "good grammar."

Perhaps partly as a reaction to the increasing variation in the language, the prescriptive movement continued to gather steam at the end of the eighteenth century. Latin and Greek, and to a lesser degree French, still had a firm place in the educational curriculum in schools and universities in Britain, and the grammarians treated Latin as a sort of ideal language. Imagining that Latin's grammar had an inherent internal logic that English lacked, they invented several "rules" of English grammar that were intended to force speakers into more Latin-like patterns. One such example is the famous prohibition on stranding a preposition, as in *Who did you talk to?* Because Latin indicates the meaning of the preposition *to* with a suffix on the Latin equivalent of *who*, rather than as a separate phonological word, it is in fact impossible to separate the noun and the preposition in the corresponding Latin sentence. In English, however, it's often very awkward *not* to strand prepositions. When chastised by an editor for stranding a preposition, Winston Churchill is rumoured to have replied, "That is the sort of English up with which I will not put." A similar "rule" of Latin, imported into English, is the famous prohibition against splitting infinitives; again, because Latin infinitival verb forms are a single phonological word, there is no way to interpolate anything into a Latin infinitive. But in English, it's quite natural to boldly insert adverbs between "to" and the verb, because "to" can be its own phonological word.

The grammarians wrote widely adopted textbooks of grammar, prescribing certain forms of speech and proscribing others, and mixing genuinely helpful guidelines for clarity of presentation and flow with arcane regulations on the use of pronouns and prepositions. Some of their edicts survive to this day. Certainly the attitude that some varieties of English are "better" than others survives robustly, and speakers of nonstandard varieties are often made to feel ashamed of their own dialect while being taught the standard one.

9.12 English Orthography: The Latin Alphabet, the Quill Pen, the Printing Press, and the Great Vowel Shift

Old English spelling was fairly phonologically consistent. As is typical when a language is first written down alphabetically, the orthography was fairly well adapted to the needs of the language, and although there was some variation among individual scribes, by and large a given spelling transparently represented a given sound.

From 1066 until 1362, however, Norman French was the official language of England, and most literate people were French speakers, writing French and Latin. When English did get written, it was written by people who didn't know the Old English orthography. By the time English again became the official language of England, the old runic letters for the interdental fricatives, þ and ð, had begun to be replaced by their modern digraph equivalent, "th," the invention of the Norman French scribes for writing a sound they themselves were unfamiliar with. Similarly, the use of /h/ in the middle of a word to represent a velar fricative was augmented by adding a "g," so the word spelled "eahta" in line 10 of *Ohthere's Voyage* above acquired a "g" in the Middle English period, which it retains in its modern English spelling: "eight." The French scribes also began to use alternative symbols for the /k/ sound. In Old English, /k/ was invariably represented with the letter "c" (as in *scare*), but in French the symbols "k" and "qu" were also used, and began to appear in English texts as well. In Old English, the word we pronounce /kwɪk/ had been written *cwice* (with a final "e" inflection), but spellings like *cwike* and *quike* had begun to crop up as early as 1200.

> The Old English letter "thorn," þ, which stood for either inter-dental fricative, was the OE letter that lasted the longest in written English. Printers who didn't have a thorn in their stock of type would sometimes substitute a *y* as the closest thing they had, resulting in spellings like "ye" for "the" – hence the use of *Ye* to achieve a fake-archaic look in names like *Ye Olde Sweete Shoppe*. The substitution of *y* for thorn didn't last long, though, and most people reading (and writing) *Ye Olde* . . . don't realize that the *Y* was intended to be pronounced as /ð/.

The original 23 letters of the Latin alphabet had to work hard to represent the 45 or so distinct sounds of English. Besides using "th" to represent two distinct sounds, and "gh" for the unfamiliar velar fricative, the French scribes used digraphs that were already in use in French for the voiceless palatal fricative /ʃ/ "sh" and affricate /t͡ʃ/ "ch." Chaucer, the great Middle English poet, used these conventions while writing between 1370 and 1400.

The Latin alphabet had to stretch considerably to accommodate English even with these additions. The main stretch was one that had been around even in Old English – the alphabet had only five vowel symbols. Old English and Middle English had many more vowel distinctions than that, as does modern English. In particular, early English distinguished between short and long pronunciations of vowels. In Old English, the additional vowel symbol æ was available, but there were no established conventions for representing the short and long vowel distinctions. Long pronunciations sounded the same as the short pronunciations – that is, the vowel quality was the same – but they lasted just a bit longer. Scribes of Middle English sometimes used combinations of vowel letters to indicate the long/short contrast, but often they would just use a single vowel, as their Old English predecessors mostly had. In the IPA, the symbol indicating a long pronunciation is a colon placed after the vowel, so the Middle English word for "house" would be transcribed /huːs/. Scribes would sometimes write it as *hus* and sometimes *hous*, but the pronunciation intended would remain the same. Naturally, native speakers of the period didn't have problems with this – after all, they knew how the words sounded.

In the late Middle English period, in 1476, the first moveable-type press was brought to England from the Netherlands by William Caxton. He was faced with the task of choosing spellings for his English translations of work from other languages, as well as for his editions of Chaucer and other English writers. He didn't have much in the way of examples, but he did have access to manuscript versions of Chaucer's works, who died around 1400. Caxton often tried to follow Chaucer's example, as Chaucer was nationally and internationally renowned. Caxton knew that English was in a state of flux; he commented on the situation in the preface to one of his books:

> And also my lorde abbot of westmynster ded do shewe to me late certayn euydences[11] wryton in olde englysshe for to reduce it in to our englysshe now vsed. And certaynly it was wreton in suche wyse that it was more lyke to dutche than englysshe, I coude not reduce ne brynge it to be vnderstonden. And certaynly our language now vsed varyeth ferre from that, whiche was vsed and spoken whan I was borne.[12]

Caxton and the other printers' choice of spellings reflected the tendency that we have remarked on before for speakers to look to older generations for linguistic standards. Unfortunately for generations of English spellers (and IPA learners), starting around the time of Chaucer's death (late 1300s, early 1400s), a major sound change took place in English. All the long vowels moved around in the mouths of English speakers between 1400 and 1500. Spelling became standardized more or less based on spellings chosen *before* the sound change – around the time Chaucer was writing – but then the sounds changed. Thanks to Caxton and other printers, the spelling stayed the same. Consequently, the vowel sounds the spellings came to stand for in English were not the usual values those same symbols had in other languages.

From Old English times all the way through to Chaucer's day, the vowel spellings made sense in the Roman alphabet. That is, the symbols "a," "e," "i," "o," and "u" had approximately the values they have in IPA today – essentially the same values they have in Spanish, French, or Italian. But by the time most of the printing and spelling got done, the sound change was pretty much over, and the standardized spellings no longer corresponded to pronunciation in the way they had before.

We can form a general picture of what happened to the long vowels if we compare the IPA symbols for front vowel sounds to their modern English spellings:

(5) *IPA transcriptions*   *Modern English spelling*
     /fijt/   feet
     /fejt/   fate
     /fajt/   fight

Ignoring the /j/ off-glide, we can see where modern English has "e," the IPA has "i." Where modern English has "a," the IPA has "e," and where modern English has "i," the IPA has "a." If you were to read these modern English spellings *as if the letters stood for their IPA pronunciation*, you would get something like a Chaucerian pronunciation. The modern English pronunciations are the result of the vowel shift. To put it in terms of phonological features: the long mid front vowel /e/ became the high front vowel /i/, the low front vowel /a/ became the mid-front vowel /e/, and the long high front vowel /i/ became the low front diphthong /aj/.

An analogous change happened in the long back vowels, but it hasn't left such an obvious trace in the spellings of those vowels. One that is obvious is in the double "o" convention: in Modern English, a double "o" is pronounced as the high back vowel /u/, as in "goose." In Chaucer's time, that word contained a long version of the mid back vowel /o/ – "goose" was pronounced /goːsə/ – hence the spelling.

Here are some representative words that used to contain the canonical long vowels of Middle English, and have since undergone the Great Vowel Shift:

(6) Middle English long vowels:
     aː   *tame, cake, rain, sane, late, staves*
     eː   *geese, feet, meet, wreath, treat, please, sea, beet*
     iː   *knight, light, write, kite, wise, my, by*
     ɔː   *no, so, boat, dote, wrote, moat*
     oː   *goose, boot, moot, loot, root, do, to, you*
     uː   *house, louse, how, our*

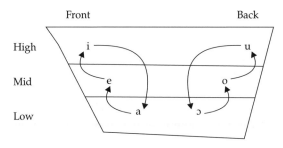

Figure 9.1 The effect of the Great Vowel Shift on vowel height in Middle English

Figure 9.1 shows the general effect of the change on vowel height.[13] All the vowels' heights increased, whether front or back – low vowels became mid vowels, and mid vowels became high vowels. High vowels couldn't raise any higher, of course; they became low, strongly diphthongized vowels – /i/ became /aj/.

This didn't happen with short vowels: the short vowels have pretty much the values, and spellings, that they had in Middle English. The correspondence between the short vowels and their IPA symbols is consequently much more straightforward:

(7) *IPA Transcriptions*   *Modern English spelling*
    /pɪt/   pit
    /pɛt/   pet
    /pæt/   pat
    /pʊt/   put
    /pɑt/   pot

We can see pairs of short and long vowels in a number of irregular verbs and their past or participial forms:

(8) *Vowel alternations derived from short/long contrast + GVS*
    a. **/ij/ ~ /ɛ/:** keep/kept, creep/crept, feel/felt, leap/leapt, sleep/slept, sweep/swept, weep/wept, bleed/bled, speed/sped, deal/dealt, kneel/knelt, breed/bred, lead/led, feed/fed, dream/dreamt, leave/left
    b. **/aj/ ~ /ɪ/:** light/lit, hide/hid, write/written, ride/ridden, slide/slid, bite/bit
    c. **/uw/ ~ /ɑ/:** shoot/shot, lose/lost

In these verbs in Middle English, the main difference between the present and the past tense form was that the vowel in the present tense was pronounced a bit longer – it otherwise sounded the same as the vowel in the past tense. But then the Great Vowel Shift occurred, and it affected only the long vowels, not the shorter ones in the past tense. So now the connection between the long vowels and their short counterparts lives on as an irregular morphophonological alternation in modern English, even though the short/long distinction is no longer made in modern English.

Understanding the Great Vowel Shift helps us to understand why the same symbol "e" is used to stand for a high front vowel, as in "keen," and a mid front vowel, as in "ken." Back in Middle English, the vowel in these two words sounded much the same; one vowel was just longer than the other. "Keen" was pronounced /keːn/; "ken" was pronounced /ken/. After the long vowels underwent the Great Vowel Shift, though, the two vowels sounded considerably different – /keːn/ became /kijn/ – though they continued to be spelled the same.

As a result of the vowel shift, we have other pairs like the following:

(9)	staves/staff	/ej/ ~ /æ/
	deep/depth	/ij/ ~ /ɛ/
	sheep/shepherd	/ij/ ~ /ɛ/
	wise/wisdom	/aj/ ~ /ɪ/
	child/children	/aj/ ~ /ɪ/
	Christ/Christmas	/aj/ ~ /ɪ/
	wide/width	/aj/ ~ /ɪ/
	know/knowledge	/ow/ ~ /ɑ/
	bone/bonfire	/ow/ ~ /ɑ/

These pairs in particular reflect an interesting phonological alternation in Old English that made a big difference in which words underwent the Great Vowel Shift in Middle English.

In Old English, as you will recall, there were many inflectional suffixes, most of which began with a vowel. Adding such a suffix to a word ending in a consonant meant that the consonant was *resyllabified* – rather than remaining as the coda of the last syllable of the stem, the final consonant became the onset in the new syllable created by adding the suffix. (We see a similar effect today in words like *dating*, which syllabifies as *da.ting*, although morphologically it is *dat-ing*.) If we take *-as*, the plural suffix we saw on *hwæl*, "whale," in our Old English text, we can see that if we add it to *hwal*, the first syllable of the word will lose its coda consonant -*l*. Similarly, adding -*as* to the stem *stæf* will take the *f* of the root out of the coda of the first syllable and put it in the onset of the second syllable.

This mattered because in Middle English, the vowel of a stressed, open syllable was *automatically* lengthened. So without any suffix, e.g. in the singular, *stæf* would be a closed syllable, and the vowel *æ* would remain short. But in the plural, the *f* would resyllabify because of the additional suffix, causing the first syllable – now *stæ* – to be open, not closed, and consequently causing the vowel *æ* to be long, not short.[14] Now we have a situation where, in the plural, the vowel is long, but in the singular, it's short. Consequently, in the plural, the vowel was subject to the Great Vowel Shift but in the singular, it wasn't – giving us the contrast between *staff/staves*. The same phenomenon is at work in *wise/wisdom*. The addition of the -*dom* suffix to the root *wis*- meant that the /s/ of the root was forced into the coda of the root syllable, so the vowel of the root was short in *wisdom*. When the root was used by itself, as an adjective, though, it would usually have had a vowel-initial suffix attached to it, agreeing in case, number and gender with the noun it was modifying. That suffix would trigger resyllabification of the -*s* in the root into the onset of the last syllable, which in turn would trigger lengthening of the vowel /i/ in the root. So the vowel was usually long in the Old English adjective *wise*, but short in the derived noun *wisdom*. Consequently, the vowel in *wise* underwent the Great Vowel Shift, changing from /iː/ to /aj/, but the vowel in the root of *wisdom* didn't.

Our spelling conventions for indicating whether or not the pronunciation of the letter "i" should be /aj/ or /ɪ/ has its roots in these phonological rules. Any vowel symbol that comes before a single consonant and a silent "e" is pronounced with its post-GVS "long" pronunciation: *kite* = /kajt/, not /kɪt/; *rate* = /ɹejt/, not /ɹæt/, etc. Any vowel symbol that comes without the silent "e" gets the short, non-GVS pronunciation, so *kit* = /kɪt/ and *rat* = /ɹæt/. The silent "e" is the last reminder of that whole enormous family of Old English suffixes that triggered resyllabification of the final consonant and consequently required lengthening of the vowel.

Similarly, the convention according to which we double the final consonants of suffixed words for "short" pronunciations of vowel symbols, (so that "rating" = /ɹejtɪŋ/ but "ratting" = /ɹætɪŋ/), was invented because of the Old English rule we discussed above: vowels in Old English syllables with codas were short, while vowels in syllables without codas were long. Doubling the consonant artificially forces an orthographic coda onto the first syllable in a word like *ratting*, and acted as a reminder Middle English speakers that the vowel in such cases was not long.

We owe some other spelling irregularities to sound changes as well. In words like *lamb, bomb,* and *thumb* the final "b" used to be pronounced, and hence was written. The phonotactic rules governing coda consonant clusters changed, however, so that voiced stops couldn't follow nasals unless both were alveolar. After that, /nd/ sequences are still pronounceable, as in *land, hand,* and *canned,* but /mb/ and /ŋg/ at the end of a word became impossible. The legacy of those formerly permissible coda clusters is still with us, though, in the form of the silent *b* at the end of these words. The same explanation applies to the silent "k" in words like *know, knit, knight,* etc.; a /kn/ onset cluster was phonotactically legitimate in Old and Middle English, but became impossible at some point in the Middle English period; consequently we have the spelling for such clusters but not the pronunciation. Phonological change also explains why the "gh" is silent in words like *light, right, thought, caught,* etc.: the velar fricative that that "gh" represented disappeared from the language sometime in the Middle English period.

Spelling irregularities in English also arose from less rule-governed sources. Spellings of Latinate words often remained very similar to the spellings they had in their original Latin or French source, and of course Latin and French had their own spelling conventions. The variation in pronunciation of *c* and *g* before front vowels (*generic* vs *garage,* or *cell* vs *cake*) is an importation from those languages, in which front vowels triggered palatalization of velar stops.

Yet another source of a few idiosyncratic spelling irregularities were the quill pens used by scribes during the Middle English period. The letters u, i, v, w, m, and n were all written using a sequence of a particular short downstroke of the quill, called a *minim* (the word *minim* itself would have been written using only minims). When several letters made of minims came in sequence, they were exceptionally hard to decipher. Was it an *i* and an *m,* or two *n*s? Figure 9.2, taken from an illustrated manuscript, shows some examples.

To assist the reader, in some frequent words spelled with sequences of minims, a convention arose whereby one of the offending vowels was changed to an *o,* so that the vowel-consonant combination was clear. In general, this caused little pronunciation difficulty, because the words were common enough that everybody could just recognize them. Some words whose spellings were affected this way

Figure 9.2 A close-up of the Ellesmere Chaucer. "Heere bigynneth the freres table / Whilom ther was dwellynge in my contree / an erchedecen a man of heigh degree / that boldely dide execucion / in punyshynge of fornication." Notice the minims in "bigy**nn**eth," "**in**," "**man**," "pu**ny**shynge," and "for**ni**cacion." Special Collections, University of Wisconsin-Milwaukee Libraries. The Ellesmere Chaucer Image is from: The Ellesmere Chaucer: Reproduced in Facsimile. Manchester, England. The University Press, 1911. 2 Volumes.

were *woman* (originally *wimman*), *come* (originally *cume*) and *love* (originally *luve*).

One final source of spelling irregularities in English dates from the inkhorn era: some zealous Latin scholars felt that not only should the spellings of newly borrowed Latin words be faithful to the Latin original, but that the spellings of some words of Latinate origin that had been borrowed hundreds of years earlier should *also* reflect the spelling of the Latin original, even when subsequent phonological change in French and/or English had caused significant alteration to the pronunciation of the Latin form. Consequently, several words with a long pedigree of English use, which had been spelled phonetically accurately according to the spelling conventions of the time, had various silent letters inserted into their spelling to indicate their etymological relationship to the Latin cognate. The silent "b" in *debt* was inserted for that reason, although it had been spelled *dette* when it was borrowed with that pronunciation from Old French, in the Middle English period. Now we can recognize *debt's* etymological connection with *debit* from its spelling, though we pay an orthographically heavy price. Similarly, a silent "p" was inserted into *receipt* for the same reason, although *conceit* and *deceit* escaped such treatment, despite being based on the same *-ceive* root – originally Latin *capĕre*, "to take." The "s" in *island* and the "c" in *indict* have this same source.

275

9.13 Summary

In this chapter, we have looked at some of the historical reasons why modern English is the way it is. The obvious and major differences between Old English and modern English, and between modern English and any other Germanic language, are largely the result of a complex series of events of English history that brought English into contact with other European languages, often as a subordinate language. Phonological change and language contact triggered the morphological changes that have made the grammar of modern English significantly different from that of Old English. Language contact and the use of English in the literary and scholarly realm resulted in the remarkable diversity of etymological sources of the modern English vocabulary. The modern English spelling system is a historical by-product of all of these events, reflecting phonological and morphological change as well as the effects of significant borrowing.

Study Problems

1. Consider the following pairs of nouns borrowed into English and their transcriptions:

candle	/ˈkændəl/
chandelier	/ʃændəˈlijɹ/
cap	/ˈkæp/
chaperon(e)	/ʃæpəˈɹown/
castle	/ˈkæsəl/
chatelaine	/ʃætəˈlejn/
chair	/ˈt͡ʃeɹ/
chaise longue	/ˈʃɛz ˈlɑŋg/
cherry	/ˈt͡ʃeri/
cerise	/səˈɹijz/
chain	/ˈt͡ʃen/
chignon	/ʃɪˈŋɑn/
catch	/ˈkɛt͡ʃ/
chase	/ˈt͡ʃejs/

    a. For each word, look it up in the *OED* and give the date it first appeared in English (for *chaperon(e)*, the date it appeared with its modern meaning, not the dates for other meanings), as well as the language from which it was borrowed *at that time.*

b. For each pair of words, give the Latin word from which they originally came.

c. For each pair of words, briefly discuss how the meaning of the first is connected to the meaning of the second. In cases where the connection is obscure, speculate briefly about the path the meaning differentiation took.

d. These words illustrate a sound change in the pronunciation of /k/ that happened in French, changing gradually from the original Latin to a different sound in Middle French to a third sound in Modern French. What sound did /k/ change into in Middle French? What sound did it then change into in Modern French? Which of the above words doesn't quite fit the pattern?

2. Consider the following pairs of words:

divine divinity
serene serenity
sane sanity
profound profundity

a. How do these pairs illustrate the Great Vowel Shift in action?

b. Similar pairs (*wise~wisdom*) were explained in the text as the result of resyllabification. This doesn't quite work with these examples. Explain why not.

3. Prehistoric Old English (before the 6th century AD) used to have a phonological rule of *umlaut*, which is illustrated in the (liberally doctored) data below. Umlaut had the effect of changing certain vowels in stems when a suffix containing /i/ was added.

The suffix was added, as always, to produce another form or meaning of the word (plural nouns, comparative adjectives, 3rd person present tense verbs, etc.). In *real* prehistoric English, the suffixes for each meaning were distinct forms – but they were all one syllable, and all contained /i/. (One plural suffix *was* just -*i*.) Here, you have the stem form plus a single pretend -*i* affix to illustrate the phonological process that was going on. You'll have to imagine the full range of suffix forms. (In addition to changing all the suffixes to simple -*i*, the stems have been altered slightly in a couple of cases to make the relationship to the modern words clearer.)

	Stem	Stem+i		Stem	Stem+i
flow	/flo:w/	/fle:wi/	*full*	/ful/	/fili/
grow	/gɹo:w/	/gɹe:wi/	*drunk*	/druŋk/	/driŋki/
foot	/fo:t/	/fe:ti/	*knot*	/knut/	/kniti[16]/
tooth	/to:θ/	/te:θi/	*mouse*	/mus/	/misi/
brother	/bro:ðoɹ/	bre:ðeɹi[18]	*know*	/kna:w/	/knæ:wi/
food	/fo:d/	/fe:d/	*rose*	/ra:s/	/ræ:ri/[15]
			whole	/ha:l/	/hæ:li/[17]
			drive	/dɹa:f/	/dɹæ:fi/

a. Figure out the umlaut rule by consulting your vowel chart, from Chapter 2. Recall that vowels can be defined as "high," "mid," or "low," depending on the height of the tongue body in the mouth, and also as "front" or "back," depending on the location (front or back) of the mass of the tongue body in the mouth. Describe in those terms what the umlaut rule did, considering only the data in the chart above (don't look at the data in (b) yet).

b. Here are some more products of the umlaut rule. Can the characterization you made in (a) above account for them? If not, why not?

	Stem	Stem+i
drink	/dɹaŋk/	/dɹeŋki/
man	/mann/	/menni/
stink	/staŋk/	/steŋki/
swing	/swaŋg/	/sweŋgi/

It's important to realize that although here we only see cases in which a relic of the umlaut rule has survived into Modern English, this rule applied to *every* appropriate stem+affix combination in prehistoric English. That is, umlaut was a regular phonotactic rule of the language.

Further Reading

Aitchison, Jean (1991) *Language Change: Progress Or Decay?* 2nd edn. Cambridge: Cambridge University Press.

Crystal, David (1995) *The Cambridge Encyclopedia of the English Language.* Cambridge: Cambridge University Press.

Freeborn, Dennis (1998) *From Old English to Standard English: A Coursebook in Language Variation Across Time*. 2nd edn. Ottawa: University of Ottawa Press.

Hogg, Richard (ed.) (1992) *The Cambridge History of the English Language*. Cambridge: Cambridge University Press (technical!).

Hughes, Geoffrey (2000) *A History of English Words*. Oxford: Blackwell.

Millward, C. M. (1988) *A Biography of the English Language*. Fort Worth, TX: Harcourt Brace.

Smith, Jeremy (1996) *An Historical Study of English: Function, Form and Change*. London & New York: Routledge.

Notes

1   Text from Cassidy and Ringler. Translation based on that of John Tucker, http://web.uvic.ca/hrd/worldcall_2003/oldenglish/index.htm and glosses from Grant Chevalier, http://www.ucalgary.ca/UofC/eduweb/engl401/texts/ohthfram.htm.

2   Of course, a more accurate translation here would be "paid," but I've used the modern cognate of *gylda*, "yielded," because it's still occasionally used with the meaning of "giving" or "rendering," and it illustrates the pronunciation of the letter "g" as /j/ next to front vowels – the OE root and the modern English root don't sound as different as they look. Plus, the OE spelling reveals the connection between *yield* and other related words whose "g"s didn't undergo palatalization, like *gold, gild*, "to put gold on," and the former Dutch currency, the *guilder*.

3   Again, a better translation would be "made," rather than "wrought" – but "wrought" is still occasionally used in modern English. It's cognate with the word "work" and to the "wright" in words like "playwright" or "shipwright."

4   To be strictly accurate, it's indicating gender and declension class as well.

5   Weirdly, *oþer$_{26}$*, which became the modern English adjective *other*, originally meant what modern English *either* means, as you can see from its use in this text.

6   As in *soothsayer*.

7   /kɛlts/.

8   "Norman" and "Normandy" are derived from "North-man," "Norse-man."

9   *Disaster* contains the same root as *asterisk* and *asteroid*: *aster*, Latin for "star."

10 The borrowing of *skipper* created another *sh/sk* pair in English – *skipper* is formed on the Dutch root meaning "ship." The English equivalent, spelled "scip" in our Old English text, had lost its /k/ several hundred years earlier.

11 Another modern English letter was introduced around this period, or rather, acquired its modern pronunciation. Before this the labial consonant

/v/ had been written with the same symbols as the labial (rounded) vowel /u/; the letters "v" and "u" were used as symbols for either the vowel or the consonant, with a semi-convention of using "v" when either was the first symbol in a word, and "u" in the middle of words. The string "euydences" is Caxton's spelling of the word "evidences" "vsed" is his spelling for "used."

12 Excerpted from Bolton (1982: 173). Here is a free modern English paraphrase of this excerpt: "My Lord the Abbot of Westminster showed me some documents written in Old English, with the idea that I might produce a version of them in our current English. The Old English was written so that it looked more like German than English; I could not translate it or understand it. Certainly, English as spoken now varies greatly from that which was used and spoken when I was born."

13 This picture is somewhat oversimplified; for a more complete account, see some of the "Further Reading" sources at the end of the chapter.

14 Incidentally, the /f/ between two vowels became voiced here, turning into /v/, as we saw in Chapter 5.

15 Source of ModE *rear* (as in what a horse does).

16 Source of ModE *knit*.

17 Source of ModE *heal*.

18 Source of ModE *brethren*.

Glossary

The key words in the Glossary are shown in bold on their first occurrence in the text.

adjective A content word that modifies a noun, occurring after a determiner and before the noun in a noun phrase. Most adjectives can appear in the *comparative* and *superlative* forms, like *happier* or *most intelligent*.

affix A bound morpheme that must be attached to a stem; a *suffix* or a *prefix*.

affricate A consonant produced by combining a stop and a fricative tongue gesture: complete closure followed by release with enough constriction to create turbulence. In English, /t͡ʃ/ and /d͡ʒ/ are affricates.

allomorph An alternative pronunciation of a morpheme that depends on the phonological context the morpheme appears in. In English, /t/, /əd/, and /d/ are allomorphs of the past-tense morpheme /d/ (-*ed*).

allophone A variant pronunciation of a phoneme in certain phonological contexts. In American English, the phoneme /t/ has the allophones [tʰ] as the onset of a stressed syllable (as in *top*), [ʔ] between stressed syllable and (unstressed) syllabic /n/ (as in *cotton*), [ɾ] between a stressed and unstressed syllable (as in *potter*), [t˺] in the coda of a word-final syllable (as in *pot*), [t] elsewhere (as in *stop* or *tomorrow*).

alveolar A consonant produced just behind the teeth, on the *alveolar ridge* between the teeth and the palate. In English, /t/ and /s/ are alveolar consonants.

anapest A foot made up of two weak (unstressed) syllables followed by a strong syllable. The words *intercede*, *understand*, and *entertain* are examples of anapests.

argument The entities that have to participate in the action or state described by a relational concept, usually a verb. In *John loves Mary*,

John and *Mary* are the arguments of *love*. In *Susan laughed, Susan* is the argument of *laugh*. In *Mary sold John a horse, Mary, John,* and *a horse* are arguments of *sell*.

argument structure   A description of how many arguments a verb can have, and what their general properties or roles are in the event or state described by the verb. For example, the argument structure of the verb *hit* is (Agent, Theme).

article   See *determiner*.

aspiration   Voiceless consonants in English are pronounced with an extra expulsion of air when they form the onset of a stressed syllable, as in *top* or *pot*, [tʰap] and [pʰat]. This extra puff of air is termed *aspiration*.

assimilation   When a phoneme changes its place or manner of pronunciation to be more like that of a neighboring phoneme. In words like *triumph*, the /m/ often changes from being a bilabial nasal to a labiodental nasal, under the influence of labiodental /f/ next to it.

auxiliary (verb)   A "helper" verb that shows up along with the main verb in some tenses and moods. Usually *be* or *have* in sentences like *John is running* or *Mary has eaten*, but also elements like *will, can, must,* and *may*.

blocking   When a more specific, homosemous morpheme or word prevents the appearance of a general morpheme or word. Irregular inflection like *-i* on *alumn-i* blocks regular inflection, preventing *alumnuses*.

bound morpheme   A morpheme that cannot appear as a phonological word on its own. All affixes are bound morphemes, but roots can be bound as well: *electr-* in *electr-ic* and *electr-ify* is a bound root.

category   See *part of speech*.

clause   Roughly, a sentence; a phrase that expresses a complete thought or proposition – a relationship between a subject and a predicate. Sentences are clauses, but can also contain other clauses. For example, in *Mary thought that he left*, the phrase [*(that) he left*] is an embedded clause. See also *relative clause*.

closed syllable   A syllable that ends in a consonant – that has one or more consonants in its coda. *Cat* is an example of a closed syllable.

cognate   Two words from different languages are cognate if they each developed from of a single word in the ancestor language. English *father* and Spanish *padre* are cognate, both having descended from a single Proto-Indo-European word with the same meaning.

comparative   A greater degree of an adjective, expressing that something is more adjectiv-y than something else. *Happier* is the comparative of *happy; more intelligent* is the comparative of *intelligent*.

complementizer   A function word that introduces a complement clause. *That, if* and *whether* are all complementizers of English.

compositional   When the meaning of an expression made up of one or more morphemes is completely determined by the meanings of those morphemes, the expression is compositional – its meaning is composed of the meanings of its parts. The meaning of the word *teacher* is compositional, as is the meaning of the phrase *eat a sandwich*, but the meaning of the word *slider* (the baseball pitch) or the phrase *eat crow* (accept a defeat or reversal) is not.

compound   A phonological word containing more than one *root*.

conjunction   A function word that joins two words or phrases of the same category. *And, but* and *or* are all conjunctions of English.

consonant   A sound made by partial or complete closure of the vocal tract. Consonants have a *manner* (kind of closure) and a *place* (location of closure) of articulation.

content   Content listemes convey the main meaning of the word or phrase they are contained in. Headlines often are made up only of content listemes.

contraction   A contraction is a single phonological word that is created when a listeme that can be pronounced as an independent phonological word is reduced and attached to another independent word, as in *can't* for *can not*, *I'm* for *I am*, or *it's* for *it is*.

coronal   A consonant produced with the tip (or "crown") of the tongue. In English, /s/ and /t/ are examples of coronal consonants.

cran-morph   A morpheme which has no meaning on its own, independent of a particular context. *Gamut* in *run the gamut* is a cran-morph, as is *-duce* in *reduce* and *deduce*.

deictic   An expression is *deictic* if its interpretation depends entirely or partly on the context of the conversation. Words like *here, there, now, tomorrow,* and *that* are deictic, as are words like *come, go, me, them, your,* and so on.

deixis   Context-dependence. See *deictic*.

demonstrative   The determiners *this, that, these,* and *those* are the demonstratives of English, used to pick out and emphasize salient entities in the conversation.

derivational   Derivational affixes produce a new stem, to which inflectional affixes can attach. Derivational affixes are not grammatically obligatory. They often change the part of speech of the stem to which they attach, and carry more content-type meaning than inflectional morphemes. Examples of derivational affixes are *-al* as in *derivational*, *-er* as in *teacher* or *-ize* as in *winterize*.

determiner A determiner is a function word that co-occurs with a noun, specifying its status with respect to the context (definite vs. indefinite) and conveying information about quantity. *The, a, every, many, much, some,* and *this* are all determiners.

digraph A sequence of two letters that represents a single phoneme. The sequences "sh" for /ʃ/, or "th" for /θ/, in English, are digraphs.

entailment An assertion that logically follows from another assertion. The sentence *Flossie is a brown cow* has the sentence *Flossie is brown* as an entailment.

first person The grammatical status of the person in a conversation who is the speaker. *I, me, our, myself,* and *we* are all examples of first person pronouns in English.

flap A voiced consonant formed by a single quick tap of the tongue to the alveolar ridge, transcribed [ɾ]. The flap is an *allophone* of /t/ and /d/ in American English in words like *butter* and *padded.*

foot A phonological unit made up of one or more syllables, one of which bears a strong stress and the others of which do not. Types of feet are determined by where the stressed syllable falls; examples are *iambs, trochees* and *anapests.* Poetic meter is described in terms of feet.

fricative A consonant produced by creating a very small opening in the oral tract, through which air flows turbulently. Some fricatives of English are /s/, /v/, and /ð/.

function Function listemes convey grammatical meanings, fitting content listemes together into phrases and sentences. They are the glue that holds the sentence together. They are often left out in "telegraphic" communication, as in a headline.

Germanic Refers to a language family descended from Proto-Indo-European which eventually spread throughout northwestern Europe, the ancestor of modern English, German, Swedish, Icelandic and Dutch, among others.

glide A consonant produced with an almost vowel-like gesture, putting the tongue in position for one of the vowels /i/ or /u/, but then quickly released, resulting in /j/ or /w/, respectively.

homophone A listeme which sounds identical to another listeme, but is semantically unrelated to it. *Dear* (the affectionate term) and *deer,* the wild ungulate, are homophones.

homoseme A listeme which expresses the same idea as another listeme, but is phonologically unrelated to it. The appearance of a homoseme rather than the default is usually determined by the stem to which it attaches. In *alumni*, the plural of *alumnus*, the suffix -*i* is a homoseme with the regular plural suffix -*s*. See also *irregular* and *suppletion*.

iamb A metrical foot made up of a weak (unstressed) syllable followed by a strong (stressed) syllable. The words *escape, today* and *arrive* are examples of iambs.

idiom A phrase whose meaning is not compositional, like *kit and caboodle* or *let the cat out of the bag*.

idiomatization The process by which a formerly compositional complex word or phrase undergoes meaning drift to become a single listeme of its own.

inflectional Inflectional affixes are required to attach to a stem in a certain grammatical context. They are *function* listemes. Past tense -*ed* and plural -*s* are inflectional affixes.

intervocalic A consonant that occurs between two vowels is intervocalic. The /t/ in *attack* is intervocalic.

IPA An abbreviation for the *International Phonetic Alphabet*, the standardized system for transcribing linguistic sounds.

irregular A root or stem that requires a special form to represent some grammatical meaning, that is, one that does not take the regular inflection. The verbs *sleep* and *run* are irregular in the past tense, because they require the forms *slept* and *ran* rather than *sleeped* and *runned*. Irregular affixes are *homosemes* with their corresponding regular suffixes.

Italic Refers to a language family descended from *Proto-Indo-European* which spread throughout southwestern Europe, the ancestor of modern Italian, French, Spanish and Portuguese, among others. Latin is the common ancestor of all these modern languages, and a daughter language of PIE.

labial A consonant produced with the lips. In English, /w/ and /p/ are examples of labial consonants.

larynx The boxy bone-and-cartilage structure at the top of the windpipe, containing the vocal folds. Also sometimes called the voice box. The tip of the larynx forms the Adam's apple.

Latinate Describes the language family descended from Latin. See *Italic*.

liquid A voiced consonant made with airflow in the mouth only partially obstructed but less so than with a fricative. The phonemes /l/ and /ɹ/ are the liquids of English.

listeme A morpheme or group of morphemes which has to be listed in the mental lexicon – something about the unit must be memorized, rather than figured out from its parts. In the word *rewrite*, re- and *write* are listemes. In the sentence *Mary kicked the bucket,* meaning "Mary died," *Mary, -ed,* and *kick the bucket* are listemes. In the sentence *Mary kicked the bucket* meaning "Mary kicked the bucket," *Mary, -ed, kick, the,* and *bucket* are listemes. See also *idiom.*

meronomy The "part-of" relation: something that is a part of something else is a meronym of it. In *John has a big nose,* the relationship between *John* and *a big nose* is *meronymy.*

monomorphemic Made up of only one morpheme.

morpheme A listeme smaller than or equal to a phonological word in size. Affixes like *-s* or *un-* are morphemes, and so are roots like *cat, love,* etc.

morphology The internal structure of a phonological word, or the study of the structure of phonological words.

nasal A sound made with airflow passing over the lowered velum through the nasal cavity. The phoneme /m/ as in *mop* is a nasal.

neologism A newly formed word, one coined just at the moment of speech.

nominalization A verb or adjective has been nominalized when it has a suffix attached that causes it to become a noun. The nominalization of *consume* is *consumption;* of *reduce* is *reduction,* of *electric* is *electricity.*

noun A content word that can usually have the plural *-s* suffix attached, and occurs to the right of determiners such as *the* or *this.*

noun phrase A sequence of words made up of a noun, any modifiers of the noun, and its determiner (if it has any). In the sentence *John would like the fresh chocolate cream pie,* the phrase *the fresh chocolate cream pie* is a noun phrase.

obstruent Consonant sounds made with a greater degree of obstruction of airflow than liquids, glides or nasals. Oral stops, affricates and fricatives are obstruents.

OED The usual abbreviation for the *Oxford English Dictionary,* the most complete source of information on the history and uses of English words.

open syllable A syllable that ends in a vowel – one that has no coda. *Hi* is an example of an open syllable.

oral tract The oral tract includes all the space from the larynx up to behind the lips – basically the mouth and upper part of the throat. Specifically excludes the nasal passages above the velum.

orthography A writing system, or, simply, writing.

palatal A consonant produced at the (hard) palate, just behind the alveolar ridge. In English, /j/ is an example of a palatal consonant.

parsing The process of analyzing and understanding speech.

part of speech   A categorization of words that sorts them into groups according to their distribution in sentences. *Noun, verb,* and *adjective* are parts of speech of content words; *determiner, complementizer,* and *auxiliary* are parts of speech of function words.

participle   The form of the main verb that shows up in combination with an auxiliary verb, as in *John has eaten cookies* or *Mary is running.* Participles often also function as adjectives, as in *the eaten cookies* or *the running woman.*

periphrastic   A multi-word expression that has a meaning that is expressed by a single-word construction in other circumstances. *More intelligent* is a periphrastic comparative, compared to *smarter.*

person   "Person" describes the role a referent is playing in a conversation: The speaker is *first person,* the hearer or addressee is *second person,* and anyone or anything else is *third person.* Person determines which pronoun will be used to refer to someone.

phoneme   The smallest contrastive unit of sound in a language. It may have several actual variants in pronunciation, or *allophones.* In American English, the phoneme /t/ has the allophones [tʰ] (as in *top*), [t] (as in *stop*), [ɾ] (as in *potter*), [ʔ] (as in *cotton*), and [t˥] (as in *pot*).

phonological word   A unit of pronunciation made up of one or more syllables, organized into one or more feet. May contain one listeme (as in *cat*), several listemes (as in *writers*) or zero (as in *gamut*) listemes.

phonology   The sound system of a language, or the study of sound systems.

phonotactics   The rules which govern the way the *phonological words* of a language may be formed. The phonotactics of modern English prevent phonological words from ending in /mb/, for instance.

phrase   A sequence of words that forms a subpart of a sentence.

prefix   A bound morpheme attached to the beginning of a stem. The morpheme *re-* is a prefix in English.

preposition   A word that combines with a noun phrase, usually expressing a locational or temporal relation. *With, before, to, of,* and *under* are all prepositions.

presupposition   An unspoken assumption that is part of the meaning of some expression. In *Who went to the store?* the presupposition is that *somebody* went to the store. In *Have you stopped calling John?* the presupposition is that you have been calling John.

productive   (Derivational) affixes which are regularly used to form new words are called *productive*: *-ing, un-,* and *-less* are all productive morphemes in English. The affixes *-al* and *dis-* are not generally productive.

Proto-Indo-European   Once a single language spoken by people living somewhere in Central Europe, this language is the ancestor of most modern European languages, including English, and also the ancestor of Persian, Hindi and other related languages to the east.

quantifier   A determiner which specifies the quantity of the noun its modifying. In *Mary patted every dog, every* is a quantifier. Other quantifiers of English are *some, most, many, all,* and *much.*

readjustment rule   A rule which alters the sound of a stem when a certain affix attaches to it. The change in stress and pronunciation of the "c" in *electric/electricity* is the result of a readjustment rule that goes with *-ity.*

regular   A root or stem that takes the default inflectional markings of the language. *Walk* is a regular verb in English; *cat* is a regular noun.

relative clause   A clause which modifies a noun, usually introduced by *that* or *which.* In "A clause which modifies a noun," *which modifies a noun* is a relative clause.

root   The morpheme conveying the main meaning in a word. In *cats, cat* is the root. In *teacher, teach* is the root. In *economics* and *economy, econom-* is the root.

second person   The grammatical status of the person or persons in a conversation who is the addressee or hearer. *You* and *your* are second person pronouns in English.

semantics   The meaning of an expression, or the study of meaning.

stem   A group of one or more morphemes, containing a root, to which another morpheme can be attached. In *competitive, competit-* is a stem for *-ive.*

stop   A consonant produced by a usually brief but complete blockage of airflow through the oral tract. Some stops of English are /p/, /g/, and /t/.

suffix   A bound morpheme attached to the end of a stem. The morpheme *-ed* is a suffix in English.

superlative   The absolute degree of an adjective, the very most adjectiv-y anything can be. *Happiest* is the superlative of *happy; most intelligent* is the superlative of *intelligent.*

suppletion   An *irregular* form of a root which bears no phonological relationship to the basic form. The past tense of the verb *go* is suppletive, because *went* shares no phonology with *go.* Similarly for the superlative of *good* (*best*) and the plural past tense of *be* (*were*). Suppletion is a type of *homosemy* in roots.

syntax   The structure of a sentence or phrase, or the study of sentence structure.

taxonomy Classification by the "is-a" relation. Sorting things into classes of like items which are all examples of the same bigger category is creating a taxonomy, as one would do in saying "St. Bernards, chihuahuas, and poodles are all dogs."

tense Expresses the temporal relationship between the moment of speech and the event or state described by the sentence. Past tense typically means "happened before the moment of speech"; future tense typically means "will happen after the moment of speech"; present tense typically means "happening at the moment of speech."

third person The grammatical status of some person(s) or thing(s) referred to in a conversation who is neither the speaker nor the hearer. The pronouns *he, she, them,* and *it* are examples of third person pronouns.

transitive (math) Any semantic relation or concept which takes two arguments and has the following entailment: If *X relation Y,* and *Y relation Z,* then *X relation Z.* The predicate *is above* is a transitive relation, and so is *precede,* but *is beside* is not transitive, and neither is *love.*

transitive (syntax) Any verb which occurs with both a subject and an object. The verb *pat* is transitive; so are the verbs *like* and *wrap.*

trochee A metrical foot made up of a strong (stressed) syllable followed by a weak (unstressed) syllable. The words *happy, toddler,* and *sofa* (and *trochee*) are trochees. The most frequent multisyllabic words in English tend to be trochees.

truth conditions The crucial things that would have to be real facts about the world to make a given sentence true. To make *John patted a cat* true, the individual named John would have had to purposely bring his hand into gentle contact with a small feline, i.e., John would have had to pat a cat. To make *Mary likes John* true, Mary would have to like John.

velar A consonant produced at the velum (or soft palate), toward the back of the mouth. In English, /g/ and /k/ are velar consonants.

verb A content word that can have the *-ing* suffix attached to it, and can occur to the right of auxiliaries such as *be, can, will,* and *must.*

verb phrase A sequence of words made up of a verb, its object and indirect object (if it has any) and any modifiers of the verb. In the sentence *Susan often gives toys to children,* the phrase *often gives toys to children* is a verb phrase headed by the verb *give.*

voice box See *larynx.*

vowel A sound produced with unimpeded flow of air through the vocal tract and with vibration of the vocal cords.

Works Consulted

Many articles and books informed the presentation of the material in this book; some are mentioned in the Further Reading sections at the end of each chapter. Here are a few more which need particular mention as they have directly provided results or analyses discussed in the text.

Aronoff, Mark (1994) *Morphology by Itself: Stems and Inflectional Classes.* Cambridge, MA: MIT Press.

Bloom, Paul (2000) *How Children Learn the Meanings of Words.* Cambridge, MA: MIT Press.

Bolton, W. F. (1982) *A Living Language: The History and Structure of English.* New York: Random House.

Fabb, Nigel (1988) "English suffixation is constrained only by selectional restrictions," *Natural Language and Linguistic Theory* 6, 527–39.

Hammond, Michael (1999) *The Phonology of English.* Oxford: Oxford University Press.

Jusczyk, Peter W. (2001) "Bootstrapping from the signal: some further directions," in Jürgen Weissenborn and Barbara Höhle (eds), *Approaches to Bootstrapping: Phonological, Lexical, Syntactic and Neurophysiological Aspects of Early Language Acquisition,* vol. 1. Amsterdam: John Benjamins, pp. 3–23.

Mattys, Sven L. and Jusczyk, Peter W. (2001) "Phonotactic cues for segmentation of fluent speech by infants," *Cognition,* 78, 91–121.

Saffran, Jenny R., Aslin, Richard N. and Newport, Elissa L. (1996) "Statistical learning by 8-month-old infants," *Science* 274, 1926–8.

Siegel, Dorothy (1974) "Topics in English morphology," PhD thesis. MIT.

Index

Page numbers in **bold** refer to the Glossary.